CHARLES DARWIN

CHARLES DARWIN

CYRIL AYDON

CONSTABLE • LONDON

Constable & Robinson Ltd
3 The Lanchesters
162 Fulham Palace Road
London W6 9ER
www.constablerobinson.com

First published in the UK by Constable,
an imprint of Constable & Robinson Ltd

A copy of the British Library Cataloguing in
Publication Data is available from the British Library

ISBN 1-84119-567-7

Printed and bound in the EU

For Deborah
who started it
and Sue
who kept the faith

Contents

———·—◆—·———

Illustrations

———•—•—•———

Fanny Myddleton-Biddulph (nee Fanny Owen), by Mrs Barrable from a miniature at Chirk Castle, painted in 1852, photographed by Christopher Gallagher (© The National Trust Photographic Library)

Darwin's rooms in Cambridge (Author's collection)

Reverend John S. Henslow, by an unknown artist (Ipswich Borough Council Museums and Galleries)

HMS *Beagle* in the Murray Narrows, by Conrad Martens (Author's collection)

Vice Admiral Robert Fitzroy, by Samuel Lane

From a portrait in the Royal Naval College, Greenwich, London (Bridgeman Art Library, London)

HMS *Beagle*: Plan and Cross-section, drawn by Midshipman Philip King

From the 1912 edition of Darwin's *Journal of Researches* (Author's collection)

Land Iguana (*Amblyrhyncus demarlii)* and *Rhea Darwinii*, both from *Zoology of the Beagle* (English Heritage Photographic Library)

Between pages 198 and 199

Darwin, aged 31, by George Richmond RA (G. P. Darwin, on behalf of Darwin Heirlooms Trust) (English Heritage Photo Library)

Emma Darwin, aged 31, by George Richmond RA (G. P. Darwin, on behalf of Darwin Heirlooms Trust) (English Heritage Photo Library)

Images nos 3a, 4a, 5a, 6a, 11a, 12a, 13 and 16 are reproduced from *Order of the Proceedings at the Darwin Celebration held at Cambridge, 22-24 June 1909*, Cambridge University Press 1909

Maps

Pages xviii to xxii

THE DARWIN – WEDGWOOD CONNECTION

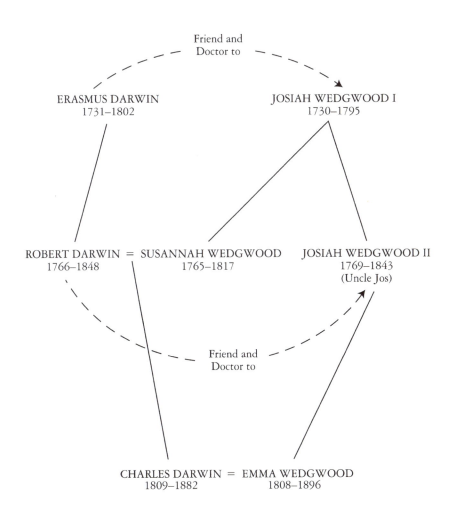

Friend and
Doctor to

ERASMUS DARWIN
1731–1802

JOSIAH WEDGWOOD I
1730–1795

ROBERT DARWIN = SUSANNAH WEDGWOOD
1766–1848   1765–1817

JOSIAH WEDGWOOD II
1769–1843
(Uncle Jos)

Friend and
Doctor to

CHARLES DARWIN = EMMA WEDGWOOD
1809–1882   1808–1896

Acknowledgements

'I have gathered a bunch of other men's flowers:
Only the ribbon that binds them is my own'

These words of Montaigne's have never been far from my mind during the writing of this book. All Darwin biographers are the beneficiaries of what has come to be called 'The Darwin Industry'; and as the latest in a long line, I am indebted to the researches of those who have gone before. Three writers in particular have smoothed my path. Adrian Desmond and James Moore set new standards of excellence when they published their *Darwin*; and their book remains unsurpassed in its analysis of the social and intellectual background. Janet Browne has performed the seemingly impossible in producing, in her two-volume *Charles Darwin*, a biography of comparable stature, without treading the same ground.

I owe a similar debt to the professional scientists who have written the many excellent expositions of Darwinian theory which are now available to the lay reader. The books listed in my Further Reading Appendix have provided particular enlightenment, and pleasure I would wish to share. I have in addition been greatly helped by my reading of the following texts:

The Autobiography of Charles Darwin, edited by Nora Barlow; *Charles Darwin and the Voyage of the Beagle – Unpublished Letters and Notebooks*, edited by Nora Barlow; *Charles Darwin – Evolution by Natural Selection*, by Gavin de Beer; *Charles Darwin – A New Biography*, by John Bowlby; *Charles Darwin – A Man of Enlarged Curiosity*, by Peter Brent; *The Survival of Charles Darwin*, by Ronald W. Clark; *The Life and Letters of Charles Darwin*, edited by Francis Darwin; *More Letters of Charles Darwin*, by Francis Darwin and A.C. Seward; *Darwin's Dangerous Idea*, by Daniel C. Dennett; *Darwin – A Life in Science*, by John Gribbin and Michael White; *The Lying Stones of Marrakech*, by Stephen Jay Gould; *Erasmus Darwin*, by Desmond King-Hele: *Fitzroy of the Beagle*, by H.E.L. Mellersh; *Evolution*, by Colin Patterson; *The Wedgwood Circle – 1730–1897*, by Barbara and Hensleigh Wedgwood; and *Charles Darwin*, by Geoffrey West.

For permission to quote from copyright material, I am grateful to Cambridge University Press, for the extracts from *Charles Darwin's Beagle Diary*, edited by Richard Keynes, and the extracts from *Charles Darwin's Letters – A Selection 1825–1859*, edited by Frederick Burkhardt; and The Folio Society, for the extracts from Robert Fitzroy's *Narrative*, as reproduced in *A Narrative of the Voyage of H.M.S. Beagle*, edited by David Stanbury. I am indebted to J.F.C. Harrison, author of *Early Victorian Britain, 1832–51*, for having led me to the letter quoted from Anna Maria Fay's *Victorian Days in England*.

Without the help I have received from the staff of the Oxfordshire County Library Service in Banbury and Oxford, my book would have been impossible. I have also received valuable assistance from the staff of the British Library, the Public Record Office, the Shropshire County Records Service, and Down House Museum; Jean Button, Librarian of the Warriner School, Bloxham; Sally Drummer of Ipswich Museum; Sue Gwilliam, Librarian of Lancing College; Kate Mayne, formerly House Steward at Chirk Castle; Lynn Miller of the Wedgwood Museum Trust; and Paul Smith of Newcastle-under-Lyme Library. Michael Roberts put me right on several matters concerning Darwin's early life.

Among the friends and colleagues who have helped to create whatever merits this book has, I must give pride of place to Jim Honeybone. It is a lucky writer who has access to an assessor who is able to offer such a combination of sound judgement, informed criticism and enthusiasm for the project in hand.

Deborah and Sue Aydon have supplied moral support and professional expertise, as well as commenting on substantial portions of the manuscript. Others who have helped with comments on the text, and with the shaping of the book, include Alec Muir, Maurice Edgington, Mike Fenner and Margaret Gwilliam. Friends who provided help in other ways include Malcolm Craig, Gerry Crossan, Frank Davis, John Hodgkins, Tina Smith and Tony Swann.

Carol O'Brien has been the sort of editor every writer should have. Her belief in the project provided the validation a first-time biographer needed; and her commitment to it has been a continual source of strength. I am also grateful to Sarah Smith, the Desk Editor at Constable, for the skill and enthusiasm she has brought to the task of turning my manuscript into a real book.

Finally, I would like to thank my wife Joyce for the support and help she has provided during the writing of this book.

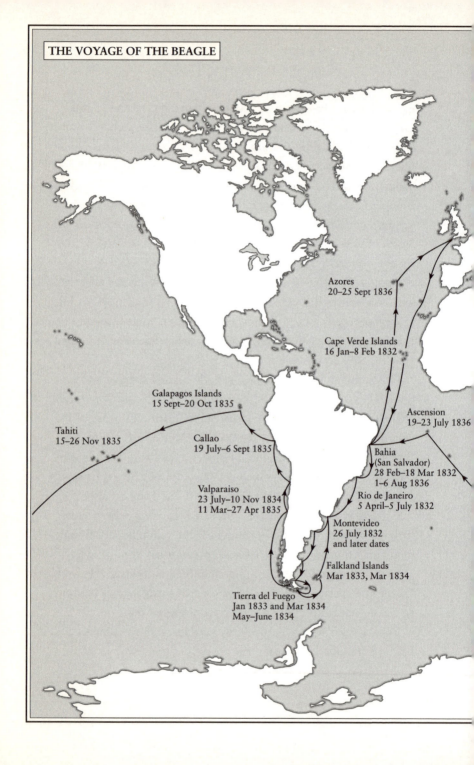

THE VOYAGE OF THE BEAGLE

Azores
20–25 Sept 1836

Cape Verde Islands
16 Jan–8 Feb 1832

Galapagos Islands
15 Sept–20 Oct 1835

Ascension
19–23 July 1836

Tahiti
15–26 Nov 1835

Callao
19 July–6 Sept 1835

Bahia
(San Salvador)
28 Feb–18 Mar 1832
1–6 Aug 1836

Valparaiso
23 July–10 Nov 1834
11 Mar–27 Apr 1835

Rio de Janeiro
5 April–5 July 1832

Montevideo
26 July 1832
and later dates

Falkland Islands
Mar 1833, Mar 1834

Tierra del Fuego
Jan 1833 and Mar 1834
May–June 1834

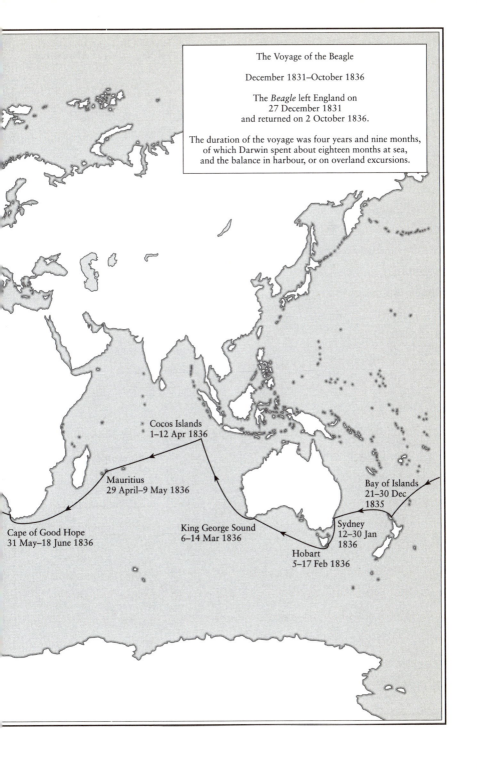

The Voyage of the Beagle

December 1831–October 1836

The *Beagle* left England on
27 December 1831
and returned on 2 October 1836.

The duration of the voyage was four years and nine months,
of which Darwin spent about eighteen months at sea,
and the balance in harbour, or on overland excursions.

Cocos Islands
1–12 Apr 1836

Mauritius
29 April–9 May 1836

Bay of Islands
21–30 Dec
1835

Cape of Good Hope
31 May–18 June 1836

King George Sound
6–14 Mar 1836

Sydney
12–30 Jan
1836

Hobart
5–17 Feb 1836

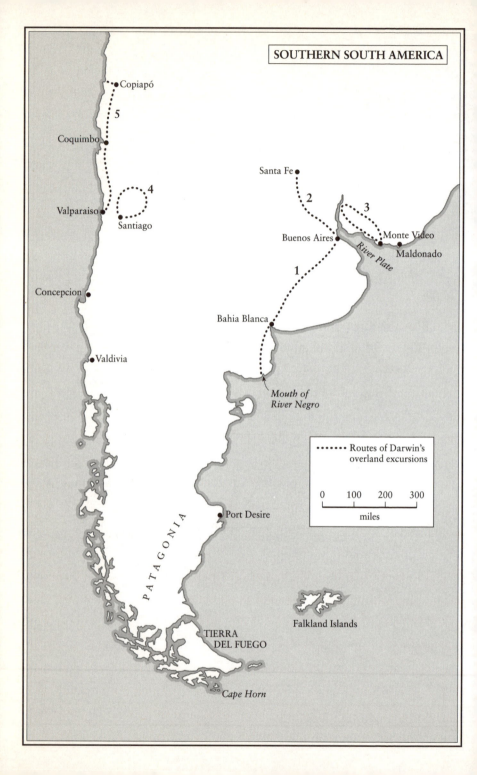

SOUTHERN SOUTH AMERICA

Copiapó

5

Coquimbo

Santa Fe

2   3

4

Valparaiso   Buenos Aires   Monte Video

Santiago   Maldonado

River Plate

Concepcion

1

Bahia Blanca

Valdivia

Mouth of
River Negro

.... Routes of Darwin's
           overland excursions

0   100   200   300

miles

Port Desire

PATAGONIA

TIERRA
DEL FUEGO

Falkland Islands

Cape Horn

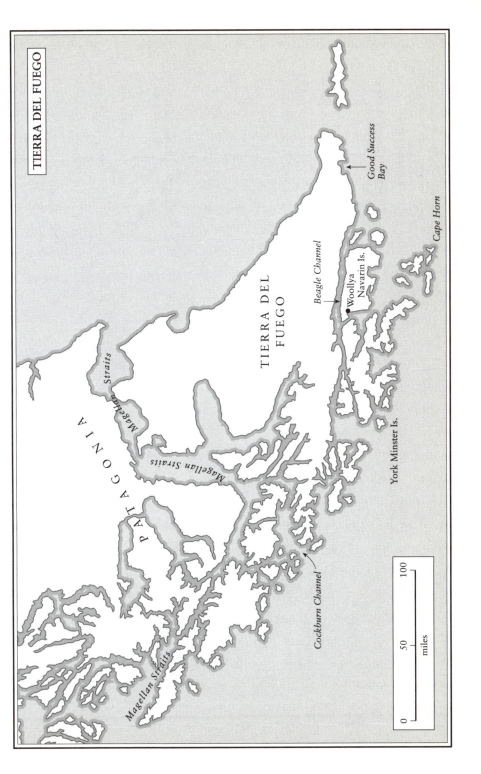

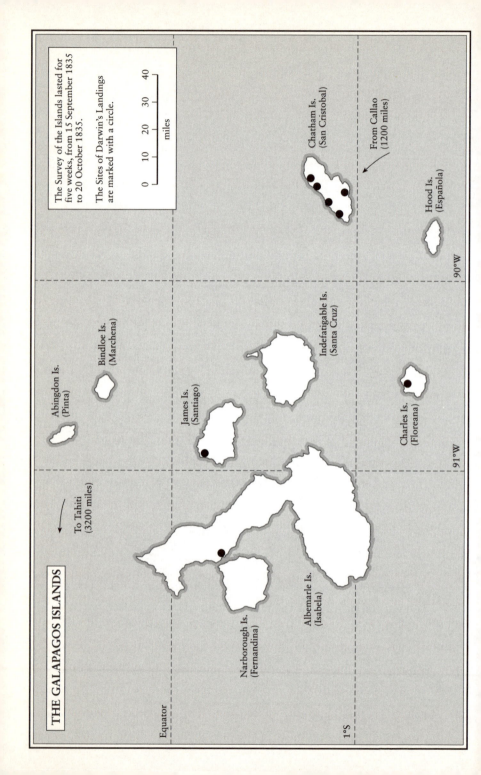

THE GALAPAGOS ISLANDS

The Survey of the Islands lasted for five weeks, from 15 September 1835 to 20 October 1835.

The Sites of Darwin's Landings are marked with a circle.

miles
0   10   20   30   40

Equator

1°S

91°W

90°W

To Tahiti
(3200 miles)

Abingdon Is.
(Pinta)

Bindloe Is.
(Marchena)

James Is.
(Santiago)

Indefatigable Is.
(Santa Cruz)

Narborough Is.
(Fernandina)

Albemarle Is.
(Isabela)

Charles Is.
(Floreana)

Chatham Is.
(San Cristobal)

From Callao
(1200 miles)

Hood Is.
(Española)

Introduction

He was one of the luckiest men who ever lived. His grandfathers were two of the most famous men in England. Thanks to them, he was from his earliest years accustomed to the company of clever and artistic people. He grew up in a comfortable home, filled with affection, in which his imagination was left free to roam. His father was a wealthy man, and in his late teens he realized that he would never have to do anything he did not want to do. For the rest of his life he did exactly as he pleased. And to the end of his days, he was surrounded by the same atmosphere of love and protection he had known as a child.

His early life was dominated by two enthusiasms: field sports and natural history. As the years passed, sport lost its attraction; but natural history fascinated him until the day he died. On his graduation, at the age of twenty-two, he took – at his father's expense – not one 'gap year', but five, on a round-the-world trip as the gentleman companion of the captain of His Majesty's Survey Ship *Beagle*. In South America, he covered more than 2,000 miles on horseback: acquiring specimens which form the core of several present-day museum collections, and making observations which provided him with the material for a library of groundbreaking works in geology, ecology and evolutionary theory. Intensely ambitious, he decided early in life that he had it in his power to do important work in the natural sciences; and he devoted himself single-mindedly to achieving this aim. For twenty years he held off from publishing his most explosive theory; and he only summoned up the courage to do so when he realized that another man was about to go public with the same idea.

Hating confrontation of any kind, he left his disciples to fight his battles for him. He died rich and famous, honoured throughout the world, and just in time to avoid seeing his ideas once more under attack from questions to which he had never been able to find an answer.

But even this favourite of fortune did not pass through life unscathed. At the age of forty-two, he suffered the loss of a darling ten-year-old daughter, whose death destroyed what remained of the religious faith in which he had been raised. And for forty years he was the pitiable victim of debilitating illness: illness which has never been properly explained, which turned what would in any case have been a magnificent life's work into an achievement of positively heroic dimensions.

His name was Charles Robert Darwin, and this is the story of his life, his work and his ultimate vindication.

A Note on Money Values

O ne of the problems of writing and reading history is the effect of inflation on money values. There was such a huge fall in the purchasing power of money during the twentieth century that accounts of transactions expressed in the money of earlier times have lost all meaning for the modern reader. They are in effect written in a foreign language. If they are to be understood, they must be translated. Fortunately for the purposes of this book, a simple equation will do the trick. Any sum quoted in the following pages should be multiplied by fifty to obtain its equivalent in today's money. This is, of course, a rough and ready measure. Not all prices change at the same rate. But without some such rule of thumb, past transactions are unintelligible.

In considering property values, a further point should be borne in mind. England is a more crowded country today than it was in the nineteenth century, and the price of property has risen much faster than prices generally. While it is reasonable to treat the £30,000 that Robert Darwin lent his brother-in-law Josiah Wedgwood to buy his country estate at Maer as being equivalent to £1,500,000 in today's money, a property which £30,000 could buy then would today cost many times £1,500,000.

When dealing with small sums, there is another problem resulting from the decimalization of sterling in 1971. Before that date, a pound was divided into twenty shillings. Using the 50:1 ratio suggested above, the fifteen shillings which the bookshops asked for *The Origin of Species*, when it was published in 1859, converts to £37.50 in today's money. This figure is perhaps over-precise; but it gives some idea of the book's likely readership in an age when great numbers of people were unsure where the price of their next loaf of bread was coming from.

Prologue

————•◆•————

I n the late eighteenth century, the town of Shrewsbury was
a proud and prosperous place. Commanding a crossing of
the River Severn, in the border country between England and
Wales, it had grown rich on the trade in Welsh wool, and its
wealth showed in the fine black-and-white half-timber houses
that lined its streets. In these streets life went on much as it had
in Shakespeare's day, two centuries before; and the town clocks
still kept Shrewsbury time, which was different from the time
elsewhere. But in the countryside around the town changes
were afoot. Roads were being made – the first proper roads
since the Roman legions had left. Along these roads the new
mail coaches raced at eight miles an hour – twice as fast as the
stagecoaches they were displacing. Ten miles down river from
Shrewsbury, around the village of Coalbrookdale, the night
sky was lit up by the glow of blast furnaces, and visitors came
from far afield to see the world's first iron bridge which soared

above the river in a single span of a hundred feet.

One day in the summer of 1786, two men – a young doctor and his older brother – rode into the town. The name of the younger man was Robert Darwin, and he had come to Shrewsbury because his father, who was also a doctor, had decided that this busy market town was an ideal place for a professional man to make his mark. Although Robert was only twenty years of age, he quickly built up a successful practice. Within six months of his arrival he had forty or fifty patients, and his fees were sufficient to support a servant and two horses. His reputation was enhanced by his election, at the age of twenty-one, to membership of London's elite Royal Society. The fact that this honour derived from his father's status as a Fellow of the Society, and a close friend of its President, rather than from any special merit of his own, is unlikely to have troubled him, any more than it would have troubled his patients.

His father, Erasmus Darwin, was one of the most famous men in England. King George III had offered him the post of Royal Physician: a post he had declined, because he did not wish to leave the little city of Lichfield where he then lived. But his reputation as a doctor was only one of his claims to fame. He had written a book called *The Botanic Garden*, which set out the whole of current botanical knowledge in the form of an extended poem. It had taken literary London by storm. He later wrote a massive work on animal life, entitled *Zoonomia*, in which he put forward a theory of what would later come to be called evolution. The *Zoonomia* was one of the most talked-about books of its day. It was paid the compliment of being pirated in New York, and the even greater compliment of being placed on the Papal Index.

Erasmus Darwin's passion for natural history was matched by his enthusiasm for science and technology. While living in Lichfield, he had been one of a group of men who met regularly in Birmingham to discuss matters of common interest in science, industry and politics. As these were the days of highwaymen and footpads, their meetings were timed to coincide with the full moon, and they called themselves the Lunar Society. This small but select group included the factory-owner Matthew Boulton, his partner James Watt, the chemist Joseph Priestley and Benjamin Franklin, who was at that time Agent for the American Colonies in London. The Secretary of the Society was the astronomer William Small. Small had formerly been a teacher at William and Mary College in Virginia, where one of his students was Thomas Jefferson, the future President of the United States. It was Franklin who had introduced Boulton to Small when the latter arrived in England; and the friendship between these two was the glue that held the Society together.

Another attender at these gatherings was the great potter Josiah Wedgwood, Erasmus Darwin's friend and soulmate. They had met when they were about thirty years of age, and the bond formed then endured for the rest of their lives. Their backgrounds could hardly have been more different. Erasmus was a graduate of the universities of Cambridge and Edinburgh: grounded in the classics, and trained in medicine. Josiah was a working potter who had left school when he was nine and at fifteen had been apprenticed to his elder brother. But they were men of great gifts and wide interests, and they were both fascinated by science and invention. They also shared the same radical politics. They were leading figures in the anti-slavery movement; they supported the American Revolution; and they rejoiced in the Revolution in France, even though it reduced the demand for Josiah's products.

Josiah had married well and with his wife's money and his own ability he had created a great business. In his factory at Burslem, near Stoke-on-Trent, he employed one of the largest workforces in Europe. In 1765 Queen Charlotte had ordered one of his tea sets, giving him the right to style himself 'Potter to Her Majesty'; and in 1774 he had supplied a dinner service of 952 pieces to Catherine the Great of Russia for the huge sum of £2,000. He was a pioneer in the application of gears and belts to lines of machines; and in 1782, on Erasmus Darwin's suggestion, he became the first factory-owner in the world to use a steam engine to power machinery. It was with Erasmus's encouragement too that he became an active promoter of canals, which enabled him to bring china clay cheaply from Cornwall, and to transport his fragile products to the seaports from which they could be sent to London and exported around the world.

Erasmus Darwin was not only Josiah Wedgwood's friend and scientific collaborator, he was also his doctor. They had both had the misfortune to contract smallpox. For Erasmus the disease had meant disfigurement; for Josiah the consequence was a crippled leg. In 1768, when Josiah was thirty-seven, Erasmus had had the distressing duty of overseeing an operation to remove his friend's damaged limb. Like all operations then, it was performed without the benefit of an anaesthetic. For the rest of his life Josiah walked on a peg leg.

In 1789, when Erasmus had put the finishing touches to his poetic masterpiece *The Botanic Garden*, he sent an advance copy to Josiah. Later in the same year Josiah repaid the compliment by presenting Erasmus with the first perfect copy of his famous Portland Vase, the product of twenty years of determined experimentation.

This friendship between the Royal Potter and the nearly Royal Physician extended to their families. Josiah's oldest and favourite child was his daughter Susannah, whose family name was Sukey. Sukey was a particular favourite of Erasmus, to whom she gave piano lessons. Robert Darwin was her childhood friend and schoolmate. As they moved through their teens, an understanding grew up that they would marry when Robert was established in a career. Sukey's father Josiah had himself married a childhood friend – a cousin – and his consciousness of the happiness this marriage had brought him must have added to the pleasure with which he contemplated the union of his beloved daughter and the son of his dearest friend.

He did not, alas, live to see their wedding. They were married in 1796, the year after he died, when Robert was thirty and Susannah was thirty-one.

ONE

A Man of Substance

———◆———

A country doctor with a wealthy clientele needed a proper house. With his wife's inheritance of £25,000, Robert Darwin could afford one. He purchased a plot of land on the edge of town, on a small hill called the Mount, overlooking the river. Here he built a house suitable for a professional gentleman and the large family it was reasonable for them to expect; and in 1800 they moved in with their two-year-old daughter. In the next three years two more daughters were born, and in 1804 Susannah gave birth to a son, who was named Erasmus, after Robert's father.

Among the interests which Robert's father and his friend Josiah had shared had been a love of flowers. It was a love they had passed on to their children. Robert and Susannah created a beautiful garden, filled with rare plants and exotic trees. Inside the house Robert built up a splendid library. He accumulated a fine collection of china, with portrait busts of Benjamin Franklin and George Washington, and a first edition of his father-in-law's Portland Vase. Susanna, who was competent, lively and artistic, created a comfortable home and, like her mother before her, acted as her husband's secretary. She had been well educated at home. She played the harpsichord; she spoke French; and she was skilled in the keeping of accounts. In the words of a London journalist, Eliza Meteyard, who later wrote a book about the Wedgwoods:

> She entered zealously into all her husband's pursuits; and as he took almost as much interest in botany and zoology as his father . . . their gardens and grounds became noted for their choicest shrubs and flowers.
>
> . . . But the wife of a leading physician of an important provincial city like Shrewsbury had . . . a multitude of other duties . . . to receive, sometimes to entertain, high-class patients in her husband's absence; to give dinner and supper parties; to be on visiting terms with the gentry of a wide neighbourhood; to take an interest in the town and town-folks; and not to omit what was one of the established customs of the place, two great half-yearly feasts to the chief medical practitioners of town and country.

As the years went by, Robert's practice prospered. His reputation spread, and he worked long hours. As a consequence, he became one of the highest-earning doctors – possibly the highest-earning – outside London. He was known throughout Shropshire and in many places beyond. He was a big man, always smartly turned-out. He favoured shades of yellow and beige, and rode in a bright yellow chaise, drawn by two black horses. He was a man of great practical intelligence but, unlike his father, he was not in the least intellectual. The difference in their mental lives was displayed in their manner of travelling. Erasmus had never wasted a minute. His carriage had been furnished as a mobile writing cabinet, and his enormous literary output owed much to his habit of writing on the move. Robert, by contrast, was a talker, not a writer. He hardly ever put pen to paper, either travelling or at home; and his long hours on the road were spent sitting bolt upright, with no diversion except his own thoughts.

Robert Darwin was a man of great sensitivity and human sympathy, and these qualities won him friends and much respect. But some people found him intimidating. This was partly due to the forcefulness of his personality and partly to the massiveness of his presence. A contemporary was later to remember him as 'the biggest man I ever saw out of a show . . . When he entered the room it was like the door coming upon you broadside on.' He was six feet two inches tall, and the passing years brought a matching increase in his girth. His father had become so corpulent in later life that he had been compelled to have a segment cut out of his dining table in order that he might continue to reach his food. Robert, in early middle age, began to go the same way. When he tipped the scales at 24 stone (336 pounds), he stopped counting, but he continued eating, with the consequence that, as his son Charles later wrote, 'he afterwards increased much in weight.'

As well as being a successful doctor, Robert Darwin was a

clever man of business. His investments were many and varied, and it is doubtful if he ever made a serious mistake. As a resident of Shrewsbury, he was ideally placed to participate in the developments which were transforming British industry. When he set up practice in the town, the villages of Shropshire were already producing a quarter of all the iron made in Britain, and more than was made in any other country in the world. In the year after he arrived, the town's citizens turned out to witness the launching of the world's first iron barge. The products of the local iron industry were becoming heavier and difficult to transport on the still mostly execrable roads. If they could be floated down the Severn to Bristol, they could be transhipped and not only sent round the coast to other parts of Britain but, like Josiah's china, exported anywhere in the world. A local ironmaster, John Wilkinson, whose enthusiasm for his product had earned him the nickname of 'Iron-mad' Wilkinson, had conceived the idea of the iron barge as a solution to this problem. When the day of its launching arrived, crowds lined the riverbank. Some had come to marvel, but many had come to mock. To the delight of Wilkinson's supporters, and the disappointment of his detractors, the barge did not sink and the iron industry of Shropshire entered a new era of prosperity.

As Robert's income expanded, he took advantage of such developments to increase his wealth still further. Whenever a scheme for a new road or a canal was floated, his name would be found in the list of subscribers. He also acquired property. Many of the local gentry were his patients, and some were also his debtors, as a result of loans he had advanced against the security of their estates.

One such gentleman who turned to Robert for help was his wife's brother, Josiah Wedgwood II, whose family name was Jos. Jos had taken over the management of the pottery when his father, Josiah I, had retired in 1793; and he had inherited the business on Josiah's death two years later, when he himself was still only twenty-six. He had never wanted to be a potter, and he had no wish to be a factory manager. Like many sons of manufacturers, he resented the snobbery with which the landed class regarded those engaged in 'trade', and he aspired to join their ranks. He had sold the family home, Etruria Hall, and decamped to Dorset with his wife Bessie, to live the life of a country squire: planting trees by the thousand and driving around in a coach with four white horses, with a coachman, postillion and footmen, all in handsome red livery. Unfortunately, this new life proved more costly than he expected, leaving him in debt to the firm; and the firm itself, deprived of proper supervision, entered into a decline.

Faced with the possible loss of the family fortune, Jos was forced to involve himself once more in the management of the business. But his aspirations had not changed, and he looked around for a suitable property, within reach of the factory, but far enough removed from it. His choice lighted upon Maer Hall, an Elizabethan mansion in Staffordshire, just nine miles from the Burslem factory, and thirty miles from Shrewsbury. With its lake and game-filled woods and its thousand-acre park, it was the perfect base for the two or three days a week he intended to devote to the company's affairs. The only problem was the price – £30,000 – which, for a second home, was beyond his means. It was, however, well within the doctor's. Robert, who had a high regard for his brother-in-law, was happy to help, and pleased to have him back within visiting distance.

Had Robert managed the pottery, it would probably have prospered. He was a real entrepreneur, whereas Jos was merely the son of the founder. But under the family's management, and in the difficult circumstances of a war with France, its finances continued to deteriorate. Robert, operating at arm's length as the firm's auditor and financial adviser, was unable to arrest the decline; but he was at least able to persuade Jos to dispose of his Dorset estate and to involve himself in the business full-time.

The Wedgwoods and their six children moved into Maer in 1807. In the years that followed, the Darwins of the Mount and the Wedgwoods of Maer became one extended family, exchanging visits and sharing opinions and, as far as the younger members were concerned, effectively growing up together. It was at Maer, in May 1808, that the Wedgwoods' seventh and last child was born, a daughter called Emma. Nine months later, on 9 February 1809, in the comfortable surroundings of the Mount, Susannah Darwin gave birth to her fifth child and second son. She named him Charles Robert.

TWO

A Golden Childhood

———◆•◆———

Fifteen months after Charles was born, Susannah Darwin gave birth to her sixth and last child, a daughter called Catherine. The family now consisted of the three older girls, Marianne, Caroline and Susan, their brother Erasmus known at home as Eras and the babies, Charles and Catherine. Susannah was often unwell and when she was well her other duties limited the time she could spend with the children. Much of the responsibility for Charles and Catherine fell upon the older girls. It was a childhood full of affection. Charles was doted on by his older sisters, to whom he was their little Bobby. When the time came for him and Catherine to begin their education, Caroline became their teacher. When lessons were over, if the weather was fine, there were the gardens to play in and on the side of the house, overlooking the river, there was a terrace walk with a chestnut tree in which Charles and Catherine had their own special seats. For the older girls life was brightened by visits to, and by, their Wedgwood cousins.

This happy life continued for several years. Occasionally, there were trips farther afield. One such excursion took place in 1816, when Susannah and the two older girls – Marianne, seventeen, and Caroline, fifteen – joined the Wedgwoods for a fortnight in Bath, which was then at the height of its reputation as a fashionable resort. It was the last holiday the girls and their mother took together. In March 1817 Robert ended a letter to Jos with the words, 'Your sister sends her love. I am sorry to say that she has been indifferent of late.' Four months later she was dead.

Robert was inconsolable. They had been childhood playmates, and they had been married for twenty-one years. He had learned from his father a habit of not talking about sad feelings. In his pain, alone with the children and the servants in the home which he and Susannah had created together, he could not bear to talk about her. The children, out of consideration for his feelings, did not talk about her either. They all, father and children alike, carried their grief inside them. For Robert it was almost more than he could bear. Susannah's death brought back memories of earlier losses. His own mother had died when he was four. When he was twelve, his eldest brother, who was a medical student in Edinburgh, had died from an infection caught while dissecting a child's brain. When he was thirty-three, his other brother – the one who had accompanied him to Shrewsbury on that summer day in 1786 – had drowned himself. And now his childhood friend and life companion had been taken from him.

He coped with his grief in the only way he knew: by

throwing himself even more strenuously into his work. He was a compulsive care-giver. He felt the pain and unhappiness of others, and he took his responsibilities seriously. Some of his patients lived fifty miles away and it was not unusual for him to be away for fifteen hours at a stretch. In cases of serious illness, he would stay overnight, sometimes for several nights in succession. When he was at home, mealtimes could be a trial. He was a pleasant, good-hearted man, with a store of practical wisdom and any number of amusing stories, and his company was valued by his contemporaries. But he had got used to being listened to and young people found his need to be in control of conversation oppressive. Now, with only the children for company, his monologues would sometimes go on for an hour or more. The strain of listening was made greater by his soft, high-pitched voice, which was in such contrast to his massive frame, and by the stammer he had inherited from his father. An unfortunate consequence for the older girls was that they saw less of their Wedgwood cousins, who no longer looked forward to visits to Shrewsbury in the way they had when their aunt had been there to ease the strain.

For the eight-year-old Charles one consequence of his mother's death was an increase in the attention he received from his sisters. The tenderness persisted, but there was now a constant pressure towards diligence and good behaviour: understandable in sisters forced into a parental role, but irksome to a growing boy.

Charles's brother Eras was a boarder at the boys' school in the town, leaving him with no male company near his own age.

Whenever he could, he would escape into the garden to enjoy the company of old Abberley, the gardener. He also spent long, happy hours on the riverbank, fishing, and got into a habit of solitary walks.

When Robert was at home, he liked to share his love of plants with Charles. Some of the plants in the garden had belonged to his father, and he took pleasure in showing them off to his own son in turn. When the weather was bad, Charles would immerse himself in a book from his father's library. Sometimes Robert would take him with him on his rounds. It must have been a tight squeeze, given the doctor's size, and the fact that the sulky, as the little carriage was called, was only meant for one. But he took pleasure in the boy's company, and Charles was happy chatting about his childish interests as they rode along and listening to his father's stories.

These visits with his father introduced him to a wide variety of households. Many of the doctor's more distant patients were well-to-do; but he had others in the poorer part of the town, almost on his own doorstep. Some of these could not have afforded his fees, had he charged them. He treated them nonetheless, and he preserved their dignity by making them pay for the bottles in which their medicines were dispensed. In the very poorest houses, his coachman would sometimes cross the threshold first, to ensure that the floor was strong enough to bear his weight.

Shortly before his tenth birthday, Charles joined Eras as a boarder at Shrewsbury School. Originally founded in the sixteenth century, the school was now housed in a new building in the town centre, about a mile from the Darwins' front door. Its pupils were mostly drawn from the gentry of the surrounding district. Unlike his brother, who was fourteen and happy to remain in school, Charles would run home when lessons were over to spend an hour or two with his sisters. The delights of these hours away from the school were given an added spice by the small margin of time he would allow himself for the run back, which had to be accomplished before the evening bell if punishment were to be avoided.

The curriculum at Shrewsbury School was a traditional one, based almost wholly on Latin and Greek. For the young Charles it held no attractions, and he did the minimum amount of work needed to keep him out of trouble. His enthusiasm was reserved for natural history. He was passionately interested in beetles and insects, and around this time he discovered the joy of bird watching. He read that most famous of British natural history books, the Rev. Gilbert White's *Natural History of Selborne*, published twenty years before he was born; and as he later wrote, 'I could not understand why every gentleman was not an ornithologist.'

Charles was devoted to his older brother; and as he approached his teens, the four-year gap between them mattered less. When he was eleven, they rode forty miles into Wales to see the famous waterfall of Pistyll Rhaeadr. The following year they crossed North Wales, in the company of two of their Wedgwood cousins, to see Thomas Telford's great suspension bridge which was being built across the Menai Straits, a ten-day journey of 255 miles. Telford's career as a road-builder had actually begun in Shrewsbury, as surveyor of public works to the county of Shropshire in the year that Robert Darwin had set up in practice there; and the Holyhead Road, which the bridge was being built to carry, was one of the many projects in which the doctor was an investor.

Later that summer, with Caroline and Catherine, Charles and Eras paid a visit to Woodhouse, thirteen miles north of Shrewsbury, as guests of the Owen family. William Owen was a friend of the doctor, and one of his greatest admirers. Like many Shropshire gentlemen, he was also in debt to him. He had a large and rather raucous family, of a similar age to the Darwins. For the latter, the liveliness and freedom of Woodhouse made it a welcome change from the more restrained atmosphere of the Mount. Charles and Erasmus were young men of considerable charm and easy, courteous manners, and they were welcome guests. For Charles, in particular, Woodhouse was to become, like the Wedgwood house at Maer, a home from home: full of young company – including pretty female company – and offering the companionship of an older man who could give him what his own father could not.

Despite his size, Robert Darwin was an active and agile man, but he abhorred sport. As Charles moved through his teens, shooting became an obsession. The gardens at the Mount remained a delight, but the only weapon which could safely be deployed there was a catapult. Woodhouse and Maer, on the other hand, were extensive properties, abounding in rabbits and hares, and generously stocked with pheasants and partridges. For a teenager discovering the joy of killing things, and the challenge of the skill required, they were a paradise. Uncle Jos and William Owen – keen sportsmen both – were his heroes, and they in turn came to treat him almost as another son. Of the fever which shooting aroused in him in his teens, he was later to write:

> I do not believe that anyone could have shown more zeal for the most holy cause than I did for shooting birds. How well I remember killing my first snipe, and my excitement was so great that I had much difficulty in reloading my gun from the trembling of my hands.

Who was, and who was not, permitted to pursue game was one of the great social classifiers in nineteenth-century England, and Charles's liberty to indulge his passion for shooting placed him firmly in the ranks of the rich and privileged. For the poor, the taking of game was a perilous activity. In the late 1820s and early 1830s about one in every seven of all criminal convictions in England were under the Game Laws which underwrote the property rights of the landed gentry. Under the Game Law of 1816 a cottager taking a hare or a rabbit could be transported for seven years; and as these same gentry were, in their capacity as magistrates, the enforcers of the law, clemency was not to be expected.

A picture of life in the hunting and shooting classes is given in a letter written by a young New York woman, Anna Maria Fay, later in the century, reproduced in a book called *Victorian Days in England*. Describing the dinner table conversation at another Shropshire house, Moor Park, where she was visiting her uncle, she said:

I cannot imagine what English country gentlemen would do were there no poachers. Mention the word and you set Mr Betton off . . . He enlarges upon the villainy of poachers, the ingratitude of poachers, tells anecdotes about poachers, until you grow so nervous that you expect to see a poacher start up and seize the bird upon your plate. Naturally, the conversation turns upon the day's sport, and you hear . . . how many cock pheasants were shot, how many hen pheasants were deprived of life . . . whose cock pheasant fell with his tail up, whose hen pheasant fell with her tail down . . . Then the meet of the previous day takes its turn – who fell in leaping over this hurdle, who in taking that hedge . . . where the fox was found, and where killed . . . how cold it was, how cold it is, and how cold it is going to be . . . and then you rise from the table and you leave the gentlemen to discuss poaching, shooting, hunting, and the cold, unrestrained by female company. After a while they come into the drawing-room and the card-table is taken out, the gentlemen cut to play and the rest look on. They are not a very intellectual set, these country gentlemen, but they are very sociable and pleasant.

Conversation at the Wedgwood and Owen dinner tables was, presumably, more varied than this; but the picture drawn by this visiting American makes it easy to understand the distaste with which Robert regarded the possibility that his younger son might become, in his words, 'an idle sporting man'.

The thought that he would one day be rich enough to live this sort of life had not yet occurred to Charles. It was not something the doctor was going to point out. His own wealth had not made him idle, and he had no wish to encourage idleness in his son. His thoughts therefore turned to the question of what that son's future was to be. It was clear that he was wasting his time at school. It may have been around this time that Robert delivered himself of the exasperated comment which Charles recalled years later, when setting down his recollections for his own children: 'You care for nothing but shooting, dogs and rat-catching; and you will be a disgrace to yourself and all your family.'

In the summer following his sixteenth birthday, Charles again accompanied his father on his rounds, and this time Robert gave him some patients of his own. Impressed with the way he handled his cases, his father concluded that he had the makings of a good physician. It was a convenient discovery. Charles's brother Erasmus was already on his way to qualifying as a doctor. He had graduated from Cambridge, and was going to Edinburgh for six months of hospital training. If Charles were to accompany him, several problems would be solved. He would no longer be kicking his heels at school; he would not be exposed to idle sporting temptations; he would have the prospect of a respectable career; and he would be under the watchful eye of a responsible older brother.

Charles was not convinced of his suitability for the career

his father had chosen for him, but he was in no position to refuse. And his father had one final, clinching argument. With a whimsical irony, which belied the dour image some people had of him, he ended the discussion with the observation that, 'It will at least give the wild life of these parts a chance to replenish their numbers.'

THREE

False Starts

———•—◆—•———

The city in which the sixteen-year-old Charles and the twenty-year-old Erasmus found themselves in October 1825 was unlike anything they had known before. Their home town of Shrewsbury and the city of Cambridge where Erasmus had passed the previous three years were both places of consequence, but neither held much more than 20,000 people. Edinburgh was a bustling metropolis, with a population of 150,000. Architecturally, it was two cities in one. Around the Castle Mound was the Old Town, with its winding alleyways and tall tenement blocks. Below it was the elegant New Town, with its public gardens and fine houses. Charles and Eras found themselves a comfortable apartment, four floors up in the Old Town, and set about exploring their new surroundings. Their father and their grandfather had been medical students there; and they came armed with introductions which ensured that they did not go short of either dinner invitations or help with making the most of the city's attractions.

Two well-to-do young men, alone together in such circumstances, might well have gone wild but, as the doctor had hoped, they were a good influence on one another. They enjoyed evenings at the theatre, but their principal recreations were wandering about the town and reading, either in local hostelries or by their own fireside. They enrolled for a few courses, but such studies as they embarked upon were neither strenuous nor systematic. In Charles's case, any temptation he might have felt to apply himself more seriously was dissolved by a discovery he made early on, a discovery that was, for him personally, one of the most important of his whole life.

Two months after their arrival in Edinburgh Erasmus came of age and came into his share of his mother's marriage settlement. Until then, Charles had not had cause to think about the wealth which underpinned the spacious way of life he took for granted. But it now dawned upon him that, as he later wrote in his *Autobiography*, 'my father would leave me enough property to subsist on with some comfort', a realization which, in his own words, 'was sufficient to check any strenuous effort to learn medicine'. And any interest he retained in a medical career evaporated when he witnessed, and fled from, two very bad operations which were carried out, as his grandfather Josiah's had been forty years before, without the benefit of chloroform.

He found the lectures almost as distasteful as the practical demonstrations. Those in geology were so tedious that he formed a resolution 'never to read a book on geology, or in any way to study the science'. The only lectures which held any interest for him were those in chemistry, which revived the enthusiasm for the subject which he and Erasmus had shared as boys, when they had their own expensively furnished laboratory in a garden shed at home.

But if his formal education languished, his self-education proceeded apace. He read widely, and he pursued his interest in natural history. Erasmus left Edinburgh in March, but Charles stayed on until the end of April, for the conclusion of the chemistry course. In May he was back at the Mount, with one thought uppermost in his mind: how to avoid confronting his father with the impossibility of a medical career. As the summer progressed, he used one excuse after another to keep out of his father's way. In June he went on a walking tour in Wales with two friends of his own age. In August he escaped to Maer ten days before the shooting season began. And when his stay at Maer ended, it was the turn of the Owens at Woodhouse to provide him with sport and an excuse to be away from home.

When he looked back in later life, these two houses shone like beacons out of his student years, and the memory of the happiness he found there during six long summers never left him. It was not only the shooting, and the company of these two older men, with whom he had so much in common, and who held him in such high regard. Equally important were the hours spent among young people of high spirits and sociable dispositions, which made his teens and early twenties a time of unalloyed delight. Woodhouse was the nearer, and the noisier. There something uproarious could always be relied upon. On one occasion the peppery Squire Owen, exasperated by comings

and goings in the small hours, placed a pile of crockery at the top
of the stairs in the hope of catching whoever was disturbing his
sleep. Getting up in the night, he forgot his own trap, sending
the crockery flying and waking the household, which drove his
wife into such a fit of uncontrollable laughter that he threatened
to kick her out of bed. For the teenage Charles, the lively air of
Woodhouse provided a welcome change from the more ordered
atmosphere of the Mount, and its attractions were enhanced
by the presence there of the pretty and high-spirited Fanny
Owen who became the first young woman to awaken his
admiration, when he saw her fire a shotgun without flinching
from the recoil, although it left her shoulder black and blue.
Sportswoman, tomboy and belle of every ball, she was a year
older than Charles, and they shared a very special friendship,
full of fun and tender affection. In Charles's eyes, she was, as
he wrote to a male cousin, 'the prettiest, plumpest charming
Personage that Shropshire possesses', and she was the first love
of his young life.

The atmosphere at the Wedgwood house at Maer was less
hectic. Uncle Jos was a quiet, serious-minded man. His sons
were not interested in sport, and his daughters were less naturally
boisterous than either the Owen girls or Charles's sisters. But the
happiness Charles found there in his youth led him to christen
the house 'Bliss Castle'. To quote his own description, written
many years later:

> Life there was perfectly free; the country was very pleasant
> for walking or riding; and in the evening there was much

very agreeable conversation . . . together with music. In the summer the whole family used often to sit on the steps of the old portico, with the flower garden, with here and there a fish rising or a water bird paddling about in front, and with the steep wooded bank opposite the house reflected in the lake.

The music that was such a feature of life at Maer included the piano playing of his easy-going, warm-hearted cousin Emma, who had taken lessons with Chopin. She and Fanny Owen were the same age – a few months older than Charles himself – but they were very different. Fanny was forward and flirtatious. She loved riding and fox-hunting and, when not thus engaged, her thoughts tended to run on balls and marriages. Emma was a complete contrast. She had a lively sense of humour but, like her father and brothers, she was somewhat reserved, keeping her emotions well hidden. She too liked to ride, but riding to hounds held no appeal. Sport and fashion alike meant nothing to her. So little, indeed, did she care about appearances that she had earned the childhood nickname of Little Miss Slip-Slop. She was open and affectionate, and the security of the Wedgwood money freed her from the preoccupation with marriage that was the lot of most young women of her class. She was bookish and well educated, speaking good French and passable German and Italian. She was not intellectual, and had no interest in science, but her wide reading, her travels and the conversation of the artists, writers and politicians who frequented her parents' house had expanded her mental horizons. Her friendship with Charles was one of easy, warm companionship, without the sexual frisson of his friendship with Fanny.

One outcome of the orgy of sporting activity that he engaged in during his first university summer was an improvement in his marksmanship. Hitherto his shooting had been noted more for its enthusiasm than its accuracy. A visit to an uncle, Samuel Galton, in the previous year, had provoked the comment that the birds had 'laughed at him from the trees'; but by determined application he had become a good shot, able to hold his own in the company of William Owen and Uncle Jos.

Somehow he got through to October without the dreaded confrontation with his father, and in November he was back in Edinburgh for another session of not studying to be a doctor. He was now on his own. Erasmus was in London, studying anatomy, but with no intention of ever practising medicine. Charles, alone with his guilty secret, settled down to read the books which appealed to him, and to indulge his love of natural history. He made the acquaintance of several like-minded students, and he attached himself to a couple of professors who could enlarge his knowledge and experience. He became an active member of the Plinian Society, a student body devoted to natural science. He sailed on the dredgers from the fishing village of Newhaven to study marine life at close quarters. He took lessons in taxidermy from John Edmonstone, a freed slave who had accompanied Charles Waterton on his South American explorations. During this second year at university he treated his official studies with spectacular neglect, but he was certainly not idle.

When he returned home in the summer of 1827, he was

unable to conceal the truth any longer. His sisters had enlightened their father as to his feelings about medicine, and the doctor insisted on a decision. He was not going to force any son of his to become a doctor. He had himself only become one as a result of his own father's insistence, and he still could not stand the sight of blood. He was, admittedly, disappointed. He was in his sixties, and he had been looking forward to the day when at least one son would share the burden of the practice. It seemed unlikely now that this would ever happen. But while he could understand an aversion to medicine, uselessness was something much less acceptable. Erasmus was beyond his influence, but Charles was still a minor, and he was not prepared to see his second son drift into an aimless life, if he could prevent it. Medicine was out. The Army, the Navy and the Law had never been conceivable. That left, in the doctor's eyes, only the Church.

Charles was at first no more enamoured of becoming a clergyman than he had been of becoming a doctor, and there was the problem of belief. From what little he had thought on the subject he had scruples about declaring his belief in all the dogmas of the Church of England; though otherwise he liked the thought of being a country clergyman. To enter the Church, he would need a degree from Oxford or Cambridge. To graduate from either, he would have to affirm his belief in the Thirty-Nine Articles of the Anglican faith. For the doctor, who was, like his own father, an unbeliever, such things were of no consequence. In his eyes, it was more a matter of commerce than of conscience. Many a country living was in the gift of the local squire, and many more were bought as investments by wealthy parents wishing to purchase social status, and a steady income, for their younger sons. Charles's uncle Jos had installed a nephew as vicar of Maer, and Robert's wealth could do the same for his son. England was full of fox-hunting parsons and beetle-collecting curates, and no other occupation offered so much scope for the pursuit of Charles's real interests. On reflection, it seemed a tempting prospect, and as nothing remotely as attractive was on the horizon, he set about studying the beliefs to which he would have to subscribe.

Faith was not something which had hitherto greatly exercised his mind. The whole business of religion had largely passed him by. He had taken it for granted, like the air he breathed. Now he was being asked to think about it for the first time in his life. Fortunately, none of the propositions to which he was required to assent presented an insuperable obstacle; so for the second time in his life, he reconciled himself to a vocation of his father's choosing.

The question as to which university he should attend answered itself. His grandfather Erasmus had been at Cambridge. So had his brother. A cousin, William Darwin Fox, was in residence at Christ's College, and there would always be a place there for any Darwin who could meet the university's not-very-demanding entrance requirements. This was not, however, something that he could readily do. He had forgotten his Greek, and his grasp of mathematics had always been fragile. He was therefore forced to spend the autumn with a private tutor, and it was not until January 1828, just before his nineteenth birthday, that he was able to join his cousin at Christ's College. Because of his late start, there was no room for him in the college itself, and he found lodgings nearby, until accommodation came available at the beginning of the next academic year. In October he moved into a suite of rooms which looked out on to the college's first court, and these became his home for the remainder of his time in Cambridge.

The rooms into which he moved his books and beetles in that autumn of 1828 were the very set which the renowned theologian William Paley had occupied as an undergraduate half a century earlier. Paley's *Natural Theology*, published in 1802, was one of the most influential books of the age, and candidates for the BA degree were expected to display a familiarity with its arguments. The most famous of these was the one with which the book opened: the Argument from Design. Suppose, said Paley, that someone wandering across a heath should find a watch lying in his path. He would know at once that it was a manufactured object, from the intricacy of its design. Such an object could not have arisen by chance. Design implied a designer. As it was with the watch, so it was with the natural world. Something so elaborate, so perfectly functioning, could not have been produced by the operation of aimless natural forces; there must have been a Creator.

For many educated people in the first half of the nineteenth century, this was a knock-down, drag-out argument to which there was no answer. But it did not only drive the unbelievers from the field; it also provided a justification for bug-hunters everywhere. To study nature was to study the work of Nature's

Architect. Beetle-collecting was lifted from a mere pastime almost to a religious obligation. Darwin was entranced. He found the logic irresistible, and he read Paley's book with the enthusiasm of a disciple, rather than the diligence of a student. Had he raised the matter in Shrewsbury, with his unbelieving father, he would have met with a sceptical reaction. But among his acquaintances in Cambridge there was no dissenting voice to cause him to question what he read.

The three-and-a-half years he spent in Cambridge were, in his own words, 'the most joyful in my happy life'. The academic standard expected of the general run of students was not high, and Charles behaved much as he had in Edinburgh. Natural history was still a passion, but in his second year he acquired a horse and cross-country riding came to rival beetles in his affections. He also enjoyed an active social life, characterized by convivial drinking, eating and card-playing.

One of the great glories of Cambridge University was the choral singing in the college chapels. Darwin himself was the most unmusical of men. He had so little sense of tune that he could not recognize 'God Save the King' if it were played with an unusual rhythm. But he took great pleasure in the college singing, and he would sometimes join with other students to hire choristers to sing in his rooms. In the autumn of 1829, he went with his Wedgwood cousins to a music meeting in Birmingham to hear the great soprano Malibran. His delight in the experience showed in a letter to his cousin Fox, to whom he wrote: 'nothing will do after Malibran . . . a person's heart must have been made of stone not to have lost it to her.' But he ended his letter with the words: 'It knocked me up most dreadfully, and I will never attempt again to do two things the same day.' It was a strange way for an active young man to react to a musical entertainment. It was an even stranger way for a young man to talk.

Early in his Cambridge career he made the acquaintance of the Rev. John Stevens Henslow, the thirty-three-year-old Professor of Botany. Henslow saw something exceptional in the young Darwin. They became friends, and Darwin became known as 'the man who walks with Henslow'. On Darwin's part the feeling was one of hero-worship. Out of doors he displayed a childlike enthusiasm on field trips, causing Henslow to say, more than once, 'What a fellow that Darwin is for asking questions.' Indoors, much amusement was generated in the student body by the rivalry which developed between him and another student as to who could get first into the room to set up the equipment for Henslow's lectures.

His final examinations were due in January 1831 and, as 1830 drew to a close, it dawned upon him that he was in serious danger of failing. Thanks to some last-minute cramming, and a generous amount of personal tuition from Henslow, the situation was retrieved. When the results were published, he was delighted to discover that he had been placed tenth out of 178 in the list of those not offering themselves for honours.

Although he had passed his examinations, he had not yet fulfilled the requirements for the BA degree. Because he had not gone up to Cambridge until January in his first academic year, it was necessary for him to remain in residence until June.

With many of his university friends gone, and no formal study called for, he embarked on a programme of reading for pure pleasure. In the course of this, he worked his way through two books that would profoundly influence the course of his life. The first of these was the recently published *Preliminary Discourse on the Study of Natural Philosophy*, by the astronomer John Herschel, which filled him with an ambition to make his own contribution to scientific knowledge. Even more exciting was the *Personal Narrative* of the explorer Alexander von Humboldt, describing five years of travel in South America between 1796 and 1801. Darwin had first come across this book as a teenager in his father's library. Now it absorbed him totally. He carried one or other of its seven volumes with him wherever he went. Those of his friends who remained in Cambridge got used to sitting around while he read passages aloud. Most of all, he was captivated by Humboldt's description of the island of Tenerife, and he determined to organize an expedition to the island. Such expeditions were not unusual among men of Darwin's age and class at this time. In the eighteenth century, it had been customary for Englishmen of good family to complete their education with a tour of the antiquities of Europe. Now, in this age of enthusiasm for natural history, they were travelling abroad to study the treasures of the natural world.

The plan was for Darwin and two or three friends to sail for Tenerife in July, and to spend three weeks geologizing and botanizing there. There was, however, a little matter of money to be attended to first. His student life had left him with some impressive debts, and excursions to Tenerife did not come cheap. A visit to Shrewsbury at Easter solved both problems. His father gave him a £200 note to take care of his debts, and expressed his willingness to meet the costs of the trip. Back in Cambridge, with finance assured, he applied himself to the expedition's planning and preparation with the thoroughness that characterized every enterprise that caught his imagination. He started learning Spanish, and set about enlarging his understanding of geology. Henslow was insistent that the benefit to be obtained from the expedition would be proportional to the knowledge with which Darwin was equipped before he embarked upon it. He therefore arranged for his protégé to be given a crash course by a master of the subject, Adam Sedgwick, Professor of Geology and President of the Geological Society of London. Sedgwick was planning a visit to North Wales to clear up some problems relating to the geology of the region. On Henslow's recommendation he offered to take Darwin along as his assistant and pupil.

At this point Darwin discovered that transport to Tenerife was only available in the month of June, which left insufficient time to make the necessary arrangements. His expedition would have to be postponed until the following year. There was, however, no reason why he should not accompany Sedgwick to North Wales. He was determined to acquit himself well; and the student who had once resolved 'never to read a book on geology again', and who had not attended any of Sedgwick's very popular lectures, now, in his own words, 'worked like a tiger at geology' during the month of July.

They set off from the Mount in Sedgwick's gig on 5 August,

and spent a week working their way across North Wales. In the field they travelled on parallel routes, meeting in the evenings to compare notes and record their findings. Day by day, Darwin's pleasure and self-confidence increased, as Sedgwick praised the quality of his work and explained the significance of his findings. Towards the end of the trip he explored the wild mountain valley of Cwm Idwal, where he spent several hours examining the rocks for fossils. Situated only a mile from the new Holyhead Road, where it cut through the heart of Snowdonia, Cwm Idwal was a geological textbook in itself. Hanging valleys and glacial moraines surrounded him on every hand. But in the state of knowledge at that time, it was a text he was unable to see, let alone understand. Recalling that day many years later, but forgetting that Sedgwick had not been there, he said:

> . . . neither of us saw a trace of the . . . glacial phenomena all around us . . . the plainly scored rocks, the perched boulders, the lateral and terminal moraines . . . a house burnt down by fire did not tell its story more plainly than did this valley. If it had still been filled with a glacier, the phenomena would have been less distinct than they now are.

Unaware of the geological treasures that had been within his grasp, and having parted with Sedgwick, who had business in Dublin, Darwin now embarked on a geological excursion of his own devising, crossing some of the wildest and loneliest mountain country in Britain. Using map and compass, and noting rock formations as he went, he headed for the little fishing village of Barmouth to join a reading party of his university friends.

The next two weeks would have passed all too quickly, and the temptation to linger must have been strong. His moment of truth was approaching. He had an understanding with his father that he was to enter the Church, and if he returned home, further procrastination would be impossible. But, as always, the call of sport outweighed other considerations. The first day of September was the start of the shooting season. With luck, he would be able to collect his gun and escape to Maer, without getting involved in a discussion about his future.

When he arrived home on the evening of 29 August, there was a package waiting for him, bearing a London postmark. Its contents left his brain reeling.

FOUR

Enter Fitzroy

———— ◆ ————

The package which awaited the twenty-two-year-old Darwin on that August evening contained two letters. One was in Henslow's familiar handwriting:

Cambridge, 24 August 1831

My Dear Darwin,

. . . I shall hope to see you shortly, fully expecting that you will eagerly catch at the offer which is likely to be made you of a trip to Tierra del Fuego, and home by the East Indies. I have been asked by Peacock . . . to recommend him a naturalist as companion to Captain Fitz-Roy, employed by Government to survey the southern extremity of America. I have stated that I consider you to be the best qualified person I know of who is likely to undertake such a situation. I state this not in the supposition of your being a finished naturalist, but as amply qualified for collecting, observing, and noting, anything worthy to be noted in Natural History . . .

Captain Fitz-Roy wants a man (I understand) more as a companion than a mere collector, and would not take any one, however good a naturalist, who was not recommended to him likewise as a *gentleman* . . . The voyage is to last two years, and if you take plenty of books with you, anything you please may be done . . . Don't put on any modest doubts or fears about your disqualifications, for I assure you I think you are the very man they are in search of . . . your affectionate friend

J.S. HENSLOW

The expedition is to sail on 25th September (at earliest) so there is no time to be lost.

Henslow's letter was accompanied by a covering letter from one of his Cambridge colleagues – the mathematician George Peacock – who was a great friend of Captain Fitzroy:

My Dear Sir,
I received Henslow's letter last night too late to forward it to you by the post; a circumstance which I do not regret, as it has given me an opportunity of seeing Captain Beaufort at the Admiralty (the Hydrographer), and of stating to him the offer which I have to make to you. He entirely approves of it, and you may consider the situation as at your absolute disposal . . .

Captain Fitz-Roy (a nephew of the Duke of Grafton) sails at the end of September, in a ship to survey, in the first instance, the South Coast of Tierra del Fuego, afterwards to visit the South Sea Islands, and to return by the Indian Archipelago to England. The expedition is entirely for scientific purposes, and the ship will generally wait your leisure for researches in Natural History, etc. Captain Fitz-Roy is a public-spirited and zealous officer, of delightful manners, and greatly beloved by all his brother officers . . . You may be sure, therefore, of having a very pleasant companion, who will enter heartily into all your views.

The ship sails about the end of September, and you must lose no time in making known your acceptance to Captain Beaufort. I have had a good deal of correspondence about this matter [with Henslow] who feels, in common with myself, the greatest anxiety that you should go . . .

Believe me, my dear Sir,

Very truly yours,

GEORGE PEACOCK

For the young Darwin, there was only one possible response. From his early schooldays, when he had first read another boy's copy of *The Wonders of the World*, he had longed to travel in remote countries. Now he was being offered a chance to emulate his hero Humboldt, combining exotic travel with scientific discovery. If it was a choice between a country parsonage and a round-the-world trip as a naturalist, there was no contest. He went to bed with his mind made up to accept. But he woke to

41

the reality of his situation: he was not in a position to accept any such offer without his father's approval.

When he came downstairs, his sisters had already briefed the doctor, and Robert was ready with his answer. In his opinion, it was a madcap scheme: a frivolous distraction from the career already decided upon. Charles was bitterly disappointed. But even if he had been temperamentally capable of defying his father, he lacked the financial independence to make defiance possible. With a heavy heart, he sat down to compose a letter to Peacock, declining the invitation. That done, he wrote to Henslow, explaining his reasons:

> Shrewsbury, Tuesday [30 August 1831]
>
> My Dear Sir,
>
> Mr Peacock's letter arrived on Saturday, 27th and I received it late yesterday evening. As far as my own mind is concerned, I should, I think *certainly*, most gladly have accepted the opportunity which you so kindly have offered me. But my father, although he does not decidedly refuse me, gives such strong advice against going, that I should not be comfortable if I did not follow it . . .
>
> Yours most sincerely,
>
> My dear Sir,
>
> CH. DARWIN

The following morning he got ready to go to Maer. Before he left, his father, conscious of his son's disappointment, added a rider to his previous day's refusal. If Charles could find 'any man of common sense' who thought he should go, he would give his consent. He also enclosed a note on the matter with a prescription Jos had requested.

Charles knew that one man above all others fitted the description of a 'man of common sense' in his father's eyes. As soon as he reached Maer, he unburdened himself to his uncle and to his Wedgwood cousins. They were united in their opinion: he must accept. Emboldened by their reaction, he penned a last desperate appeal to his father, enclosing a letter of support from Jos:

> My Dear Father,
> I am afraid I am going to make you again very uncomfort-
> able. But, upon consideration, I think you will excuse me
> once again, stating my opinions on the offer of the voyage.
> My excuse and reason is the different way all the Wedg-
> woods view the subject from what you and my sisters do.
> I have given Uncle Jos what I fervently trust is an accu-
> rate and full list of your objections, and he is kind enough
> to give his opinions on all . . . may I beg of you one favour,
> it will be doing me the greatest kindness, if you will send
> me a decided answer, yes or no? If the latter, I should be
> most ungrateful if I did not implicitly yield to your better
> judgement, and to the kindest indulgence you have shown
> me all through my life; and you may rely upon it I will
> never mention the subject again . . . The danger appears
> to me and all the Wedgwoods not great. The expense can
> not be serious, and time I do not think, anyhow, would
> be more thrown away than if I stayed at home. But pray

do not consider that I am so bent on going that I would for one *single moment* hesitate, if you thought that after a short period you should continue uncomfortable . . .
Believe me, my dear father,
Your affectionate son,
CHARLES DARWIN

He had listed his father's objections:

1 Disreputable to my character as a Clergyman hereafter.
2 A wild scheme.
3 That they must have offered to many others before me the place of Naturalist.
4 And from its not being accepted there must be some serious objection to the vessel or expedition.
5 That I should never settle down to a steady life hereafter.
6 That my accommodations would be most uncomfortable.
7 That you [i.e. Dr Darwin] should consider it as again changing my profession.
8 That it would be a useless undertaking.

Jos had addressed himself to each objection in turn:

My Dear Doctor,
I feel the responsibility of your application to me on the offer that has been made to Charles as being weighty, but as you have desired Charles to consult me, I cannot refuse to give the result of such consideration as I have been able

to [give] it. Charles has put down what he conceives to be your principal objections, and I think the best course I can take will be to state what occurs to me upon each of them.

1   I should not think that it would be in any degree disreputable to his character as a Clergyman. I should on the contrary think the offer honourable to him; and the pursuit of Natural History, though certainly not professional, is very suitable to a clergyman.

2   I hardly know how to meet this objection, but he would have definite objects upon which to employ himself, and might acquire and strengthen habits of application, and I should think would be as likely to do so as in any way in which he is likely to pass the next two years at home.

3   The notion did not occur to me in reading the letters; and on reading them again with that object in my mind I see no ground for it.

4   I cannot conceive that the Admiralty would send out a bad vessel on such a service. As to objections to the expedition, they will differ in each man's case, and nothing would, I think, be inferred in Charles's case, if it were known that others had objected.

5   You are a much better judge of Charles's character than I can be. If on comparing this mode of spending the next two years with the way in which he will probably spend them, if he does not accept this offer, you think him more likely to be rendered unsteady and unable to

settle it is undoubtedly a weighty objection. Is it not the case that sailors are prone to settle in domestic and quiet habits?

6 I can form no opinion on this further than that if appointed by the Admiralty he will have a claim to be as well accommodated as the vessel will allow.

7 If I saw Charles now absorbed in professional studies I should probably think it would not be advisable to interrupt him. His present pursuit of knowledge is in the same track as he would have to follow in the expedition.

8 The undertaking would be useless as regards his profession, but looking upon him as a man of enlarged curiosity, it affords him such an opportunity of seeing men and things as happens to few.

You will bear in mind that I have had very little time for consideration, and that you and Charles are the persons who must decide.

I am,

My dear Doctor,

Affectionately yours,

JOSIAH WEDGWOOD

The letters went off in a carriage the next morning, and Charles was out early, to vent his anxiety on the bird life of Maer. At ten o'clock, when he had just shot his first partridge, a servant brought a message from his uncle Jos, offering to drive him to Shrewsbury. By the time they arrived Robert had read their letters and was ready to withdraw his opposition.

What had promised to be a fraught debate became a discussion of ways and means. Charles's contribution to the discussion was the observation that he would be deuced clever to overspend his allowance while at sea. His father, with his son's overspending at Cambridge fresh in his mind, replied, 'But they tell me you are very clever.' In this exchange – as in Charles's earlier comment that 'the expense can not be serious' – can be heard the authentic voice of the indulged child, and the relaxed response of the wealthy parent, for whom the cost of a two-or-three-year voyage around the world was a minor consideration.

But having refused the invitation, was he now too late to accept? Snatching a few hours sleep, he was up again at three a.m. to catch the express coach to London, which took him to within fifty miles of Cambridge. Hiring carriages for these last fifty miles, he arrived late that same night. From his hotel he wrote a quick note to Henslow:

My Dear Sir,

I am just arrived; you will guess the reason. My father has changed his mind. I trust the place is not given away. I am very much fatigued, and am going to bed. I dare say you have not yet got my second letter. How soon shall I come to you in the morning?

Send a verbal answer.

Good night,

Yours,

C. DARWIN

The next two days were spent with Henslow. From him, he learned that the invitation had previously been extended to another Cambridge man, a married clergyman, who had had his bags packed before deciding that he could not desert his family. He learned too that Henslow himself had been close to accepting, and that his wife had given her consent, but that she had looked so miserable that he had decided against going.

By now Darwin's mind was in a whirl: one moment desperate to go, the next, fearful of the implications of such a journey. Uncertain of the outcome, he wrote to his sister Susan: 'Tell nobody in Shropshire yet . . . in case I should not go, it will make it more flat.' But twenty-four hours later, and only three days after leaving home, he was writing to her from his London lodgings, next door to the Admiralty, all caution cast aside, and semi-literate in his excitement:

> . . . Captain Fitzroy is [in] town, and I have seen him; it is no use trying to praise him as much as I feel inclined to do, for you would not believe me . . .
>
> We stop a week at [the] Madeira Islands, and shall see most of [the] big cities in South America. Captain Beaufort is drawing up the track through the South Sea . . . There is indeed a tide in the affairs of man, and I have experienced it, and I had entirely given it up till one today.

Writing to Henslow, his excitement bubbled over:

> *Gloria in Excelsis* is the most moderate beginning I

can think of . . . Captain Fitzroy is everything that is delightful . . . Till one today I was building castles in the air about hunting foxes in Shropshire, now llamas in South America.

Darwin was not the only person pleased with the outcome. Fitzroy also had every reason to be delighted at the way things had turned out; although, as befitted the twenty-six-year-old nephew of a duke – and a hardened sailor – he was less puppy-dog-like in his enthusiasm. The truth of the matter was that he was desperate to find a congenial companion. With only three weeks to the expected date of departure, it was unlikely that he would find anyone else who was both acceptable to him and able to commit to such a voyage. But the prospect of setting out without a companion was one he did not care to contemplate. The position of captain of a man-of-war was a lonely one in any circumstances. The responsibilities were great, and a distance had to be kept between a captain and his junior officers. But the strains of this expedition were likely to be exceptional. The ship was going to be away for a long time, and some of that time was going to be spent in the most inhospitable seas in the world. The *Beagle*'s previous commander had shot himself, and died a slow and painful death in those same waters. As if this were not enough, there was the shadow of an uncle, Viscount Castlereagh, who had slit his throat in a fit of depression. It must have been with enormous relief that he made the acquaintance of the modest, gentlemanly, cheerful Darwin on that September day.

Late that evening, while Darwin was writing his ecstatic

letters to Henslow and to his sister Susan, Fitzroy was recording his own reactions in a letter to Captain Beaufort at the Admiralty:

> I have seen a good deal of Mr Darwin, today having had nearly two hours' conversation in the morning and having since dined with him.
>
> I like what I see and hear of him, much, and I now request that you will apply for him to accompany me as a Naturalist. I can and will make him comfortable on board more so perhaps than you or he would expect, and I will contrive to stow away his goods and chattels of all kinds and give him a workshop.
>
> Upon consideration, I feel confident that he will have a much wider field for his exertions than I was inclined to anticipate on Friday last.

The following day was the coronation of King William IV, and Darwin paid for a seat to watch the procession. When the shops reopened, he confirmed his commitment to the voyage by buying a rifle, a telescope and a compass. Twenty-four hours later, he and Fitzroy boarded the steam packet bound for Plymouth to inspect the vessel which he expected to be his home for the next three years.

These three days at sea provided an opportunity for the two men to get to know one another in circumstances similar to those that would apply on the voyage. They also gave Darwin a chance to learn more about the expedition, and about the background of its commander. Fitzroy was a descendant of King Charles II and his mistress Barbara Villiers. His father had been a professional soldier and had finished up a general. In addition to his uncle the duke, and the cabinet minister Castlereagh, he had a third uncle who had served in the naval battle of the Glorious First of June, and risen to be an admiral. Fitzroy himself had been a star pupil at the Royal Naval College, winning a Gold Medal and becoming the first student to obtain full marks in all his examinations. In 1828, when he was still only twenty-three, he had been appointed captain of the *Beagle*, one of two ships engaged in a survey of the West Coast of South America. He had continued the survey, often in appalling conditions, for a further two years, before returning to England in September 1830. Twelve months later, and still only twenty-six, he was preparing his ship for a return visit.

The story of how this second voyage had come about was one that Darwin must have found intriguing. While surveying the coast of Tierra del Fuego, one of Fitzroy's whaleboats had been stolen. In the course of an expedition to recover it, he had taken three Fuegians hostage, in the mistaken belief that this would result in its return. He had later 'acquired' a fourth, for reasons never clearly explained, in a transaction involving a quantity of buttons and beads, as a result of which the unfortunate native had been christened Jemmy Button. It had then occurred to Fitzroy that his captives might be made to serve a Higher Purpose. He was an intensely religious young man, for whom there could be no worthier enterprise than to aid the spread of Christianity to places where it was still unknown. He accordingly resolved to take his prisoners back to England, to educate them and to return them as missionaries to their own people. He had written to his commanding officer, Captain King, explaining:

Beagle, at sea, 12 September 1830

SIR,

I have the honour of reporting to you that there are now on board of Her Majesty's Sloop, under my command, four natives of Tierra del Fuego.

Their names and estimated ages are:

York Minster 26
Boat Memory 20
James Button 14
Fuegia Basket (a girl) 9

I have maintained them entirely at my own expense, and hold myself responsible for their comfort while away from, and their safe return to, their own country: and I have now to request that, as senior officer of the expedition, you will consider of the possibility, of some public advantage being derived from this circumstance; and of the propriety of offering them, with that view, to His Majesty's Government . . .

They have lived, and have been clothed, like the seamen, and are now, and have been always, in excellent health and very happy. They understand why they were taken, and look forward with pleasure to seeing our country, as well as returning to their own.

Should not His Majesty's Government direct otherwise, I shall procure for these people a suitable education, and after two or three years, shall send or take them back to their country, with as large a stock as I can collect of those articles . . . most likely to improve the condition of their countrymen, who are now scarcely superior to the brute creation.

ROBERT FITZROY

Captain King had forwarded this letter to the Secretary of the Admiralty, and had received the following reply:

Admiralty Office, 19 October 1830

SIR,

Having laid before my Lords Commissioners of the Admiralty your letter and its enclosure from Commander Fitzroy, of the Beagle, relative to the four Indians whom he had brought from Tierra del Fuego . . . I am . . . to acquaint you that their Lordships will not interfere with Commander Fitzroy's personal superintendence of, or benevolent intentions towards, these four people, but they will afford him any facilities towards maintaining and educating them in England, and will give them a passage home again.

JOHN BARROW

On reaching England, the Fuegians had been placed in the care of a schoolmaster in London. One of them, Boat Memory, had died within weeks as the result of a smallpox vaccination, but the others had thrived. They had been taught English, the elements of Christianity, and basic skills – such as gardening and the use of simple tools – of a kind thought likely to be of use on their return. They had also been presented at Court.

Fitzroy had hoped that the South American survey would be continued, but when he had learned that this was unlikely to happen, he had become anxious about the return of his protégés. He had accordingly chartered a ship, at his own expense, to take himself and five companions, plus the Fuegians and a number of goats, back to South America. But a conversation with his naval uncle, who was in a position to exert influence at the Admiralty, had resulted in his being commissioned, not only to carry out a further survey, but to do so in his old ship, the *Beagle*.

All of this was familiar to Darwin by the time they reached Plymouth. But nothing he had heard had prepared him for the shock that awaited him in the naval dockyard in nearby Devonport. The *Beagle* was a ten-gun brig, not a pleasure cruiser, and naval vessels in 1831 were designed as fighting machines, not as mobile homes for itinerant naturalists. The ship was a mere ninety feet long by thirty feet wide. Within these dimensions room had to be found for ten guns and their ammunition; surveying equipment and chronometers; working space – and sleeping space – for sixty-five officers and crew, plus nine supernumeraries; and food and drinking water for seventy-four people for several months at a time. For someone accustomed to the spaciousness of the Darwin home in Shrewsbury, the shock was severe.

There were only two cabins on the ship, the poop cabin, at

the rear end of the upper deck, and a smaller one nearby, on the deck below. To Darwin's relief, his name went up on the larger, while the smaller was taken by Fitzroy. But 'larger' in this context did not mean much. The poop cabin measured only eleven feet by ten, and much of this space was taken up by the chart table where the maps were drawn. Nor was the remaining space Darwin's alone. During the day he would be sharing the cabin with nineteen-year-old John Lort Stokes, the Assistant Surveyor (the Captain was 'Commander and Surveyor'), and a fourteen-year-old midshipman, Philip King, the son of Fitzroy's commander on the previous expedition. Darwin would be sleeping in a hammock slung above the chart table, Stokes in a cubicle just outside the cabin door, and the young midshipman below decks. Space was so restricted that the top drawer had to be removed from Darwin's clothes cabinet, so that one end of his hammock could be secured within it. His only luxury was a very small cabin for his specimens, under the forecastle. His height – close on six feet – did not help. Fortunately he had inherited only his father's height. Had he taken after his father and grandfather in his other dimensions, the situation would have been impossible. But if his initial reaction was one of dismay, it quickly wore off. Nothing could take away his excitement and delight at the prospect before him.

Three days after reaching Plymouth, with the expected sailing date fast approaching, he took the coach back to London. From London, he travelled to Cambridge, where he spent two more days picking Henslow's brains. He then returned to Shrewsbury to satisfy his sisters' curiosity, and to make his farewells, not only to his own family, but to those other families which had for so long provided him with a home-from-home. A visit to Maer was followed by a weekend with the Owens at Woodhouse, where he experienced a disappointment. Fanny, the person he would most have wished to see, had broken off a recently announced engagement and by a cruel irony had fled to Exeter, only fifty miles from where the *Beagle* was lying. Whatever words they might have exchanged that weekend would never now be spoken.

When he returned home, there was a note waiting from Fitzroy to say that sailing had been postponed by another week. He had a few precious extra days to complete his preparations and to savour the atmosphere of the childhood home that he would never experience in the same way again. On 2 October 1831 he said goodbye to his father and sisters, and walked out of the Mount. It would be five years before he saw it, or them, again.

FIVE

The Great Adventure

———————◆•◆•◆———————

He did not go straight to Devonport. He had much to learn, and most of the people who could teach him were in London. He returned to the lodgings where he had stayed four weeks earlier, close to the Admiralty. Armed with introductions from Henslow, he made daily sorties to confer with experts on the many skills he would need if he were to send his trophies home in good condition. He learned how to dry and mount plants; how to kill and preserve sea anemones and small sea creatures; how to pickle crabs; and how to pack animal skins. He went shopping for the paraphernalia of the travelling naturalist: microscope, geological hammer, barometer, specimen jars, boots, breeches. He wrote to Fitzroy, to say that, if necessary, there were two cases marked 'To be left behind'. A message came back informing him of another postponement, until 4 November.

By now, he was raring to go. Writing to Fitzroy, he said: 'I am daily more anxious to be off, and, if I am so, you must be in a perfect fever. What a glorious day the 4th of November will be to me! My second life will then commence, and it shall be as a birthday for the rest of my life.'

On 23 October, having seen his packing cases off on a coastal steamer, he took the coach to Plymouth. In Devonport he joined Fitzroy in lodgings on the quayside. There now followed several weeks of frustration, as preparations continued. Many of the ship's timbers were rotten, and it was effectively being rebuilt. To the relief of the six-foot-tall Darwin, this included replacing and raising the deck, providing welcome, if still limited, head-room below. The ship's hull was being sheathed with new two-inch fir planks. Two of its original guns had been exchanged for brass cannons to avoid interference with magnetic observations and, despite Admiralty scepticism, lightning conductors were being fitted to the masts. In a specially created room next to Fitzroy's cabin there were twenty-two chronometers, packed in sawdust, six of which he had paid for himself. Wherever Admiralty specifications fell short of what he thought necessary, he was dipping into his own pocket to fund the expense involved.

The repeated postponements affected Darwin's nerves, and his mental state showed in physical symptoms. He developed a rash around his mouth, and experienced chest pains and palpitations. Believing he had heart disease, and convinced that any request for medical advice would result in his being declared unfit for the voyage, he kept his concerns to himself. As far as his companions were aware, he remained carefree and eager to go.

On 13 November, the three natives of Tierra del Fuego arrived from London, accompanied by Richard Matthews, the young missionary who was returning with them to South America. The oldest, York Minster, was about twenty-seven, and Jemmy Button about fifteen. The girl, Fuegia Basket, was thought to be about twelve. They could all speak English. Fuegia, who was clearly very bright, spoke it fluently. Their baggage brought forth caustic comments from the crew members who had to unload it. Well-wishers, whose piety was more evident than their understanding of life in Tierra del Fuego, had laden them with 'useful' goods, including beaver hats, table napkins and whole services of china.

The next day Fitzroy moved his chronometers on board, and set up the ship's library in the poop cabin: 145 volumes, including an excellent selection of the most up-to-date scientific books. In the evening, the ship's orders arrived, containing detailed instructions for the task ahead.

The voyage had two principal objectives. The first of these was to complete the survey of the coast of southern South America which had been begun by the previous expedition, and to prepare detailed maps of the coast and the adjacent islands. This was of pressing importance. The states of the newly independent Argentinean federation were free of their centuries-old obligation to trade with Spain, and the unexplored coast of southern South America had as a result acquired great commercial and naval importance. To ensure that the survey's valuable results would not be lost through shipwreck, maps were to be drawn en route, and despatched to London as they were completed.

The survey's other principal objective was to fix the latitude and longitude of every location visited during the voyage. Maps were no use on the open ocean. Ships could only be safely navigated if their navigators knew at all times exactly where they were, and the precise latitude and longitude of the places they were heading for. It was easy to ascertain latitude – the position of a place relative to the equator – by measuring the height of the sun or stars above the horizon. The determination of longitude – position in an east–west direction – was much more difficult. It involved measuring the difference between local noon and the simultaneous time at Greenwich, and this could only be known if a ship's chronometers were set to Greenwich time, and were capable of extreme accuracy over long periods. Given that a one-minute error in timekeeping at the equator meant an error of seventeen miles in east–west distance, the performance of the *Beagle*'s chronometers was clearly going to be a crucial factor in the success or failure of its mission.

The extreme busyness of everyone around him reminded Darwin just how irrelevant he was to the real purposes of the expedition. He was the Captain's travelling companion, not a member of the crew. He had no official role. The advantages of this arrangement were considerable. He was not under orders, and he was free to leave the ship, and make his own way home, at any stage of the voyage. Equally important, any specimens he collected were his property, to dispose of as he pleased. It was to ensure his independence that his father had declined to pursue the possibility of his being paid a salary out of Admiralty funds. Darwin was sure that observing and collecting would keep him fully occupied once he was at sea; but at this stage there really was little he could do, other than try to keep out of the way. He did his best to look occupied by repeatedly re-arranging his belongings. Writing to Henslow, he said: 'My chief employment is to go on board the *Beagle*, and try to look as much like a sailor as I can. I have no evidence of having taken in man, woman or child.'

His 'birthday' continued to recede into the future. On 5 December a gale pinned them down for four days. On the 10th Fitzroy gave the order to hoist sail, and the frustration of the past weeks was forgotten as the crew leapt into action. As the ship sailed into the Channel, Darwin's suffering began. The breakfast he had eaten disappeared over the side. Every attempt to eat produced the same reaction. By evening the seas were mountainous. The next morning Fitzroy gave the order to turn back. On 21 December he made another attempt – and ran aground. By the time the ship was free, another gale had struck.

Christmas Day found them still in harbour. For all the crew knew, it might be the last Christmas they would ever see. They decided to make it a memorable one. They came back on board drunk and obstreperous. On Boxing Day the weather conditions were perfect. The condition of the crew was somewhat less than perfect. Some were in irons, and many were unfit to man their posts. Darwin noted in his diary: 'the ship has been all day in a state of anarchy . . . Several have paid the penalty for insolence, by sitting for eight or nine hours in heavy chains.' And in an unconscious comment on the advantages of being born into the officer class, he added: 'Dined in the gun-room & had a pleasant evening.'

Fortunately, 27 December was another fine day. At eleven a.m., the *Beagle* weighed anchor. While the crew guided the vessel towards the open sea, Fitzroy and Darwin dined on mutton chops and champagne on the Harbour Commissioner's yacht. At two o'clock they joined the ship. Darwin studied the disappearing coastline, and congratulated himself on retaining his lunch.

His self-satisfaction did not last long. As they sailed into the Atlantic, seasickness overwhelmed him. Helpless in his hammock, he listened to the screams outside his cabin, as the Christmas Day revellers took their punishment. Fitzroy was a just and caring commander, but he was unflinching in the administration of the discipline necessary to preserve good order. It was going to be a long voyage, and he was determined that a memorable example would be set at the outset. His log recorded the pain inflicted:

Elias Davis: 31 lashes for reported neglect of duty
David Russel: 34 lashes for breaking his leave and dis-
                         obeying orders
James Phipps: 44 lashes for breaking his leave, drunken-
                         ness and insolence

Darwin had expected his first day at sea to be a day to remember. It was turning out to be one he would rather forget.

In the next nine days he enjoyed only one afternoon free

of seasickness. Fitzroy watched over him like a brother. On Darwin's one good day, he read to him in his own cabin. On one of Darwin's worst days, Fitzroy arranged his hammock with his own hands: an act which, when reported back to Shrewsbury, brought tears to the doctor's eyes.

At last, on 5 January, he began to feel better. When he came on deck, the weather was warm, and there was a gentle swell on the sea. The English winter was 1,300 miles behind him. Tenerife was a mere hundred miles ahead. The landfall he had dreamed about as a student was about to be realized. Or so he thought. But he had forgotten the cholera raging behind them in England. As they prepared to drop anchor, the harbour-master's boat came alongside to inform them that they must perform a rigorous quarantine of twelve days. Fitzroy would have none of it. He ordered all sail to be set and a course made for the Cape Verde Islands.

Darwin's disappointment at not visiting Tenerife was soon forgotten. Light winds and a gentle sea gave his stomach a rest. He was able to take an interest in his surroundings, and to begin the work he had come to do. He made a plankton net and trailed it behind the ship. It yielded a fascinating haul of sea creatures for him to study.

The ship's company was now in tropical clothing, and in the evenings it was warm enough to sit out on deck, chatting to whoever was off duty. A question of etiquette now arose. How was he to be addressed? To the Captain he was Darwin, just as the Captain was Fitzroy in return. But this not possible for the junior officers. On the other hand, no officer could be expected to call him Mr Darwin. That was a form of address more suited to common sailors. One day, Fitzroy called him 'Philosopher'. It was perfect. 'Philos' he became, for the rest of the voyage.

The young officers treated him with respect; but he was their own age, and he came in for some good-humoured ribbing. They took particular pleasure in teasing him about religion. His beliefs were still those that his sister Caroline had instilled in him as a child, and he displayed an acceptance of the Bible's moral teaching which his irreverent shipmates found amusing. It was on the *Beagle* that he first heard someone express doubt concerning the biblical story of the Flood, and the experience came as a shock.

It was during this passage that Darwin and Fitzroy established the routine they would follow whenever they were at sea. Breakfast was taken without formality. Darwin would spend the morning at the chart table. At one o'clock, they dined together, but did not linger. Afternoons were devoted to the writing-up of diaries and notebooks, and the Captain's log. If the seas were heavy, Darwin would rest in his hammock, with a volume from the ship's library. After tea was their time for talk. Their conversation was wide-ranging, and almost invariably good-humoured. It was also clear-headed. There was no wine at the Captain's table.

Darwin and Fitzroy had read and loved the same books, and they shared a keen interest in geology and natural history. One book, in particular, fascinated them. It was *The Principles of Geology* by Charles Lyell, Professor of Geology at King's College, London, the first volume of which had recently been published. Geology was a young discipline, which was just establishing its fundamental propositions, and it was the most glamorous of the natural sciences. For Fitzroy and Darwin, geology, and Lyell's volume in particular, were at the cutting-edge of scientific knowledge. Lyell was an advocate of what he called Uniformitarianism. This was a clumsy word for a simple proposition. The key to understanding earth history, in Lyell's view, was to assume that the processes which had governed the earth's past were those which operated in the present day: erosion by wind and water; deposition of material on the seabed; earthquakes and volcanoes. This in turn implied that geological change, and related changes in the living conditions of animals and plants, was the consequence of relatively modest changes accumulating over long periods of time. The opposing view, which was called Catastrophism, saw change as being driven primarily by infrequent but catastrophic events, such as the biblical Flood, and earthquakes and volcanic eruptions operating on a global scale. Fitzroy had shown his regard for his new friend by presenting him with a copy of Lyell's book before the *Beagle* had sailed, and they looked forward with impatience to seeing whether the geology of South America would provide evidence to support Lyell's theories.

The two dining companions did not only share a common attitude to science; their religious views were also essentially the same. Only politics divided them. Fitzroy was a High Tory, whereas Darwin remained true to his family's Whig tradition. Back home in England the debates in parliament over the Great Reform Bill were being conducted in a climate of near revolution. But these two courteous and level-headed young men, who supported opposing sides in these debates, had the good sense to make a joke of their differing backgrounds, and violent argument was avoided.

One subject that regularly featured in their conversations was the relationship between science and religion. Fitzroy was an intelligent man, with a firm belief in the ability of science to explain the natural world. But he was also a devout one; and he believed that scientific enquiry, properly conducted, was not necessarily the enemy of religious faith. It was his hope that the voyage would yield discoveries that would provide evidence of Benevolent Design. This was not a hope that Darwin felt any need to question. In so far as he had thought about religion at all at this stage of his life, he saw no reason why science and religion should be at odds.

From time to time his routine was varied by an invitation to join the junior officers in the gun-room. As he got to know them better, he came to value the good-heartedness behind their schoolboy manners. Two of them in particular, the First Lieutenant, Clements Wickham, and the Second Lieutenant, Bartholomew Sullivan, became his close friends. He also spent many evenings sitting out on the boom, chatting to his day-time cabin companion, the fourteen-year-old Midshipman Philip King.

On 16 January 1832 the *Beagle* made landfall on the Cape Verde island of St Iago. It was at first sight almost completely barren, but it contained rich pockets of tropical vegetation.

In the rock pools were live corals. They alone would have been worth the journey. But for an observant geologist there were greater treasures. Wherever he looked there were signs of volcanic activity, and layers of rock that had obviously been laid down on the seabed before being uplifted and folded. He had spent much of the previous fortnight immersed in Lyell's *Principles*, and now, here before his eyes, was evidence of the truth of Lyell's view of the earth's history. Everything spoke of long periods of time during which gradual, but massive, change had been brought about by the operation of processes which still continued. It was a moment of intellectual awakening he would remember for the rest of his life. As he sat on the beach, eating a lunch of tamarind and biscuits, it occurred to him that he might one day 'write a book on the geology of the various countries visited, and this made me thrill with delight'. His diary entry for his first day on the island ended with the words: 'It has been for me a glorious day, like giving to a blind man eyes – he is overwhelmed with what he sees & cannot comprehend it – Such are my feelings, & such may they remain.'

After a three-week stay to enable Fitzroy to complete his measurements, and to appraise the trading potential of the islands, they set sail for South America. On the morning of 28 February a bright green strip – the coast of Brazil – stretched out before them. At eleven a.m. they sailed into the bay of All Saints and tied up in the spacious harbour of Bahia, or San Salvador. If the bay itself was a place of beauty, its surroundings almost defied description. Darwin was overwhelmed. After wandering alone in his first tropical forest, he tried to pin down his sensations:

delight is . . . a weak term for such transports of pleasure . . .
To a person fond of natural history such a day as this
brings with it pleasure more acute than he ever may again
experience . . . Brazilian scenery is nothing more nor less
than a view in the Arabian Nights, with the advantage
of reality.

But if the natural beauty of Bahia brought out the poet in him,
its social foundations revolted him, and his revulsion brought
about the first breach in his relations with Fitzroy. Anyone
reading their recorded comments on the subject of slavery would
have had difficulty in finding cause for a falling-out.

I have no doubt the actual state of the greater part of the
slave population is far happier than one would previously
be inclined to believe . . . But it is utterly false . . . that . . .
even the very best treated, do not wish to return to their
countries.

Fitzroy in his *Narrative*, said:

Could the Brazilians see clearly their own position, unani-
mously condemn and prevent the selfish conduct of
individuals, emancipate the slaves now in their country,
and . . . prevent the introduction of more, Brazil would
commence a career of prosperity, and her population would
increase to an unlimited degree.

But they were two proud and prickly young men, and it needed only one false word to set them on their high horses.

Fitzroy was noted for his quick temper, and it was the custom for an officer coming on duty to ask whether much 'hot coffee' had been spilt on the previous watch or, alternatively, whether 'much sugar' had been served with it. This was the accepted code for enquiring after the Captain's mood. It was now Darwin's turn to upset the pot. During one of their teatime conversations, he alluded to the local situation in disparaging terms. Fitzroy countered that slaves had assured him that they were perfectly happy with their situation. Darwin's response was to ask if their masters had been present and, if so, what other reply could have been expected? Fitzroy was incensed. Since Darwin doubted his word, he said, it would not be possible for them to continue to live together. Darwin, who was used to speaking his mind in the company of men of consequence, was unrepentant; but he felt sure he would have to leave the ship. When the junior officers learned of the falling-out, they invited him to dine with them in the gun-room. But if Fitzroy had an aristocrat's pride, he could display a matching magnanimity. Within hours he sent a gracious apology, accompanied by a request that Darwin should 'continue to live with him'.

Their next port of call, Rio de Janeiro, had special associations for Fitzroy. He had visited it as a young midshipman, and it was there that he had later been promoted to the command of the *Beagle*. Remembering his own first sight of the harbour, he waited until daylight, so that the crew might enjoy the experience to the full, and his ship might arrive in style. On the morning of 5 April, they entered the harbour, carrying every possible yard of sail, and with a lively following breeze. Darwin's pride in the ship showed in his letter home:

> We came, in first-rate style, alongside the admiral's ship, and we, to their astonishment, took in every inch of canvas, and then immediately set it again. A sounding ship doing such a perfect manoeuvre with such certainty and rapidity is an event hitherto unknown in that class.

Their 'perfect manoeuvre' had required all hands, including Darwin himself, who at one point had a rope in each hand and another in his teeth. 'The feat could not have been performed without me,' he told his shipmates afterwards. In the midst of this display, a bundle of letters arrived on board. 'Send them below,' thundered Wickham, the First Lieutenant. 'Every fool is looking at them and neglecting his duty.'

Darwin was not under orders, so he was able to follow the letters below and feast on his. His sister Caroline had written him a loving letter, which called forth an outpouring of his own love and gratitude in return. Charlotte Wedgwood, his cousin Emma's sister, announced her impending marriage to a clergyman, and expressed her desire to see Charles settled in his own parsonage with a wife of his own. His sister Catherine sent news of another marriage that knocked him sideways. His teenage sweetheart, Fanny Owen, had made a romantic match with a young member of parliament shortly after the *Beagle* had sailed, and was now married, and living in a castle on the Welsh border. Catherine understood the importance of what she was writing:

> I hope it won't be a great grief to you, dearest Charley . . . You may be perfectly sure that Fanny will always continue to be as friendly and affectionate to you as ever, and rejoiced to see you again, though I fear it will be but poor comfort to you, my dear Charles.

He was at a loss as to whether to laugh with delight at the remembrance of family and friends, or to weep for the loss of past happiness now beyond recall. His letter to Caroline ended with the words: 'Between laughing and crying, I bid you all goodnight.' He suddenly felt a long way from home.

Rio de Janeiro did not impress him. The local officials, with what he called their 'insolence of office', impressed him even less. But he desperately wanted a passport for the interior and, as he confided to his diary: 'The prospect of wild forests tenanted by beautiful birds, Monkeys & Sloths, and Lakes by Cavies and Alligators, will make any naturalist lick the dust even from the foot of a Brazilian.' The reward for his foot-licking was an eighteen-day excursion, as the guest of a local rancher, through tropical forests, filled with large and beautiful butterflies and strange parasitic plants, and anthills twelve feet high. He returned to the ship replete with new experiences, and with a fine collection of insects and reptiles acquired along the way.

Just after his return, he was given an opportunity to become a temporary resident. Fitzroy had discovered a difference of four miles of longitude between his estimate of the distance from Bahia to Rio and that of the noted French navigator Baron Roussin. As all his future determinations of longitude in South America would be measured from Rio de Janeiro, he felt obliged to obtain confirmation of his own results. The only way to obtain this was to return to Bahia – a round journey of 1,800 miles – and to repeat his observations. There was no need for Darwin to make the journey, so he rented rooms in a delightful house in the seaside village of Botofogo, and he and the ship's artist Augustus Earle lived there for the next two months. It was within walking distance of the city and Earle, who knew Rio, was able to show him the sights.

Darwin now had the best of two worlds: simple living in his cottage by the sea, and dinners at the English Minister's house, or with Rear Admiral Sir Thomas Baker, the Commander of the British South American Station, on his flagship. With the pleasures of city life, the beauty of his surroundings and firm ground under his feet, these two months were like a holiday, and he looked forward with apprehension to going back on board.

When the *Beagle* returned, it brought confirmation of Fitzroy's calculations, but it had other news that extinguished any desire to celebrate. Before the ship had left for Bahia, eight of the crew had gone snipe-shooting. Within four days of sailing, they had gone down with malaria. By the time the ship returned, three of them had died. Darwin had had a lucky escape. If his memory of his first snipe had tempted him to join the party, he might have been one of the dead.

On 5 July, the *Beagle* left Rio, bound for Buenos Aires. As they sailed out of the harbour, past two great fighting ships, the *Warspite* and the *Samarang*, they were greeted with three cheers from the crews manning the rigging, while a band played 'Cheer up, my lads, 'tis to glory you steer'. It was a remarkable tribute to a small ship setting out on a peacetime assignment, and it brought a glow of pride to all on board.

Darwin shared his shipmates' pride; but he also had his own reasons to feel good about himself that morning. It was six months to the day since he had emerged into the tropical sunlight, after his first terrible week of seasickness. He had not always been well during these months, but there had been enough days on land, and enough calm days at sea, for him to be able to savour the experiences which they had afforded. There had been his geological awakening on St Iago, and his first experience of a tropical forest. He had had the excitement of seeing, and collecting, hundreds of new varieties of plant and animal life, on land and on the water. And all the while he had been on an intellectual journey, his speculations nourished by the sights he had witnessed and by the books he was reading. If the voyage had ended there and then, he would have had memories enough and ideas to last a lifetime.

SIX

Southern Lands

———————•—◆—•———————

In the face of adverse winds, the 1,300-mile passage to Buenos
Aires took four weeks. Within two days of leaving Rio,
Darwin was ill again. Even when the wind abated, there was
a long swell on the sea, which caused him hour after hour of
sickness. As they continued south, the temperature dropped.
Tropical kit was put away and beards began to sprout. The talk
now was all about the coast of Patagonia, and the sport they
would have hunting ostriches and the llama-like guanacos.

In Buenos Aires they were delayed by an incident with a
guard ship, caused by fear that the *Beagle* might be bringing
cholera from England. When this was resolved, they were further
delayed by a request from the authorities for help in suppressing
an insurrection, during which Darwin's boyish hunger for
adventure was nourished by the excitement of participating
in heavily armed patrols through the city streets.

September found them 500 miles further south, near the

military settlement of Bahia Blanca. Here they remained for six weeks, while Fitzroy made preparations for a survey of the coast of Patagonia. Darwin lived on board, but made daily excursions with members of the crew, including seventeen-year-old Syms Covington, who was acting as a servant to both him and Fitzroy. This six-week stay was a blessed relief from seasickness, and it also provided some memorable experiences. As he recorded in his diary:

> I am spending September in Patagonia much in the same manner as I should in England, viz in shooting; in this case however there is the extra satisfaction of knowing that one gives fresh provisions to the ship's company. Today I shot another deer & an Agouti or Cavy. The latter weighs more than 20 pounds; & affords the very best meat I ever tasted.

On 22 September, in the course of a cruise around the bay, he noticed a cliff near a promontory known as Punta Alta from which a large number of shells and fossil bones protruded. The next day he and Covington returned with pickaxes. They were rewarded with the discovery of the massive head of an unknown creature, which Darwin took to be something akin to a rhinoceros. It took them three hours to dig it out, and it was after dark when they got it on board. For a twenty-three-year-old, who twelve months before had been looking for fossil seashells in North Wales, it was the stuff of dreams. Two weeks later, eager for more fossils, he returned to Punta Alta, where he made further finds, including a jawbone which his books led him to believe belonged to a Megatherium, or giant sloth. This was an extinct creature of which the only examples in Europe were in the King's Museum in Madrid. He could hardly believe his luck.

These discoveries, thrilling as they were, were only one element in an existence that daily delivered up fresh delights. He was not only fulfilling his boyhood dreams of foreign travel, he was indulging his enthusiasm for riding, shooting and collecting. His marksmanship made him a valued member of the hunting parties sent out to find fresh food for the crew. It also enabled him to secure specimens of bird and animal life for shipping back to London. Suddenly, everything he had done in his life seemed like a preparation for the task he was now engaged on. The shooting on his Uncle Jos's estate; the beetle-hunting around Cambridge; the botanizing with Henslow, and the geologizing with Sedgwick; the lessons in taxidermy from John Edmonstone in Edinburgh; and the hours of reading travel books in his father's library – all the seemingly aimless activities which had filled his days between the ages of twelve and twenty-two – now came together in a glorious unity, in which work and recreation were indistinguishable, and every day was like a birthday.

An essential feature of his new life was the support system operating on his behalf in England. The most important aspect of this was the financial back-up provided by his father. He needed money continuously. While he was at sea, he was enjoying services that had to be paid for by regular instalments. When he was in harbour, there was personal shopping to be done. If he wished to explore, he had to hire horses and guides. And where his letters of introduction could not open doors, he had to pay for accommodation. At no time did he have to give a thought as to how he was to meet these expenses. He knew that he could write cheques – or in the terminology of the time, draw bills – in any large town he entered, and that these would be cashed without question and honoured by his father's bankers, with his father's ready acquiescence. But as well as financial support, his family provided him with essential emotional underpinning. His sisters took it in turns to write, and they made sure that a steady stream of news, gossip and loving thoughts followed him wherever he went. In return, he sent them fascinating letters and regular instalments of his diary, which were read out at home and passed around among friends and relations.

While his family in Shrewsbury concerned themselves with his personal welfare, his old tutor Henslow, in Cambridge, and his brother Erasmus, in London, attended to his scientific needs. His cases of specimens were addressed to Henslow, who saw that they were placed in the care of the experts best qualified to deal with them. In addition, Henslow was arranging for extracts from his letters to be read before scientific gatherings, ensuring that, although Darwin himself was thousands of miles away, his name was becoming well-known in scientific circles at home. And while Henslow acted as his agent for the disposition of his collections, his brother Erasmus was an equally reliable agent for buying books he wished to read, and supplying scientific and field equipment he was unable to obtain on his travels.

An essential element in this scientific support system was

the generous assistance he received from his shipmates. The example was set by Fitzroy. Although Darwin was a private individual with no official role, the ship's movements, except in moments of emergency, were at all times arranged to fit in with his convenience. The other officers, who were all making natural history collections, gave him every assistance, and often put his collecting needs before their own. His messy and sometimes repellent specimens were treated with amused tolerance, and were permitted to pollute the hallowed precincts of the quarterdeck while he dealt with them. And the bulky cases he was regularly despatching to England, which should have been transported at his own expense, were treated, on Fitzroy's authority, as official Admiralty cargo. The indulgence he enjoyed owed much to his personal charm; but it owed even more to the courtesy and scientific curiosity of his host.

In mid-October, the *Beagle* headed back to Buenos Aires, to lay in the stores needed for the months ahead in the seas around Tierra del Fuego. Like condemned men savouring their last meal, Darwin and his shipmates wandered the streets of the city, shopping, looking at churches and ogling the elegant señoritas, whose charms were magnified by the knowledge that they were the last fashionable females they would see for a long time. Their week in Buenos Aires was followed by ten days in Monte Video for more supplies and one last taste of city living: a grand ball, a night at the theatre to hear Rossini's *Cenerentola*, and then, on 27 November, they were on the open ocean, carrying enough provisions to last for eight months.

Seven weeks after leaving the civilized delights of Monte

Video, on the morning of 17 December, they rounded the south-eastern corner of Tierra del Fuego, at the southern tip of South America. They dropped anchor in the shelter of Good Success Bay, the site of Captain Cook's landfall sixty-three years before. As they entered the bay, they were greeted with shouts from a group of natives on a nearby headland who, when their shouts were ignored, lit a fire to attract their attention. It was the first of what were to be many occasions when Fitzroy was amazed at the ability of the local inhabitants to produce instant fire in that wet climate, when his own crews would sometimes take two hours to achieve the same result.

The next day, a boat party was sent ashore to make contact. Darwin's first meeting with the people of Tierra del Fuego came as a shock. The hours he had spent in the company of the clean and clever Fuegia, with her facility for languages, and the teenage Jemmy, with his kid gloves and button boots, had left him ill-prepared for these unkempt creatures with painted faces, wearing only a guanaco skin draped over one shoulder. In his diary entry for the day, he said: 'I would not have believed how entire the difference between savage and civilised man is. – It is greater than between a wild and domesticated animal . . .'

Their next destination was York Minster Island, a hundred miles to the west, and the designated site of the proposed mission. It was the home country of York Minster and the young Fuegia, who were now man and wife, having been married by Fitzroy at their request.

A month or two earlier a hundred miles would have been a day's run, but their little ship was now in the stormiest seas in the world. Three weeks after rounding Cape Horn, they were still a hundred miles away from the their destination; the only difference being that instead of a hundred miles to the east of it, they were now a hundred miles to the south. They had spent twenty-four days getting precisely nowhere, all the while wet and cold, while the ship pitched heavily in waters churned by opposing winds and currents. Darwin was in despair. During the whole three weeks, he had barely one hour free of seasickness. When they finally made it to the island on 11 January, conditions were too rough to risk a landing. For thirty-six hours they lay offshore, while the elements raged about them.

At breakfast on the 13th Darwin observed to Fitzroy that a gale was not such a terrible thing in a good sea boat, to which Fitzroy replied, 'Wait until we ship a sea.' They did not have to wait long. At one o'clock that afternoon three stupendous rollers, each equal to the biggest Fitzroy had ever seen, bore down on the ship. It rode the first without harm, but with much reduced headway. The second stopped the ship dead and turned it round. The third, catching it sideways on, forced it over, so that the rail was three feet under. Fortunately, there was no fourth wave of comparable size, and the prompt action of a carpenter in driving a spike through a porthole enabled the decks to drain, and the ship to right itself, before the next heavy sea. It had been a close call. When they assessed the damage, they found that a whaleboat had been torn away by the force of the waves but, amazingly, only one of the chronometers on board had been put out of commission.

At this point York announced that he and Fuegia would prefer to settle in Jemmy's country around Woollya Cove, halfway along the Beagle Channel, which had been named, and partly surveyed, during the previous expedition. Woollya now became the preferred site for the mission. The gusts and squalls around the islands made it unsafe for the *Beagle* to attempt the passage, so three whaleboats were fitted out for the hundred-mile journey. Darwin was one of the party selected to escort them. As they rounded the north-east corner of Navarin Island and turned into the Channel, news of their presence spread, and by the time they reached Woollya four days later, they had an escort of around forty canoes.

The weary sailors set to work to prepare the settlement where Matthews and his flock were to live. Between 23 and 28 January, three wigwams were constructed, and a garden planted with vegetables. While this work proceeded, the number of spectators continued to increase, and soon there were 300 of them, outnumbering the sailors ten to one. Fitzroy decided that a display of firepower was called for. Either from this cause or some other, the crowds later disappeared. It seemed safe to leave the settlers for a few days, so Fitzroy set off with two of the boats to survey the north-west arm of the Beagle Channel.

Ten days later, they returned to Woollya, and bad news. York and Fuegia had not been molested, but Matthews and Jemmy had been harassed day and night, and robbed of most of their property. It was clear that Matthews, if he was to escape with his life, could not be left behind. Heavily outnumbered, the small contingent managed to sneak him into a boat. Waving goodbye to Fuegia, York and Jemmy – the two latter still wearing their kid gloves and tunics – set off on their return journey to the *Beagle*.

The ship's next task was to survey the Malvinas – or as the British preferred to call them, the Falkland Islands. On 4 March 1833 they dropped anchor in Berkeley Sound on East Falkland. But the survey had hardly begun when it was interrupted by one of Fitzroy's impetuous decisions. He had met a merchant who wished to sell a schooner, a little smaller than the *Beagle*. There was no question of his being given authority to buy it. But, as always, he was prepared to spend his own money to ensure the best outcome. If another ship could accompany the *Beagle*, it could share the task of surveying, and carry additional supplies, avoiding time-consuming journeys back to port for provisioning. He agreed a price, and wrote to London to request help with the cost of manning a second vessel. On 4 April, the schooner left for Maldonado, a small town at the mouth of the River Plate, to be refitted for its new role; and three weeks later the *Beagle* followed.

In Maldonado a grateful Darwin walked off the ship and found lodgings, where he stayed for ten weeks. He settled down to a routine of shooting and collecting on one day and preserving his trophies on the next. To make the most of his opportunities, he agreed to employ Syms Covington, the servant he had been sharing with Fitzroy, full-time. He wrote home with news of this expense, trusting that it would meet with the same indulgence as the money he was drawing in every major port along his way.

In the letter informing his father of this arrangement, he

reported another development which promised to increase his comfort for the rest of the voyage:

> This . . . schooner will produce the greatest benefits to me. The Captain . . . has given me all Stokes' (who will be in the schooner) drawers in the Poop cabin, and for the future nobody will live here except myself. I absolutely revel in room: I would not change berths with anyone in the ship.

The schooner was renamed *Adventure*, in honour of the *Beagle*'s companion ship on the previous voyage. While its refit proceeded, the *Beagle*, with Darwin on board, headed south for the Rio Negro, for a rendezvous with two small boats that Fitzroy had been hiring for the survey of the Patagonian coast since the previous September. He paid their owner the rental owed to him, and took the crews back on board the *Beagle*.

Rather than make the journey back to Maldonado by ship, Darwin decided to travel overland. This would enable him to avoid five weeks at sea, to enjoy a ride of over 600 miles and to penetrate further inland than any European had yet done. The country through which he had to travel was the scene of fierce fighting between the government of Buenos Aires and the native population it was attempting to exterminate. General Rosas, the officer in command of the campaign, was encamped nearby, and was curious to meet Darwin. The meeting went well, and resulted in Darwin's obtaining a safe conduct from the general, which promised to be useful in his future explorations. With the security of his safe conduct, he set off on the first stage of his journey, which was the 200 miles to Bahia Blanca.

After a rendezvous with the *Beagle* in Bahia Blanca, Darwin obtained a guide and a passport for horses from the general and set out, suitably armed, on the 400-mile journey to Buenos Aires. Halfway there, he was met by an officer with instructions to escort him for the remainder of the distance. It was a memorable adventure. Geologizing all the way, he slept in military posts, and sometimes – in freezing temperatures – on the ground, and dined on venison from the deer he shot and on ostrich eggs, of which he found sixteen in one nest.

After a fortnight of riding across the plains, the olive groves and peach orchards of Buenos Aires were a welcome sight. Even more welcome were the comforts of the house where he spent the following week. It was the home of an English merchant, who not only proved a gracious host, but arranged for the despatch of a case of fossil bones after Darwin had left, persuading a friend to escort it, free of customs, through the port of Liverpool. It was an example of the special treatment that Darwin's gentlemanly status secured for him wherever he went.

The *Beagle* was in Monte Video, and when he learned that it was not expected to sail for at least a month, he embarked on another cross-country ride: this time to Santa Fe, 300 miles up river. He failed to find the rich repository of fossils he had heard about, but he returned with an intriguing souvenir: the fossilized tooth of a horse. Horses had been introduced to South America by the Spanish. But this fossil clearly predated the conquest. The implication was that South America had once had its own horses, which had since died out. How many other species, he wondered, had roamed these plains, and then become extinct? It was another question to add to the list of puzzles that had been presenting themselves since his first overland excursion. Why did so many of the fossils he had found seem to bear a family resemblance to animals still roaming – and peculiar to – South America? Why did a particular species – such as the rhea, or ostrich – give way to a related species as one moved from north to south, or from east to west? He had no answers at the moment, but he was beginning to suspect that the questions were important ones.

When he met up with the ship in Monte Video, it was still not ready to sail. The months of surveying had produced a vast amount of information, which had to be charted and sent to London, before further work could be done. The charting was being done in the poop cabin, and when Darwin realized that he had nowhere to work, and four weeks to kill, he set off, with a hired guide, to explore the lower reaches of the River Uruguay. By the time he got back to the ship at the end of November, he had notched up another 500 miles in the saddle.

On 7 December 1833 the *Beagle* and the *Adventure*, with twelve months' provisions, sailed out of the River Plate, bound for Patagonia and Tierra del Fuego. For four months they worked up and down the coast of Patagonia, charting a 500-mile stretch of coastline. Christmas found them at Port Desire, two-thirds of the way to Cape Horn. They camped on the shore and on Christmas Eve Darwin climbed up the rocks to view the neighbouring countryside. What he saw gave him much to think about in the months that followed:

> a great *level* plain, which extends in every direction . . . It is remarkable that on the surface of this plain there are shells of the same sort which now exist . . . the muscles even with their same blue colour . . . It is therefore certain that within no great number of centuries all this country has been beneath the sea.

But if the geology of the landscape fascinated him, it did not blind him to the sporting possibilities of the animal life grazing upon it. Lifting his gun to his shoulder, he took aim, and a short time later he returned to a hero's welcome with his contribution to the crew's Christmas dinner: a guanaco – a kind of llama – weighing in at 170 pounds. It was the first time he had used a gun in months. As he had become fascinated by the geology and natural history of the places he visited, his sporting enthusiasm had waned, and the shooting of specimens had become the job of his servant, Covington. If this should turn out to be his last kill, it would be one to remember.

In January 1834 they re-entered the Straits of Magellan. By early March they were back in Jemmy Button's country, which they had left just over a year earlier. One morning, a canoe came alongside, paddled by someone they did not at first recognize. Then they realized that the wasted, half-naked creature in it was in fact their old friend Jemmy, who had once been the dandy of the ship. He brought beautiful otter skins for two of his old friends, and some spear heads and arrows for Darwin and Fitzroy. In the course of a long conversation, Fitzroy gleaned his story. York had robbed him of his belongings – something he had apparently planned to do all along – and returned to his own country, taking Fuegia with him. Jemmy had built a canoe, and seemed to be coping. He showed no desire to return to England. As the ship got ready to depart, with Jemmy still on board, a frantic female appeared alongside, whom Jemmy explained was his wife. Darwin recorded the final parting in his diary:

> Every soul on board was sorry to shake hands with poor Jemmy for the last time . . . I hope & have little doubt that he will be as happy as if he had never left his country . . . He lighted a farewell fire as the ship stood out . . . on her course to East Falkland Island.

It was the end of Fitzroy's five-year dream of missionary endeavour.

The next four weeks were spent on East Falkland, completing the survey which had been interrupted by the purchase of the *Adventure* a year earlier, and it was not until 13 April that the *Beagle* made it back to the coast of Patagonia, near the mouth of the Santa Cruz. Here it was beached to enable its bottom to be inspected before entering the Pacific.

On 23 May they entered the Straits of Magellan for the last time, and on 10 June, two and a half years after leaving England, they were in the Cockburn Channel, ready to enter the Pacific. Leaving the only sheltered anchorage for the *Adventure*, which they assumed was close behind, they tacked backwards and forwards in a narrow strait for fourteen hours, most of them in darkness, and all of them squally. And then, in Fitzroy's words:

> When the day at last broke on the 11th, we saw the *Adventure* coming out to us from the cove where she had passed the night, and then both vessels sailed out of the Channel . . . as fast as sails could urge them. At sunset we . . . with a fresh north-west wind stood out into the Pacific, with every inch of canvas set which we could carry.

It was one of those moments that made the bad times seem worthwhile.

SEVEN

Earthquakes and Islands

Before beginning his survey of the Chilean coast, Fitzroy planned a major refit of both ships. He therefore made for Valparaiso, which they reached on 23 July 1834. The city was small, but pretty and, compared to anything they had seen during the previous eight months, it was elegance itself. Even better was the weather. After months of wind and cold and rain, they basked in warm sunshine. Darwin, whose old boy network was operative again, was delighted with Valparaiso. It was a nuisance to have to dress and shave, but roast beef and good wine were compensations. There were several English residents who were delighted to talk geology, and whose thoughts were, he snobbishly observed, 'no way connected with bales of goods and pounds shillings and pence'. One of them, Richard Corfield, had attended Shrewsbury School and been a financial customer of his father's, and his house became Darwin's base for the duration of his stay.

Of the many delights of Valparaiso, the greatest was sitting in the sun, reading letters from home. His sister Susan had written on his birthday, five months earlier, correcting his spelling and wishing him 'many happy returns, but not abroad'. The doctor was not a letter-writer, but Charles's sisters left him in no doubt of his father's continuing love, and the pride he took in his son's growing reputation among men of science back home. They also provided reassurance concerning his father's attitude to his spending. Caroline wrote that: 'My . . . father bids me say he did not growl or grumble at the last £50 you said you drew . . . he says you must not fret about money . . . but be as prudent as you can.'

It was nice to be reassured, but it had never occurred to him to do anything other than what he wanted to do, without concern for cost or consent. Writing to Susan, he said: 'My Father will believe that I *will* not draw money in crossing the Pacific, because I *can* not.' But, on second thoughts, he added: 'I verily believe I could spend money on the moon.'

Within a fortnight, he was off on another geological excursion. Over a period of six weeks, with a week's break in Santiago, he and Covington made a circular tour of some 400 miles, sometimes staying in haciendas, sometimes sleeping under the stars. It was a memorable trip, but it had an unhappy ending. As they neared Valparaiso, Darwin began to feel unwell. Whatever it was, it was clearly serious. For five weeks, he was bedridden, the enforced guest of his hospitable friend Corfield.

While he lay ill, events on the *Beagle* took a dramatic turn. Fitzroy had finally received a reply to the request for help with the cost of manning the *Adventure* that he had submitted fifteen months before. He now learned that its purchase was not approved, and that he was responsible for all its operating costs, past and future. For someone of his proud and volatile disposition it was a severe blow. He had worked to the limit of his considerable abilities for three-and-a-half years. He had prosecuted the survey magnificently, often in appalling conditions. And now he was being made to bear a substantial loss, and being reprimanded into the bargain. Convinced he was the victim of prejudice, as a known Tory serving a Whig government, he took to his cabin to brood. When he emerged, it was to consult the ship's doctor as to the possibility that he was losing his mind, and to announce that he was invaliding out, and that First-Lieutenant Clements Wickham was in command.

When Darwin heard what had happened, he decided that, as soon as he was well, he would abandon the voyage, and make a twelve-month exploration of Chile and Peru, before crossing the continent to Buenos Aires and home. It was Wickham who saved the day. He could not refuse to command the expedition, but he made it clear that he would stick to the letter of its instructions. These said that in the event of the Captain's invalidity on the west coast of South America, the *Beagle* was to be brought straight home via the Atlantic. He also pointed out that these instructions required only that the survey be carried as far as Coquimbo, 200 miles north of Valparaiso, and that coastal surveying thereafter was at the commander's discretion. These arguments, and a period of reflection, were sufficient to calm Fitzroy's mind. To the relief of Wickham and Darwin, and the joy of the crew, he withdrew his resignation. He announced that henceforth they would be doing only what was strictly required, and that they would be home within two years. The *Adventure* was sold, at a loss of £300, and its officers were taken back on to the *Beagle*.

While Fitzroy was still smarting from this humiliation, he and Darwin quarrelled, for only the second time on the voyage. The cause was their differing response to the hospitality they had received in Valparaiso. Fitzroy felt obliged to give a party, which he was not in the mood for. Darwin thought that there was no such obligation. Fitzroy reacted angrily. That was just the sort of person Darwin was, he said, to take all help and give nothing in return. Darwin, who had never been spoken to in such a manner in his life, was deeply offended. He walked out of the cabin without a word, and went back to his friend Corfield.

When he returned a few days later, it had blown over. Fitzroy, hurt as he was, had no doubt been more than usually conscious of the favours Darwin received wherever he went. As for Darwin, he would have had to be remarkably thick-skinned not to have perceived some truth in Fitzroy's accusation.

By the beginning of November the outstanding charts had been completed and despatched to London; but Fitzroy, without telling Darwin the reason, waited a further ten days until his companion was fully fit to travel. On 10 November the *Beagle* set sail to begin the survey of a thousand-mile stretch of coast to the south of Valparaiso.

Three months later, on 20 February 1835, Darwin was resting

in a wood near the town of Valdivia when the earth moved. The *Beagle*'s geologist was experiencing his first earthquake. Sailing north the following week, they recorded several further shocks. When they rode into the city of Concepcion, they found scenes of devastation. The earthquake, which in Valdivia had been a mere unpleasantness, had in Concepcion been strong enough to lay waste the city. In the nearby coastal settlement of Talcahuano, the sea had been seen to retreat three times, each time returning in great tidal waves which tossed large ships around like corks and hurled small boats inland. For Darwin, who for months had been speculating on the forces that could have raised beds of seashells high above present-day sea levels, it was like a demonstration arranged for his personal benefit.

By mid-March the ship was back in Valparaiso to pick up provisions and to collect a supply of money for the use of the citizens of Concepcion. Darwin, who had no desire to return to Concepcion, moved in with his friend Corfield. A few days later he rode to Santiago, where he re-engaged his guide from his previous expedition, and on 18 March he set out with ten mules for Portillo and Mendoza. During the next three weeks, he crossed two high mountain passes, geologizing as he went, and sampling the thin air at 10,000 feet. After crossing the second range of the Cordillera, he was struck by the great differences between the plant and animal forms on the western and eastern sides of the Andes, and the similarity of the latter to the forms he had met in Patagonia. Even more striking was the evidence of past earth movements all around him. Up here, high in the hills, were fossilized tree trunks, fifteen feet in circumference, embedded in marine strata. They had clearly once sunk below the sea, and afterwards been lifted up again. Everything told the same story, of long periods of time during which the face of the earth had undergone continuous change, and raised teasing questions concerning the relationship between these changes in the earth's surface and changes in the living forms upon it.

The journey was scientifically, as well as literally, the high point of his travels in South America. When he wrote to his sister Susan, a week after his return, he was still enraptured by the experience:

> Since leaving England, I have never made so successful a journey . . . I am sure my father would not regret it, if he could know how deeply I have enjoyed it . . . I cannot express the delight I felt at such a famous winding-up of all my geology in South America. I literally could hardly sleep at nights for thinking over my day's work.

When the *Beagle* returned to Valparaiso, Darwin was on the dockside, holding a letter addressed to Fitzroy, containing news of his promotion to the rank of captain. Hitherto, although graced with the title of captain, his actual rank had been that of commander. The promotion was some consolation for the agony he had been through.

The ship now headed north. Darwin, eager to one last excursion before he left South America, arranged to be met near Copiapó, 400 miles further along the coast. Bidding farewell to his friend Corfield, he set off again with the same guide, but this time with four horses and two mules. They travelled in their usual fashion, sometimes sleeping in the open air, cooking their own food; sometimes staying with English residents, to whose homes his letters of introduction were an infallible means of access.

This last excursion provided little in the way of geology, but he did not mind. It had avoided five weeks of possible wretchedness on board ship, and it had enabled him to enjoy healthy exercise in the open air, and sleeping on the solid earth. For all he knew, it might be the last such journey he would ever make. Ahead of him stretched 30,000 miles of ocean. It had been good to have been out of sight of the sea for a while.

Only one surveying task now remained: to map the seas around the Galapagos Islands, which straddled the equator 600 miles off the coast of Ecuador. On 15 September they anchored off Chatham Island, the easternmost island of the group. Two boats were despatched to other islands, and five weeks' intensive surveying began.

While the survey proceeded, Darwin was free to wander. He had been looking forward to the islands with excitement but, geologically speaking, they were a disappointment. He had been expecting live volcanoes. What he found was a covering of black lava and red cinders, pitted with craters, most of them extinct. But if the geology of the islands was disappointing, the animal life displayed a strangeness that exceeded his wildest imaginings. In his diary he commented that they were like 'inhabitants of some other planet'. Great lizards – marine iguanas up to four feet long and as black as the volcanic earth beneath them –

lazed on the rocks. Even more striking were the tortoises, with shells seven or eight feet in circumference. These great creatures were unfazed by the sailors' presence; so much so, that Darwin was able to ride upon the back of one without distracting it from its chosen path. He was told that five years earlier, in 1830, one had been caught which had '1786' carved into its shell, and which required six men to lift it. It had obviously already been a respectable age when the date had been incised, fifty years before, presumably because it was already too heavy for whoever found it to remove it. The locals, he was told, could tell which island a tortoise came from by merely looking at its shell. The seas around the islands swarmed with life. Fish, sharks and turtles popped their heads up everywhere. What with fish, and tortoise breast, and young tortoise soup, these weeks on the islands were a gourmet holiday for the *Beagle*'s crew, who looked forward to further treats at sea from the tortoises they captured, which they knew were capable of living for months without food or water.

The animal life of the islands presented Darwin with another puzzle to add to those he had already collected in South America. The generally accepted explanation for the variety of animal life around the globe was that animals and their environments were part of one great Creation, whereby living creatures were perfectly matched to their conditions of life. Animals in cold countries had been given fur coats, and camels that lived in deserts had been given humps. But if this were so, similar environments ought to be characterized by similar life forms. But this was clearly not the case. The geographical location and the environment of the Galapagos were similar to those of the Cape Verde Islands, but the life forms in the two island groups were dramatically different. Both animals and plants on the Galapagos bore a closer resemblance to species on the mainland of South America than they did to those on island groups elsewhere. Something did not add up.

The birds on the islands were still so unused to man that they had no instinct of flight when approached. They seemed to have no instinctive reaction to human beings whatsoever. They were not frightened when stones were thrown at them, and when Darwin came across a hawk, it refused to move until he used his gun to push it off the branch on which it was sitting. On Charles Island he watched while a small boy collected his family's lunch. Sitting by a well, the child was striking with a stick the doves which came there to drink, and in no time at all he had collected as many as he needed.

Darwin found the birds particularly interesting. Many of them were of species he had seen nowhere else, and some displayed differences peculiar to individual islands. Unfortunately, he was not sufficiently prepared in his mind to make the most of this discovery. Before landing on the islands, it had not occurred to him that such a diversity of related, but quite distinct, forms might be found within such a small area. Had he been prepared for the experience, his observing and his collecting would have been more careful and systematic. For the moment, he was too busy absorbing new impressions to think about their implications. He recorded his day-to-day experiences in his diary, but he drew no conclusions from them.

He was going to need many months of quiet reflection to work out the significance of what he had seen.

On 20 October the survey of the islands was complete and the *Beagle* was pointed west, for England and home. Under cloudless skies trade winds swept them along at a stately 150 miles a day. After three-and-a-half weeks of non-stop sailing, and 3,200 miles nearer home, the island of Tahiti came into view. Here they passed eleven delightful days, enjoying the islanders' hospitality, listening to the children singing and picnicking in the hills. But there was also work to be done. Point Venus, on the north side of the main island, was perhaps the most important location, navigationally speaking, of the whole voyage. It was here that Captain Cook had established a station to observe the transit of Venus in 1769, and Cook's measurements of the station's latitude and longitude provided a crucial validation of the *Beagle*'s own results.

Like all westbound round-the-world sailors, the *Beagle*'s crew had to lose a day somewhere, and it was on Tahiti that the sun, so to speak, caught up with them. Darwin's diary entry for 15 November was followed by one for the 17th. For him, and for his companions, 16 November 1835 would always be the day that never was. Ironically, and unknown to him, it was one of the most notable in the construction of his scientific reputation at home. As he climbed a sun-drenched mountainside on the morning of 17 November, it was evening on 16 November in Cambridge, where his old tutor John Henslow was reading out a thirty-page collation of his letters before some of the university's most eminent fellows and professors.

The journey from Tahiti to New Zealand was an uncomfortable one, and he lost many days to seasickness. But he was able to use his better days to set out in full his theory of the origins of coral reefs. Some authorities, most notably his geological hero, Charles Lyell, believed that they were the consequence of volcanic action. Darwin, despite his reverence for Lyell, was convinced that this was mistaken. He had not yet seen a reef, but he was sure that they were the result of a gradual sinking of the seabed, accompanied by a matching increase in the height of the reefs themselves, as living corals grew upon the remains of dead ones.

He was not impressed with the Maori population of New Zealand. He had been entranced by the beauty of Tahitian men, and he considered the New Zealand men to be very much their inferiors. Fitzroy found the Maoris more interesting. His own protégé, the missionary Richard Matthews, who was still on board the *Beagle*, had a brother who was a missionary in New Zealand, and it was with some sense of justification that Fitzroy left Matthews with his brother to assist with his missionary efforts.

January 1836 found them tied up in Sydney harbour. This time, Darwin *was* impressed. His twenty-six-year-old heart filled with pride as he contemplated the city that British colonial enterprise, and convict labour, had created. His admiration showed in his letter home: 'Ancient Rome, in her imperial grandeur, would not have been ashamed of such an offspring . . .

There are now men living, who came out as convicts . . . who are said to possess without doubt an income from 12 to 15,000 pounds per annum.'

He did not add that they might possibly have been transported for killing pheasants on a Shropshire estate.

Three months later they reached the Cocos Islands, a thousand miles west of Java. Here Darwin's own researches for once meshed perfectly with the expedition's objectives. The ship's instructions explicitly directed that evidence should be looked for to support or contradict the volcanic theory of the origin of coral reefs. While the crew charted currents and took soundings, Darwin waded waist-deep, examining the coral and the creatures living upon it. Everything he saw convinced him that his theory of how reefs were formed – as a result of continued growth, as the ocean bed sank – was a sound one. To find it supported by actual examination of reefs was a source of delight. It added to his growing self-confidence, and reinforced his ambition to amount to something in the world of science. His career in the Church had long since disappeared below the horizon.

On 12 April the *Beagle*, its holds filled with coconuts, pigs, poultry and turtles, set out on the next great leg of its voyage: a 3,000-mile non-stop journey across the Indian Ocean. The thoughts of all on board now centred on home. Two-and-a-half weeks sailing brought them to landfall on Mauritius. Darwin took advantage of the stop to write one last letter to his family:

The captain is daily becoming a happier man . . . He . . .

102

Erasmus Darwin
Scientist and poet

Josiah Wedgwood I
Potter and industrialist

Josiah Wedgwood I and his family, by George Stubbs
The mounted figures from left to right are Susannah (15), Josiah II (11) and John (14)

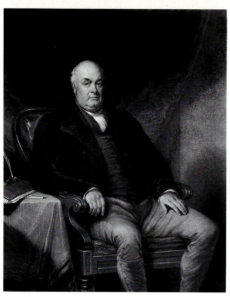

Friends and relations:

(Above) Robert Darwin and his wife
         Susannah, née Wedgwood.
         (Charles's parents)

(Left)   Susannah's brother
         and Robert's friend,
         Josiah Wedgwood II
         (Charles's Uncle Jos)

The Mount, Shrewsbury
Darwin's birthplace and childhood home

Maer Hall, Staffordshire
Home of Josiah Wedgwood II and Darwin's 'Bliss Castle'

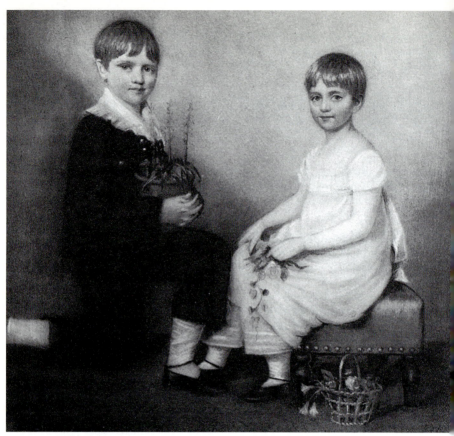

(Above) Childhood playmates:
Charles (about 7)
and Catherine (about 5)

(Left) Teenage sweetheart:
Fanny Myddleton-Biddulph
(née Fanny Owen), sketched
after her marriage

(Above) Darwin's first floor rooms in
Christ's College, Cambridge
(Front court, south side, staircase G)

(Right) His friend and tutor,
John S. Henslow,
Professor of Botany

A ship and its captain:

(Above) HMS *Beagle* in the Murra
Narrows, Tierra del Fueg

(Left) Robert Fitzroy, the *Beagle*
Commander

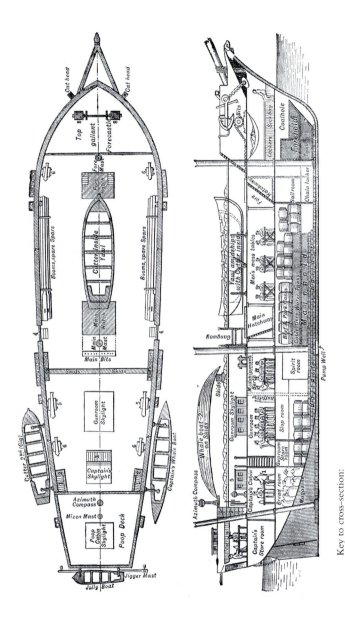

Key to cross-section:
1. Darwin's seat in the Captain's cabin 2. Darwin's seat in the poop cabin 4. Bookshelves

HMS *Beagle*, drawn by Midshipman Philip King

Reptiles Plate 12.

Amblyrynchus Demarlii Nat size

Birds Pl. 47

Zoological puzzles:

(Above)   A Land Iguana – found only
          the Galapagos

(Left)   Rhea Darwinii – a distinct f
          with its own specific range i
          South America

is busy all day in writing . . . the account of the voyage . . . He has proposed to me to join him in publishing the account . . . I look forward with no little anxiety to the time when Professor Henslow . . . shall decide on the . . . merits of my notes. If he shakes his head in a disapproving manner, I shall then know that I had better give up science, for science will have given up on me. For I have worked with every grain of energy I possess.

From Mauritius they sailed to Simonstown in South Africa. They remained there for two weeks, while Fitzroy took measurements at the observatory and conferred with the astronomers. Darwin explored a little, but found nothing to excite him. His longing for home outweighed his desire for new experiences.

As the *Beagle* turned north into the Atlantic, Darwin settled down once more to the task of converting his notes and diary entries into a form suitable for his published *Journal*. As he did so, he reflected upon what he had seen. In his Ornithological Notes he recorded the thoughts that were stirring in his mind on the subject of species and their origins. One of his less coherent entries looked back to his exploration of the Galapagos Islands in the previous October:

When I recollect the fact, that from the form of the body, shape of scales and general size, the Spaniards can at once pronounce from which isd. any tortoise may have been brought – when I see these Islands in sight of each other . . . tenanted by these birds but slightly differing in structure

103

and filling the same place in Nature, I must suspect they are only varieties. The only fact of a similar kind of which I am aware is the constant asserted difference between the wolf-like Fox of East and West Falkland Isds. – If there is the slightest foundation for these remarks the Zoology of Archipelagoes will be well worth examining; for such facts would undermine the stability of species.

What he was saying was that if the various types of tortoise, and the different kinds of birds, associated with particular islands were to be regarded as mere varieties, then they came within the range of variation allowed for in contemporary definitions of a species. But if the differences were such as to require them to be treated as separate species, then the resemblances between them, and the pattern of their distribution, raised questions which struck at the very foundation of currently accepted explanations of the origin of living forms. 'Undermine the stability of species' was the most potent phrase he had ever put on paper. But at this stage it was just a fugitive thought, flitting across his brain. He would need time, and freedom from distraction, if he were to catch it and pin it down

Five weeks after leaving Simonstown, they reached the mid-Atlantic island of Ascension. From there it should have been a straight run to England. On 23 July they put to sea, to the joy of all on board. Their elation was short-lived. As soon as the ship cleared the shore, its head was turned WSW. Fitzroy's perfectionism was taking them across the Atlantic. He had decided to make a detour to revisit Bahia, the location of his first South American landfall, to calibrate his chronometers once more.

The decision brought a cry of despair from Darwin: 'This zig-zag manner of proceeding is very grievous; it has put the finishing touch to my feelings. I loathe, I abhor the sea, and all ships which sail on it.'

His disappointment soon passed. It was at Bahia that he had first walked in a tropical forest and the emotions of that magical day four years earlier were reawakened. On 6 August, he took his last walk in South America:

> I stopped again and again to gaze on such beauties, & tried to fix them for ever in my mind . . . they will leave, like a tale told in childhood, a picture full of indistinct, but most beautiful figures.

Now, at last, they really were headed home. He settled down to draw up his balance sheet of the delights and disadvantages of ocean travel. There was no doubt what went on the debit side:

> If a person suffers much from seasickness, let him weigh it heavily in the balance . . . it is no trifling evil cured in a week . . . And what are the boasted glories of the illimitable ocean? A tedious waste, a desert of water as the Arabian calls it.

When he came to list the benefits, the disadvantages were far outweighed. Pride of place was taken by the delight afforded by the scenery of the places he had visited, especially the tropical jungle. Close behind came the sense of wonder generated by 'the first sight, in his native haunt, of a real barbarian'. The memory of his land-based expeditions remained as vivid as ever, although his sister Susan would have deplored his spelling:

> It has been said that the love of the chace is . . . a relic of an instinctive passion – if so, I am sure the pleasure of living in the open air, with the sky for a roof, and the ground for a table, is part of the same feeling . . . I always look back to our boat cruizes & my land journeys . . . with a kind of extreme delight, which no scenes of civilisation could create.

His summing-up was decisive:

> . . . I have too deeply enjoyed the voyage not to recommend to any naturalist to take all chances . . . he will meet with no difficulties or dangers (excepting in rare cases) nearly so bad as he before hand imagined . . . the effect ought to be, to teach him good humoured patience, unselfishness, the habit of acting for himself, and of making the best of everything . . . at the same time he will discover how many truly goodnatured people there are . . . ready to offer him the most disinterested assistance.

And on this happy note he effectively closed his diary. On Sunday, 2 October 1836, five years to the day after he had left the Mount, the *Beagle* entered the English Channel. In pouring rain, Fitzroy conducted his last shipboard service, to give thanks for their safe return. As they approached the Cornish coast, Darwin experienced a sense of anticlimax:

> After a tolerably short passage, but with some heavy weather, we came to anchor at Falmouth. – To my surprise and shame I confess the first sight of the shores of England inspired me with no warmer feelings, than if it had been a miserable Portugeese settlement.

The voyage had lasted four years and nine months, and it had cost his father over £1,000. He had sailed 40,000 miles and ridden more than 2,000 miles on horseback – and he was still only twenty-seven. He had 1,700 pages of zoology and geology notes; a diary of 800 pages; 4,000 labelled skins, bones and other dry specimens; and another 1,500 preserved in spirits. It had been the adventure of a lifetime. But, thank God, it was over at last. With luck, he would never be seasick again.

EIGHT

Homecoming

———•—◆—•———

For Fitzroy and his officers Falmouth was one more temporary stopover. Their voyage would not be complete until the *Beagle* dropped anchor at Greenwich, four miles down river from London Bridge. But their passenger was under no such constraint. It was, in Darwin's own words, a 'dreadfully stormy' night; but it would have taken more than a Cornish storm to keep him on board. Within hours of the ship's arrival in Falmouth, he was on the Exeter coach, bound for Shrewsbury.

The journey took two nights and two days, in the limited comfort of a succession of mail coaches. But the confined space and the bumpy ride were no hardship to a fit twenty-seven-year-old who had spent several hundred nights and days on a man-of-war. On the second day, as he rode in the *Hirondelle* – The Swallow – through the rolling countryside of the Welsh border, his spirits soared. He thought of his dining companion of the previous five years, to whom he would later write: 'I wished much for you to admire the fields, woods and orchards. I am sure we would have thoroughly agreed that the wide world does not contain so happy a prospect as the rich cultivated land of England.'

He reached Shrewsbury on the evening of 4 October. Not wishing to disturb the household, he spent the night at an inn, and it was not until breakfast-time that he walked in on his delighted family. 'Why, the shape of his head is quite altered,' said his proud but undemonstrative father. His sisters were overjoyed. Writing to a Wedgwood cousin, Caroline said:

Charles is come home so little altered in looks and not a bit changed in his own dear self. We have had the happiest morning – Charles so full of affection and delight at seeing my father looking so well and being with us once again. Now we have him really again at home, I intend to begin to be glad he went on this expedition, and now I can allow he has gained happiness and interest for the rest of his life.

The spirit of celebration embraced the entire household. As Darwin reported to Fitzroy: 'Two or three of our labourers . . . immediately set to work, and got most excessively drunk in honour of the arrival of Master Charles.' Only one inhabitant of the Mount was unmoved. When he called his dog, it set off ahead of him, on the route of their usual walk, as if he had never been away.

In the midst of this excitement, he found time to write to some of the people who had made his voyage possible. His letter to his old tutor ended with the words: 'My dear Henslow, I do long to see you; you have been the kindest friend to me that ever man possessed. I can write no more, for I am giddy with joy and confusion.' To his uncle Jos, whose influence had swung the argument on that fateful day five years before, he wrote:

My Dear Uncle,

. . . My head is quite confused with so much delight, but I cannot allow my sisters to tell you first how happy I am to see all my dear friends again.

I am obliged to return in three or four days to London when the Beagle will be paid off, and then I shall pay Shrewsbury a longer visit. I am most anxious once again to see Maer and all its inhabitants, so that in the course of two or three weeks I hope in person to thank you, as being my First Lord of the Admiralty. I am so very happy I hardly know what I am writing.

To his greatest benefactor of all, his courteous and considerate host throughout the voyage, he wrote:

My Dear Fitzroy

I arrived here yesterday morning at breakfast-time, and, thank God, found all my dear sisters and father quite well. My father appears more cheerful and very little older than when I left. My sisters assure me that I do not look the least different, and I am able to return the compliment.

Indeed all England appears changed excepting the good old town of Shrewsbury and its inhabitants, which, for all I can see to the contrary, may go on until Doomsday . . . I do assure you I am a very great man at home; the five years' voyage has certainly raised me one hundred per cent . . .

I hope you will not forget to send me a note telling me how you go on . . . If you do not receive much satisfaction for all the mental and bodily energy you have expended in His Majesty's service, you will be most hardly treated . . .

God bless you! I hope you are as happy, but much wiser, than your most sincere but unworthy philosopher,

CHAS. DARWIN

His description of his father as being 'quite well' was somewhat overstated. Now seventy years of age, Robert was no longer his former active self. He was grossly corpulent and short of breath, and he suffered severely from gout. The workload he had carried for nearly fifty years was now beyond him. Fortunately, he had been able to keep the practice in the family, without the help of his sons. His eldest daughter, Marianne, had married a doctor, whom he had taken into partnership, and to whom he had handed over most of his patients.

The news of Charles's return travelled fast. Within hours he received an invitation from his shooting mentor, William Owen, to visit Woodhouse on the following Saturday. Fanny's father was clearly expecting a renewal of their sporting partnership:

pray bring your Gun with you, for I have not forgot the amusement we used to have together, and I am anxious to see whether you are *improved by your travels* or whether I am again to be your instructor.

Incredible as it would have seemed five years earlier, such an invitation no longer held much appeal. William Owen, like Darwin's sisters, was mistaken in assuming that 'normal' life was about to be resumed. The Darwin who had come back was not the Charles who had gone away. The love of his family and the affection of old friends were delightful to return to. But the belief of family and friends, that they had got their 'old' Charles back, had no basis in reality. The physical and intellectual excitements of the voyage had changed him. On the outside, he was still the modest, agreeable young man they had always known. But beneath the unchanged exterior there burned a fierce ambition, supported by a new self-confidence, and he knew that his future lay elsewhere.

For three weeks he immersed himself in his family's happiness. Writing to his cousin Fox, he said that he had 'talked and laughed enough for years'. But he was itching to escape to where he could talk science. The necessity of attending to his specimens gave him the excuse he needed to break away. His father's agreement to make him a generous allowance, and his gift of a parcel of stocks and shares, made it possible for him to do so. By the end of October he was in Greenwich, overseeing the unloading of his treasures.

Henslow's active promotion of Darwin's letters, and displays of the specimens he had sent home, had aroused considerable interest. When news of the ship's arrival in Greenwich reached London, people began to travel out to inspect it. These visitors, who included sightseers as well as scientists, became so numerous that Fitzroy gave orders that 'respectable-looking persons only' were to be admitted by the accommodation ladder. Those who did not meet this description were to be directed to the gangway, where they had to negotiate three small projections from the ship's side, while clinging on to two ropes. One day, a rather ordinary-looking gentleman, with a pretty wife, asked for the Captain, and was directed by the sentry to this 'tradesman's' entrance, whence he was conducted below. Some time later, a less than happy Fitzroy appeared above deck, and said to the officer of the watch: 'Do you know it was the Astronomer Royal who has been treated with such scant ceremony?'

While Darwin was in Greenwich, he received a dinner invitation from the man whose writings had been his inspiration throughout the voyage: Charles Lyell. It was their first meeting, and it was the beginning of a lifelong friendship. Lyell, at nearly forty, was twelve years older than Darwin. Like Darwin, he had had a youthful passion for entomology, and for beetles in particular; but his adult life had been devoted to geology. He had just completed a year as President of the Geological Society. But on that October evening it was the older man who sat spellbound, as Darwin recounted his experiences and expounded his theory of the formation of coral reefs. It was at this dinner also that Darwin first made the acquaintance of Richard Owen, Professor at the Royal College of Surgeons, and the leading anatomist at the London Zoo. He too was fascinated by Darwin's traveller's tales.

A few days later Darwin's own status as a geologist was confirmed by his election to membership of the Geological Society, and in mid-November, in his role of ancient mariner and coming man of science, he made his long-looked-for visit to the Wedgwoods at Maer. For four days he endured an almost non-stop barrage of questions from his eager cousins and a parade of visiting relatives. Then it was back home to the Mount to receive an astonishing piece of news. While he was in London, a letter had arrived from Fitzroy, in reply to his own letter of a month earlier. Its contents bore witness to a gentlemanly discretion which was amazing even by the standards of that buttoned-up age:

I am delighted by your letter. The account of your family – & the joytipsy style of the whole letter were very pleasing. Indeed, Charles Darwin, I have *also* been *very* happy – even at the horrid place Plymouth – for that horrid place contains a *treasure* to *me* which even *you* were ignorant of!! Now guess – and think and guess again. Believe it or not, – the news is *true* – I am going to be married!!!!!!! Now you may know that I have decided on this step, long *very* long ago.

Fitzroy, it appeared, had had an understanding with the lady in question since before the *Beagle* had sailed. He and Darwin had been daily dining companions, on and off, for nearly five years and this was the first mention of her existence.

Darwin remained in Shrewsbury for two weeks, during which he found time to draw a line under a romantic episode in his own life. His teenage sweetheart, Fanny Owen, nearly five years married, was expecting her third child. They had met a few weeks earlier, when he had found her unwell. He now sent her a gift of flowers. She wrote back to thank him; but her letter showed that she was hurt by the studied formality of the mode of address – 'My Dear Mrs Biddulph' – he had adopted in his covering note. Whatever memories he carried in his heart, the newly elected Fellow of the Geological Society was clearly determined to observe the proprieties.

By the first week of December, he was back in London, where his collections were attracting great interest. It was clear that he would have to spend a lot of time there in the future, but the thought of living in 'dirty, odious London' was repellent. The obvious compromise was to live in Cambridge, which was sufficiently close, yet small enough to be pleasant, and which had the advantage of containing many notable men of science. Within a week he had secured an invitation to lodge with his old tutor. The house in which Henslow and his wife lived was comfortable, and the company was delightful, but the distraction was not conducive to work. He accordingly found a house to rent in the town centre, close to his old college, and near enough to the Henslows for him to have the best of both worlds. He moved in just before Christmas. Never having had to fend for himself in his life, it did not occur to him to do so now. His personal servant on the *Beagle*, Syms Covington, had been paid off and was looking for a position. He moved in with his former employer, as servant and scientific assistant, and they settled back into their old relationship.

Darwin was now able to involve himself in the scientific life of London. On 4 January 1837 he presented eighty preserved mammals and 450 stuffed birds to the Zoological Society. On the evening of the same day he read a paper on the Elevation of Land in South America to the Geological Society, and at the next monthly meeting he was elected to its Council.

His base in Cambridge enabled him to enjoy the social, as well as the scientific, pleasures of London life. At his brother's house in Great Marlborough Street he could hear the latest theories being discussed by clever and well-informed people. At Lyell's dinner table he could exchange ideas with Lyell himself, and with other leading men of science. Most brilliant of all were the soirées at the home of Charles Babbage, the inventor of the world's first mechanical calculator. These social and intellectual circles overlapped. It was at Erasmus's house that he made the acquaintance of Thomas Carlyle, whose *History of the French Revolution* had just been published, and it was at a dinner there that Carlyle subjected a company, including Darwin, Lyell and Babbage, to a long harangue on the Virtue of Silence. Both Lyell and Babbage were used to being listened to and they did not take kindly to being forced into the role of listeners. At the end of the evening a grim-faced Babbage thanked Carlyle for his 'interesting talk on Silence'.

These encounters with clever and interesting people created a heady atmosphere for a young man of an enquiring turn of mind, especially one who had been so long cut off from such exchanges. 'Dirty' and 'odious' London might be, but it was where the action was. If he was to make the most of the opportunities London afforded, he really could not live anywhere else. After only three months in Cambridge, he moved back to London, and rented a house in Great Marlborough Street, a few doors away from where his brother lived.

It was at Great Marlborough Street that he put the finishing touches to his *Journal of Researches into the Geology and Natural History of the Various Countries visited by HMS Beagle*. The *Journal* was an adaptation of the detailed diary he had kept during the voyage. Despite its heavyweight title, it was in fact a popular account of the events of the voyage, and of Darwin's reactions to them. Most of it had been written at sea; but preparing it for publication occupied him on and off for seven months. While still engaged in this task, he conceived the idea of a further, multi-volume work on the zoology of the voyage, for the use of future travellers. With its 150 coloured plates, it would be expensive to produce, and it was unlikely to be a commercial proposition. He put the idea to Henslow, and the old boy network swung into operation. Henslow was a personal friend of the Chancellor of the Exchequer. On 18 May, armed with letters of recommendation from eminent men of science, Darwin attended an interview at the Treasury. He emerged from this meeting with a promise of a grant of £1,000 to underwrite the costs of publication. The promise was confirmed in writing three months later, in a letter that gave him carte blanche in the spending of the money. This freedom to use the grant in whatever way he thought fit was unexpected, and he immediately made plans to stretch it to cover a volume on the geology of the voyage as well.

Shortly after this interview at the Treasury, he paid a visit to Greenwich, to bid farewell to the ship that had been his home for so long. The *Beagle* had been refitted, and was due to leave for Australia at the beginning of June, with Wickham in command. Nostalgia crept into the letter he wrote to Henslow: 'It appeared marvellously odd to see the little vessel and to think that I should not be one of the party. – If it was not for the sea sickness, I should have no objection to start again.'

While preparing his *Journal* for the printer, Darwin had reflected on his observations and discoveries in an attempt to make sense of all that he had seen. As he had done so, questions had begun to form in his mind. They were questions as exciting as they were unsettling; but they were questions he was careful to keep to himself. As the specialists began to pronounce on his specimens, these questions became more insistent. The birds and fossil mammals he had donated to the Zoological Society had caused a stir, and their examination had yielded some striking results. The first to deliver his verdict was the artist and ornithologist John Gould, who was Superintendent of Stuffed Birds at the Society. This title belied the reality of his position, which was that of a poorly paid professional of inferior status to the gentlemen amateurs who made up the Society's membership. To supplement his earnings, he had embarked on a series of magnificently illustrated books, with titles such as

Birds of Australia and *Birds of Europe*. Although he was a paid employee, his reputation stood high, and his knowledge of the bird life of the world was unequalled. If anyone could place Darwin's Galapagos finches in their proper context, Gould was the person to do it.

Darwin had not paid much attention to the birds when he had collected them. So unsuspecting was he of any exceptional significance attaching to the differences between the specimens from various islands, that he had failed to label them as to their places of origin, and he had been forced to seek help from one of the ship's officers to make good his neglect. To Gould's expert eye they were clearly not mere varieties. As soon as he received them, he put other work on one side, and within a week had come to conclusions that were as surprising to Darwin as they were to the other members of the Society. In reply to Darwin's question as to whether they were all finches, or whether they represented different species, Gould's answer was 'Yes' and 'Yes'. They were all finches, but they were of different species: twelve species in all, constituting a single group previously unknown to science. The most notable feature of this new group was the variation in the form of the beak from species to species. Even more surprising was the discovery that several species seemed to be associated with particular islands. It was a puzzle. Why should these islands share a group of related species unknown anywhere else in the world? And why should individual islands have their own unique species?

A month later, with Darwin in the audience, Lyell presented to the Geological Society the results of Richard Owen's examination of the fossil mammals. Among Darwin's treasures Owen had identified a giant ground sloth and a giant llama: two species hitherto unknown, but clearly related to smaller forms still living in the same regions. Darwin was startled. He had hoped to hear that his finds were new to science; but he had assumed that they must be related to creatures living in similar latitudes in Africa. The generally accepted view was that the various species of animals and plants had been created with characteristics to match their environments. Polar bears had been given thick coats to suit them to a life in cold countries, and camels had been given the ability to endure long periods without water to fit them for life in the desert. On this reasoning, similar creatures ought to be found in similar climates and terrain, even if their habitats were thousands of miles apart. To be told that his fossils were distinctive American types, unlike anything known elsewhere, added more questions about species and their origins to those already going round in his brain.

Lyell expressed the opinion that these findings were evidence for a Law of Succession, whereby species in a particular region were replaced over time by other, related species. In a private letter to the astronomer Herschel in the previous year, he had allowed for the possibility that evolution had taken place, but in his public pronouncements he was more circumspect. His publicly stated position was that the Providence that had created species could surely bring about their replacement by other species.

For Darwin, this comfortable conclusion was too easy. If individual species were the result of individual acts of creation, why were particular species found in one locality, but not in another? The conventional explanation, that species had been created to match their particular environments, did not make sense. If this were true, one would expect that similar species would be met with in similar circumstances in various parts of the world. But his five-year voyage had taught him exactly the opposite: that similar environments separated by great distances were notable for the *dissimilarity* of the plant and animal species inhabiting them. The most striking similarities were those between species in neighbouring regions, and between past and present species within regions, and these similarities seemed explicable only on the assumption that the species in question were somehow *related*.

The questions would not go away. In July 1837, with his *Journal* ready for the press, he opened a small brown notebook, and wrote on its title page the single word *Zoonomia*. It was the title of the book in which his grandfather Erasmus had set out his ideas on the subject of animal evolution sixty years before. Darwin had read it as a student, and found it unconvincing. His admiration had been reserved for Paley's *Natural Theology*, and its Argument from Design. But now, at twenty-eight, as he began to set down his thoughts on the subject of species and their origins, from the perspective of his five-year voyage, Paley was dismissed, and he proudly, secretly, claimed his intellectual inheritance.

He spent the summer in a fever of speculation. Ideas poured on to the pages of the little book. He drew a diagram, simple in itself, which challenged the basis of conventional thinking about the animal world. In 1837 the most widely accepted description was still the 'Great Chain of Being': a created world with a sequence of gradually more complicated, or 'higher' forms, and with human beings as its crowning glory. In this view, the word 'sequence' referred not to succession in time, but to an ordered classification of animal species existing at the same time, and the concepts of 'lower' and 'higher' were of its essence. Even those who challenged this view – people like Darwin's grandfather Erasmus – and who wished to substitute a picture of gradual evolution of species over time, operated within the same philosophical framework. They still thought in terms of 'higher' and 'lower'. They talked of a ladder, rather than a chain; but the ladder led up to 'Man' (they were all men), and the highest rung of all was occupied by white, so-called 'civilized' Man.

Darwin's little diagram was quite different, and unnerving in its implications. The picture he drew was more like a tree. The trunk was the early, shared origin of later animal forms. The limbs, and the thinning branches, were successive sub-divisions of the animal world. On a tree, one twig had no more significance than any other. The twigs as a whole did not lead anywhere: they merely spread. If this analogy were applied to the natural world, the implications were mind-blowing. Looked at in this way, the worm had equal status with the chimpanzee. All talk of 'higher' and 'lower' was meaningless. The only adjective that could be applied to species was 'different'. Human beings were located at the tip of just one of a vast number of similar twigs, all of which were of equal significance – or insignificance.

It was at this point that Darwin's own human limitations

caught up with him. As his thoughts raced ahead, his body rebelled. He had lived for twelve months at a physical and mental pitch which few men, even fit young men of his own age, could have maintained for so long. First, there had been the upheaval of his return, followed by weeks of almost constant socializing. Then there had been the coming and going associated with the disposal of his collections, and the preparation and delivery of a series of papers to audiences of the highest intellectual calibre. While so engaged, he had been preparing his *Journal* for the press and negotiating the financing of his zoology volume. He had sustained this feverish activity through a stifling hot summer, without any of the domestic comforts that a married man of his age would have had. On top of all this, he was asking his constitution to endure the nervous strain of a secret mental journey which carried with it a sense of transgression, not only against the conventions of his time, but against the sincerely held beliefs of the scientists he held in most respect. At the end of such a year, it was not surprising that a collapse should have occurred. The wonder was, when the collapse came, that it was not more serious.

When his body called a halt, the symptoms were reminiscent of those he had experienced in the weeks before the *Beagle* sailed. On 20 September he was brought up sharp with what he described as 'an uncomfortable palpitation of the heart', and his doctors warned him sternly that he must give up all work and get out of town. He did as he was told. He wrote to Henslow, enlisting his help in correcting his *Journal* proofs, saying: 'I feel I must have a little rest, else I shall break down.' He left London on 25 September and spent the next four weeks in Shrewsbury and at Maer.

It was a desperately needed holiday. But even on holiday he was unable to escape completely. While he was 'resting', a letter arrived from Henslow, asking him if he had made up his mind about an invitation to serve as Secretary of the Geological Society which had been extended some months earlier. He penned a plaintive reply, giving a list of reasons why he would not be the right person for the post:

> I doubt how far my health will stand the confinement of what I have to do, without any additional work. I merely repeat, that you may know I am not speaking idly, that when I consulted Dr Clark in town, he at first urged me to give up entirely all writing and even correcting press for some weeks. Of late anything which flurries me completely knocks me up afterwards, and brings on a violent palpitation of the heart. I can neither bear to see myself selfish and sulky, nor can I see the possibility of my taking the Secretaryship without making a sacrifice of all my plans and a good deal of comfort.
>
> . . . do not judge me by the activity of mind which you and a few others possess, for in that case the more different things in hand the pleasanter the work; but, though I hope I shall never be idle, such is not the case with me.

It was a cry from the heart – almost literally, given his symptoms. Only a masochist would have considered accepting

125

such an invitation in these circumstances. But the offer was a flattering one, and accept it he did, just four months later. The son of the workaholic Robert Darwin was behaving like his father. But the doctor, although he worked long hours, had always paced himself. Those hours spent on the road, bolt upright in his carriage, were physically tiring, but they provided an escape from stress. During these exhausting months, Darwin had no such safety valve. As he pressed on, his constitution, which had enabled him to perform such feats of endurance in South America, was being gradually undermined. In giving in to the demands which his scientific colleagues, and his own ambition, were making on him, he was overreaching his strength.

His four-week break brought him some relief; but when he returned to London on 21 October, he immediately settled down to the task of checking the remaining proofs of his *Journal*. On 4 November he wrote to Henslow: 'If I live till I am eighty years old I shall not cease to marvel at finding myself an author: in the summer before I started, if anyone had told me I would be an angel by this time, I should have thought it an equal impossibility.'

His pleasure in his newly acquired status as a writer was punctured by two broadsides from his former shipmate. He had dashed off a preface to his *Journal*, and had sent it to Fitzroy, for what he assumed would be his approval. In his customary self-absorption, he had given less credit to the ship's officers than he might reasonably have been expected to. Fitzroy was not pleased. He had earlier that year been awarded the Geographical Society's Prize, in recognition of his achievements, and though he did not say it in so many words, he did not take kindly to having those achievements belittled by his paying guest. In two letters, written on successive days, he made his feelings clear. In polite, but acid, paragraphs, he complained that his own contribution to Darwin's success had not been sufficiently recognized, and that the support Darwin had received from the other officers had received no proper mention at all. 'Most people', he added, were well aware that Darwin's journey had only been possible because of his own invitation and the sacrifice of his living space, and that the other officers had held the ladder by which Darwin had mounted to the position he now occupied. It was unpleasant medicine, but it was not unreasonably administered, and Darwin had no choice but to swallow it. He drafted a more generous preface, and the dispute was resolved. But it left a bitter taste in his mouth.

At the end of March 1838 the two men met again, when Darwin called on the Fitzroys and their new baby. In a letter written to his sister Susan, his resentment slipped out:

> I went to the Captain's yesterday evening to drink tea – it did one good to hear Mrs Fitzroy talk about her baby . . . its little voice was such charming music – The Captain is going on very well, – that is for a man, who has the most consummate skill in looking at everything & everybody in a perverted manner.

This was the same Fitzroy of whom he had said, in that earlier letter to Susan, after their first meeting: 'it is no use attempting to praise him as much as I feel inclined to, for you would not believe me.'

The day before he called on the Fitzroys, he had spent a day at the zoo. He had come away with plenty of food for thought. His reason for going had been to see Jenny the orang-utan, who had arrived there a few months earlier. She was the first great ape Darwin had seen, and one of the first ever seen in Britain. In the letter home which described his visit to the Fitzroys, he recounted the experience:

> the keeper showed her an apple, but would not give it to her, whereupon she threw herself on her back, kicked and cried, precisely like a naughty child . . . the keeper said 'Jenny if you will stop bawling & be a good girl, I will give you the apple' – she certainly understood every word of this, & though like a child, she had great work to stop whining, she . . . got the apple, with which she jumped into an armchair & began eating it, with the most contented countenance imaginable.

Shortly afterwards, he wrote in his secret notebook:

> Let man visit the ouran-outang in domestication . . . see its intelligence. Man in his arrogance thinks himself a great work . . . More humble and I believe true to consider him created from animals.

He was not only suggesting that evolution had taken place; he was now implying that humanity itself was the product of such a process. It was an idea that was anathema to most respectable scientists. His 'mental rioting', as he called it, was taking him into deep waters.

Throughout the spring and summer of 1838 he continued to overwork. He was engaged simultaneously on several books and still giving papers. He was reading widely. And all the while he was accumulating secret notes on the problem of species. Just occasionally, he would let out a hint to a close friend or colleague. To Lyell he wrote:

I have lately been sadly tempted to be idle – that is, as far as pure geology is concerned – by the delightful number of new views which have been coming in thickly and steadily . . . bearing on the question of species. Note-book after note-book has been filled with facts which begin to group themselves *clearly* under sub-laws.

Writing to his cousin Fox, he was even more daring:

I am delighted to hear you are such a good man as not to have forgotten my questions about the crossing of animals. It is my prime hobby, and I really think some day I shall be able to do something in that most intricate subject, species and varieties.

On 21 June he added to his creature comforts, and his

intellectual resources, by being elected to the Athenaeum, a gentleman's club just a short cab ride from where he was living. For city-dwelling men of Darwin's social level membership of a club was essential to their way of life. It provided a home from home, a refuge from female company, the company of like-minded contemporaries and an opportunity for networking. Some clubs were defined by their politics; some revolved around drinking and gambling. The Athenaeum was the preferred resort of scientists and men of letters. Lyell was already a member. Darwin became a member on the same day as Charles Dickens. In the months following his election, he dined there most days. He wrote his letters there, and he spent long hours in its well-stocked library.

In July he took a two-week holiday, divided between Shrewsbury and Maer, and on 1 August he travelled back to London by train – the first train journey of his life. There were no trains in Shropshire; but the line connecting London and Liverpool, which had been opened in the previous year, passed within a mile of his Uncle Jos's park gates. While he had been travelling the world in one of the oldest forms of transport – a sailing ship – Britain had gone mad over the newest – the steam-driven train. The country had been seized with a railway mania. Fortunes had been made, and lost. Many companies had gone bust, but 400 miles of railway had been laid, and there were those who forecast that the days of the mail coach were numbered. An age of rapid transit was being born. And as men of science met more frequently, the exchange of ideas speeded up.

Ideas were what Darwin now hungered for. He was reading

widely, but his reading was anything but aimless. He was engaged on a quest, and he was prepared to read anything that might – or talk to anyone who might – be able to guide him on his way. On 28 September 1838 he struck gold. It was a day he would remember all his life.

The book he picked up that day was not about geology, or zoology, or botany. It was not, on the surface, about anything remotely to do with the natural world. It was a book about economics, first published ten years before he was born. Its title was *An Essay on the Principle of Population*, and its author was the Rev. Thomas Malthus. Malthus was a Cambridge graduate, of the same age as Darwin's father. He had gone on to become Professor of History and Political Economy at the East India Company's college in Hertfordshire. His *Essay* had been published anonymously as a long pamphlet in 1798. It had gone through several editions until the massive sixth edition of 1826, which was the one that Darwin opened that day. It was not a chance discovery. Malthus was a familiar figure in the Darwin and Wedgwood circles, and Darwin was familiar with the general thrust of the book's argument. His brother Erasmus was a close friend of the novelist Harriet Martineau, who was one of Malthus's most ardent disciples.

Malthus argued that the growth of human populations would always outstrip the rate of growth of food production, and that poverty and starvation were the inevitable fate of the mass of humanity, unless population were limited by self-control, by disease, or by some other restraining factor. More precisely, population increased by a geometrical progression, whereas food production expanded only arithmetically. It was the argument that had caused Carlyle to christen economics 'the dismal science'. As an economic proposition, it was of only academic interest to Darwin. But as an analogy, it promised to provide him with the key that could unlock the box in which the secret of evolution lay hidden.

By the time he finished reading the book, on 3 October, he had, in his own words, 'a theory by which to work'. The competition for food and shelter, which Malthus saw as the basis of human existence, had its parallel in the natural world, where various kinds of plants, and various kinds of animals, competed for the means of survival. Those that were successful in this competition would be the ones most likely to survive to the stage where they were able to reproduce. The less successful would be eliminated before they could propagate their kind. At this stage, it was no more than an idea. But it was an idea that gripped his imagination, and gave a shape to his thinking. In his heart he felt sure that species *had* evolved. The specimens he had brought back from his travels seemed to be telling him that they had. Now, thanks to Malthus, he had a template on which to model a theory that might explain how such changes came about. He did not need to talk to anyone about it. Malthus had spoken to *him*.

NINE

A Married Man

Enthralling as Malthus's *Essay* was, there were other matters competing for his attention that October. His intellectual life, both public and private, was as full as anyone could have wished for. His personal life was going nowhere. All around him friends and relations were marrying and raising families. Fitzroy and his Mary were snug in their little house, with their baby boy. Fanny Owen was married, and a mother three times over. His sister Caroline had that summer married their cousin Jos – Emma's brother – Josiah Wedgwood III. And here he was, at twenty-eight, in his bachelor house, with only his manservant for company, eating at his friends' tables, envying them their comfort, and their pretty wives, and barely able to imagine the bliss they enjoyed. It was a situation that would have to be resolved, if he was to have the comfort he craved, and the peace of mind he needed to concentrate on work. Discomfort at sea was one thing; lack of comfort at home was something else. The little boy who had been petted and spoiled by a family of older sisters was in need of petting again.

When he had first started to think seriously about marriage, his thoughts had gone round in circles. Because of his naivety about money, he had assumed marriage must mean an end to his comfortable, carefree life as a gentleman naturalist. As he saw it, the responsibility of a family must mean either paid employment as a university professor, or a lifetime of scrimping and saving. It had not occurred to him that he might enjoy the blessings of a wife and family, a gentlemanly existence, *and* a good standard of living. The problem had seemed so intractable that he had confided his concerns to his father, who had explained just how unnecessary such worries were for any son of his. The doctor was now a rich man. His total wealth amounted to well over £100,000, and his annual income was around £10,000. Charles was not familiar with these numbers, and he would have had difficulty putting them in context if he had known them. As far as money was concerned, he was still the child who had never had to bother his head with such things. And his father was still the universal provider, whose loving care, and financial acumen, ensured that no member of the family would ever know what it was to want for money, or the things that money could buy.

This conversation with his father convinced him that his agonizing over money had been unnecessary. He did not have to make any painful choices. He could be married, and comfortably off, and still enjoy a gentlemanly existence. With this point settled, he addressed himself afresh to the arguments for and against the married state. He reached for a sheet of paper, and drew up two lists, headed 'Marry' and 'Not Marry':

Marry	Not Marry
Children – (if it please God) – Constant companion, (& friend in old age) who will feel interested in one, – object to be beloved and played with. – better than a dog anyhow. – Home, & someone to take care of house – Charms of music & – female chit-chat. These things good for one's health. – *but terrible loss of time.* – My God, it is intolerable to think of spending one's whole life, like a neuter bee, working, working, & nothing after all. – No, no won't do. Imagine living all one's day solitarily in smoky dirty London House. – Only picture to yourself a nice soft wife on a sofa with good fire & books & music perhaps – Compare this vision with the dingy reality of Grt. Marlbro's St.	Freedom to go where one liked – choice of Society & *little of it.* – Conversation of clever men in clubs – Not forced to visit relatives. & and to bend in every trifle. – to have the expense & anxiety of children perhaps quarelling – *Loss of time.* – cannot read in the Evenings – fatness and idleness – Anxiety & responsibility – less money for books &c – if many children forced to gain one's bread. – (But then it is very bad for one's health to work too much) Perhaps my wife wont like London: then the sentence is banishment & degradation into indolent idle fool.

By the time he reached the end of the list, he was in no doubt: 'Marry – Marry – Marry Q.E.D.' he wrote. It was a list such as many a young man must have drawn up, and thrown away. But this young man had been taking notes for too long to casually throw one away. Into the file it went.

He did not have to look far to find a candidate for the role of 'nice soft wife'. The nicest, softest, most wife-like person in his field of view was unquestionably his cousin Emma. They had always been the warmest of friends, and the happiest of companions. She had a kind, playful, easy-going personality which endeared her to everyone she met. She was pretty. Although not artistic or intellectual herself, she mixed easily with people who were. She played the piano. And she was the daughter of his inestimable uncle Jos. She was possibly beyond his reach. With her personal qualities *and* her potential dowry, she was undoubtedly a catch, and she had turned down several proposals already. He had no conceit about his own merits where women were concerned. For one thing, he felt sure he was too plain. But it was worth a try.

On 9 November 1838 – a Friday – he travelled to Maer, for the make-or-break encounter. As usual, there were other weekend guests, and Saturday passed without anything being said. There was a Sunday School in the laundry at Maer, which Emma had taught since she was fourteen. That particular Sunday, before the school began, they found themselves alone together. Charles proposed and, to his surprise and delight, was accepted. Emma went off to Sunday School, but found she was talking nonsense, and came away again. The headache Charles had been nursing since he arrived was intensified by the stress of proposing. They both looked so miserable at dinner that Emma's brother Hensleigh and his wife began to suspect that Charles had proposed and been refused. It was not until quite late in the evening that the truth finally emerged. It then transpired that, if Charles was surprised at being accepted, he was the only person who *was* surprised. His delight was shared by the whole family. His uncle Jos wept tears of joy, as he contemplated the marriage of his beloved sister's son and his treasured daughter. 'You have won a prize,' he said to Charles who saw no reason to disagree. The doctor too was delighted. 'Emma having accepted Charles gives me as great happiness as Jos having married Caroline, and I cannot say more,' he wrote to Emma's father, when he heard the news.

Charles's misgivings had, it turned out, been groundless. Emma had long since decided upon her answer, in the event of such a proposal; but she had detected nothing in his behaviour to cause her to think one likely. They had seen quite a lot of one another in London when she had been staying with her brother Hensleigh. But she had concluded that his behaviour towards her was just part of his naturally kind and friendly disposition. Writing to one of her aunts she said:

He is the most open, transparent man I ever saw, and every word expresses his real thoughts. He is particularly affectionate and very nice to his father and sisters, and perfectly sweet tempered, and possesses some minor qualities that add particularly to one's happiness, such as not being fastidious, and being humane to animals . . .

'Not being fastidious' was clearly a plus in the eyes of the Wedgwood family's 'Little Miss Slip-slop'. She had never been fussy about little things herself, and she did not want a man who was.

In his uncertainty, he had underrated his own attractions. It was true that he was not conventionally handsome. But neither was he positively ugly. And he had many qualities calculated to impress a young woman of intelligence and spirit. He had, after all, just returned from a round-the-world voyage with a store of exciting stories. He was being spoken of as someone who was going to achieve great things in science. Yet, for Emma, he was still the same cousin Charles she had known since childhood, whose gentle character was esteemed by everyone around her, her beloved father most of all.

Although Emma had accepted him so readily, she did not wish to be rushed into marriage. She wanted time to savour the happiness of being engaged, and to wind up her single life. Writing to Charles's sister Catherine, she said:

Since Charles went, I have been rather afraid of his being in too great a hurry so hope you will all hold him in a little . . .

And on the back of the letter, she added:

Tell Charles to be a good boy . . . and take things

leisurely . . . J.A. says it is the happiest time of Emma's life & it is a thousand pities it should be a very short one. Do dear Catty clog the wheels a little slow.

'J.A.' was, of course, Jane Austen, whose own *Emma* had been published twenty years earlier. It was clear who was being cast in the role of Mr Knightley.

Between Charles's impatience and Emma's caution, a compromise was arrived at: a ten-week engagement, with the wedding fixed for 24 January. One problem remained. Where were they to live? If Charles were to maintain his involvement in the scientific life of the capital, it would have to be somewhere near where he was presently living. With his brother's help, he set about house-hunting. Time was short, and the stress of the search, added to the excitement of the engagement, and on top of his other commitments, brought back his headaches and his palpitations. Emma was concerned:

I want to persuade you my dear Charley to leave town at once and get some rest. You have looked so unwell for some time that I am afraid you will be laid up . . . nothing could make me so happy as to feel that I could be of any use to my own dear Charles when he is not well . . . So don't be ill any more my dear Charley till I can be with you to nurse you.

The 'nice soft wife' was promising to be his nurse as well. This was *much* better than a dog.

139

It was at this point that the outside world intruded on their plans. His name had been put forward for membership of the Royal Society. The Society now had 800 members worldwide, and whatever it had signified in his father's case, his own election was a genuine recognition of his scientific standing. With its entry fee of £70, it was not a club for poor scholars. He yelped at the cost, but it was a price he was willing to pay for the company it would enable him to keep. The election was due to take place on the very day they had chosen for their wedding. Fortunately, only family and close friends were involved, and they were able to substitute another date.

A week before they were married, he sat down in his London club, and penned a warning note to his bride-to-be:

> Sunday Night, ATHENAEUM
>
> I do hope you may be as happy as I know I shall be: but it frightens me, as often I think of what a family you have been one of. I was thinking this morning how it came that I, who am fond of talking and am scarcely ever out of spirits, should so entirely rest my notions of happiness on quietness and a good deal of solitude . . . It is that during the five years of my voyage (and indeed I may add these two last), which from the active manner in which they have been passed may be said to be the commencement of my real life, the whole of my pleasure was derived from what passed in my mind while admiring views by myself, travelling across the wild deserts or glorious forests, or pacing the deck of the poor little Beagle at night. Excuse

this much egotism, I give it you because I think you will humanise me, and soon teach me there is greater happiness than in building theories and accumulating facts in silence and solitude.

Should it prove impossible to 'humanise' him, she was being given fair notice of the sort of life that might lie ahead. And the message was underlined by his description of his afternoon's entertainment: 'The Lyells called on me today after church . . . I was quite ashamed of myself . . . for we talked for half-an-hour unsophisticated Geology, with poor Mrs Lyell sitting by, a monument of patience.' For all his talk of 'poor Mrs Lyell', it was unlikely that the future Mrs Darwin would be treated any differently. He had never shared his intellectual life with a woman, and he was not looking for one to share it with now.

On 29 January 1839 a party of friends and relations turned out to see the twenty-nine-year-old FRS and his thirty-year-old bride married at Maer. Emma wore a dress of 'greenish-grey rich silk . . . and a white chip bonnet trimmed with blonde [lace] and flowers'. It was, in every sense, a family affair. In the little church in the grounds of the bride's family home, the two cousins were joined together by a vicar who was a cousin to both of them: a vicar who had been appointed to his living by the bride's father, who was his uncle. In the congregation was a sister of the groom who was married to a brother of the bride. For the older members of the congregation, there were echoes of another wedding, nearly half a century before, when the twenty-nine-year-old Robert Darwin, FRS, had married the thirty-one-year-old Susannah Wedgwood. Sadly, Emma's mother, who in happier times had presided over so many family celebrations, was unable to share in her daughter's happiness. She had been in failing health for some time, and was now only vaguely aware of what went on around her. To Emma's relief, she slept through the afternoon, sparing them both 'the pain of parting'.

The simple ceremony, designed to accommodate Unitarian sensibilities, was soon over. The wedding party walked back to the house, and soon afterwards, the happy, but subdued, couple left for London, carrying their wedding breakfast with them: a packet of sandwiches and a bottle of water, to be consumed on the train. They had decided to dispense with a honeymoon. Their new home was waiting for them, and that was where they wanted to be. It was a cold day, and by the time they reached London, it was dark. But the house was only a five-minute cab ride from the station. Charles had warned the housemaid that they might arrive at any time and, as Emma reported in her letter home, they found it 'blazing with fires'.

The house was one that Charles and his brother had found: number 12, Upper Gower Street, on the edge of Bloomsbury, and near to University College. It was a four-storey terraced house, neither large nor very small, built fifty years before as part of the Bedford estate: a planned development without shops, public houses or stables. The previous occupants had left behind a garish assortment of furnishings, and Charles and Emma promptly christened it 'Macaw Cottage'. Charles and his manservant had transported his books and furniture, and his geological specimens, from Great Marlborough Street, and a butler, a cook and a housemaid were already in post. For Emma, it lacked only one thing for it to be considered a home. The deficiency was soon remedied. They arrived home one day to find a van in the street, bringing a gift from Emma's father: a Broadwood piano.

It was not only their physical comfort that was now assured. Their financial needs had also been attended to. By marrying within the family, they had strengthened the ties of money binding the Darwin and Wedgwood dynasties together. Their fathers could afford to be generous in their dispositions, without fear of the seeping away of family wealth that was the dread of wealthy parents contemplating their children's marriages. The pleasure that Robert and Jos took in the marriage was reflected in the provisions they made. Jos made a capital settlement of £5,000 on Emma, with an additional £400 a year of spending money. Robert's provision for Charles matched Jos's, pound for pound.

One cloud hovered over their happiness. It could not be ignored, but they did their best to lighten the shadow it cast. The cloud was religion. Emma had held true to the belief in which she had been raised. It was not a strident faith, nor was it an intellectual one, but it was sure. Charles, on the other hand, was gradually slipping away from what remained of his own childhood beliefs. He had never been very interested in religion, so there was no drama in his letting go of it. His transition from unquestioning acceptance to tepid agnosticism had not involved any sudden change, like that experienced by the butterfly that breaks out of its chrysalis. It had not even been like the snake that casts off its outgrown skin. It had been more like the gradual change of habit of the young animal which daily strays further from its childhood home, until the day comes when it goes home no more.

When he had fretted over the arguments for and against marriage, religion had been one of the things that had given him most concern. It was a sign that he was thinking of a particular person, and not just the institution of marriage, that he sought his father's advice on this subject, as well as on the subject of money. His father, as always, had clear counsel to offer. It had been his observation, he said, that differences of religion did not usually present problems in the early years of a marriage. But he had known several cases where wives had become more concerned about such differences as time went by, putting severe strains on marriages that had once seemed secure. His advice was that Charles should keep his doubts to himself.

For once Charles had been unable to act on his father's advice. He did not have his father's ability to keep the parts of his life in watertight compartments. His open nature made him want to start married life on a basis of honesty. When the time came to ask someone to share his life, he blurted out his misgivings, and Emma's dismay was palpable. She put her feelings in writing:

When I am with you I think all melancholy thoughts keep out of my head but since you are gone some sad ones have forced themselves in, of fear that our opinions on the most important subjects should differ widely . . . I thank you from the bottom of my heart for your openness with me & I should dread the feeling that you were concealing your opinion from the fear of giving me pain . . . my own dear Charley we now do belong to each other & I cannot help being open with you. Will you do me a favour? . . . it is to read our Saviour's farewell discourse to his disciples which begins at the end of the 13th Chap. of John. It is so full of love to them & devotion & every beautiful feeling. It is the part of the New Testament I love best. This is a whim of mine it would give me great pleasure though I can hardly tell why. I don't wish you to give me your opinion about it.

She had, without knowing, chosen the very text his sister Caroline had recommended to him when he was a sixteen-year-old student in Edinburgh.

Soon after they moved in to their new home, his reputation received a further boost. His *Journal*, which he had prepared for the press two years earlier, was finally published, as part of a multi-volume set entitled *Narrative of the Surveying Voyages of HMS Adventure and Beagle Between the Years 1826 and 1836*. The agreement he had reached with Fitzroy, that their journals would be published together – with Fitzroy as editor – alongside the narrative of the *Beagle*'s earlier survey, had delayed the appearance of his own volume. Fitzroy had not only taken longer to complete his account of the voyage; he had held up publication at the proof stage to add two chapters containing his reflections on the discoveries made during the survey. The main body of his narrative dealt with his experiences in a manner which revealed an enquiring intelligence – and a breadth of reading – quite exceptional in a professional sailor. In the first of his supplementary chapters, he had interesting observations to make on the subject of the dispersion of human populations over time. He suggested, for example that North America might have been populated out of Asia, via the Aleutian Islands, which was quite a remarkable speculation for its time. But this chapter was marred by his efforts to demonstrate that the entire world had been peopled from the Near East. His final chapter was given up entirely to arguments designed to counter the anti-scriptural tendency he perceived in Darwin's record. This chapter, entitled 'A Very Few Remarks with Reference to the Deluge', set out his belief that the shells and fossils which had been found so far from the sea were evidence of the Flood described in the Book of Genesis. The two travelling companions, who had set out with almost identical views of scriptural authority, had for seven years been travelling on opposite courses, and they were now, philosophically speaking, on opposite sides of the globe.

When the reviews appeared, Darwin's volume was highly praised. Fitzroy's was either patronized or ignored. The set as a whole was not a success. It was an intimidating package, and its price was high. In August 1839 Darwin's volume was reissued separately, with the title of *Journal of Researches*. In this form it became one of the most popular books of the age. Readers who wished to know about Rome or Florence could go and see these places for themselves. But if they wished to learn about places farther afield, they were forced to rely upon travellers' tales. Darwin's traveller's tale went on to become a bestseller. Unfortunately, the terms of his contract prevented him from benefiting financially from its success.

Darwin's reputation among British scientists was already high before his *Journal of Researches* appeared. Its publication not only raised him further in the esteem of his own countrymen and women, it brought him fame abroad as well. It was praised both for its scientific content and for its literary quality, and it received the sincere flattery of being followed by a string of imitations. The sweetest praise of all came in a letter from the great Alexander von Humboldt, whose own *Narrative* had inspired Darwin's youthful dreams of foreign travel. Not only did Humboldt say: 'You have an excellent future ahead of you'; he suggested that his having been Darwin's inspiration might turn out to be his own greatest achievement. Darwin thought this was a bit over the top, but he purred nonetheless.

He was doubly blessed. While he basked in the praise of his scientific peers, he was luxuriating in his new-found happiness as a married man. Emma was pregnant, and as summer slid into autumn, they gave up parties and settled into a comfortable routine. He still had his club, and the company of his scientific friends. But he was relieved of the strain of social gatherings, which not only represented a waste of valuable time, but also played havoc with his constitution. His health was still fragile, and any kind of excitement – even an otherwise enjoyable dinner party – was liable to bring on headaches and bouts of sickness. Fortunately for him, Emma was happy at home, and her concern for his wellbeing overrode any need she had for other company.

On 27 December their happiness was completed by the birth of their first child, a son named William. Darwin's delight in the child, and his joy in parenthood, were immense. But he was still a scientist, and this was an opportunity to observe a young animal at close range. He opened another notebook, and recorded the child's development in the same detailed, speculative way in which he had once recorded the behaviour of Jenny the orang-utan.

His personal happiness and his bodily health were now set on different courses. The stress of Emma's confinement, and the upheaval of the new infant's arrival, intensified his symptoms. As 1840 dawned, his condition worsened. Writing to Lyell in February, he said: 'Dr Holland thinks he has found out what is the matter with me, and now hopes he shall be able to set me going again. Is it not mortifying, it is now nine weeks since I have done a whole day's work.'

Once again, it was Emma who was proving the stronger. In March, less than three months after her confinement, while still nursing, she sat for her portrait to the society painter George Richmond. She did so to please her father, who wanted her picture to soften the sharpness of her absence. Richmond's artistic credo was 'to show the truth, but lovingly told'. In Emma's case, he excelled himself. Her warmth, and the artless sincerity of her character, leapt from the canvas. It was a picture to gladden any father's heart.

In April Darwin travelled to Shrewsbury to seek his father's advice. When he mounted the scales, he discovered that he had lost nearly twenty pounds since his return from the voyage. Never fat, he was now positively scrawny. Under his father's care, his vomiting fits were brought to a halt; but the doctor confessed himself puzzled by his son's symptoms.

After a week's rest at the Mount, he felt well enough to return to Upper Gower Street. He resumed his scientific activities, and he and Emma began to socialize. But the excitement proved too much, and within a month he was ill again. This time his sickness and languor were serious, continuing for weeks at a stretch. Emma took him off to Maer, where they remained until the autumn. With a six-month-old baby and a sick husband, and pregnant, she was glad to be out of London and in the comfort of her childhood home. She did not mind the demands his sickness made on her. Writing to one of her aunts, she said: 'It is a great happiness to me when Charles is most unwell that he continues just as sociable as ever . . . he . . . never wants to be alone, but continues just as warm and affectionate as ever, so that I feel I am a comfort to him.'

That she was a comfort, he never ceased to tell her. His sickness brought them closer together. She could not travel with him in that world of the mind where so many of his waking hours were spent. But his need of her, and her need to be needed, created a bond that nothing could sever.

The whole of 1840, as far as science was concerned, was largely a write-off. When he felt well enough, he would do a little work on the book on coral reefs he had begun before his marriage. This was a serious academic work in which he set out to persuade fellow geologists of the correctness of his own theory of how reefs were formed. Many geologists still believed what Lyell had believed until Darwin had convinced him to the contrary, that reefs had been uplifted from the seabed as the result of volcanic action. Darwin was sure that they were formed by continued coral growth, as the ocean floor slowly sank. He was determined that his book would contain such a mass of evidence that its argument would be irresistible. He spent hours over ocean charts and read every book he could find on the topic. When he needed a change of subject, there was the bird section of the *Beagle* Zoology to be attended to for his commissioned multi-volume work. By his own standard of the previous two years, he was perhaps not accomplishing very much; but the work rate he maintained during this summer of invalidity would have satisfied many a fitter man.

As autumn turned into winter, and Emma grew heavier, they settled back into their London home. In a letter to his cousin Fox, he gave a progress report on his condition:

> My strength is gradually . . . increasing; so that I have been able to work an hour or two several days in the week . . . I am forced, however, to live very quietly and am able to see scarcely anybody & cannot even talk long with my nearest relations . . .

and he added a footnote that showed that he was still wrestling with the problem of species:

> I send you this P.S. as a memento, that I continue to

collect all kinds of facts about 'varieties and species', for my some-day work to be so entitled . . . Don't forget, if your half-bred African cat should die that I should be very much obliged for its carcase sent up in a little hamper for the skeleton; it, or any cross-bred pigeons, fowl, duck, &c, &c, will be more acceptable than the finest haunch of venison.

In referring to 'my some-day work to be so entitled', he was giving the clearest indication yet of the major work he had in mind. And in staking his claim on a dead cat, he was displaying his insatiable desire for any evidence that might be relevant.

On 2 March 1841, Emma was delivered of her second child, a girl. They named her Anne Elizabeth, but she quickly settled into Annie. Darwin delighted in her from the start. Looking forward, he anticipated that she would be their 'solace in old age'. But true to form, the stress of her arrival made him ill again.

At the first sign of summer, they left London for the clear air of Maer. While they were there, William's nursemaid took him off to Shrewsbury to meet his grandfather and his aunts. Darwin and his manservant followed soon after. As usual, he was after his father's medical opinion. But on this occasion he had something else on his mind as well. Their London house was beginning to feel cramped, now that their family was growing. They needed somewhere larger. They also wanted to get away from the city's noise and smoke. But the sort of home they aspired to was beyond their means. The question was: would the guv'nor be able to help? The answer, as always, was yes. The man who had helped Emma's father to buy her childhood home, forty years before, was not going to refuse them now. He found it difficult to believe that they could find an acceptable home without living in their preferred area first. But he was happy to advance them £3,000, as a loan against Darwin's future inheritance, and the money would be available whenever it was needed.

The knowledge that they were in a position to move whenever they wished took some of the urgency out of the decision. Darwin went back to his book on coral reefs. In January 1842 the manuscript went off to his publisher, and by the end of May *The Structure and Distribution of Coral Reefs* was in the bookshops. It had, he estimated, occupied twenty months of the four years that had elapsed since he had signed the contract for it. In his diary he listed the other work he had accomplished during this period – an unimpressive list by his reckoning – and added a forlorn note: '. . . and rest all lost by illness'.

In one respect at least, his creative powers were undiminished. As the first buds of spring opened, Emma discovered that she was pregnant again. She was due in September. They really would have to find a new home soon.

In May they were back at Maer, with the prospect of two months in the country to cheer them. Darwin was feeling better than he had for some time. With no book crying out to be finished, he turned once again to the question of species. It had never been far from his thoughts, and he had never stopped taking notes on the subject. Now he was able to sit down and arrange his ideas into a coherent shape. During those long summer days, in the idyllic setting of his uncle Jos's estate, he began to put together an outline of the theory that had taken shape in his mind over the previous five years.

This outline, written in pencil, was an attempt to bring order to his notebook jottings. He addressed himself first to the huge amount of variation found among domestic animals, from racehorses to plough-horses, and from lapdogs to gun-dogs. The process by which these varieties had arisen, as a result of deliberate breeding for desirable characteristics, he called Artificial Selection. Arguing by analogy, he suggested that something similar happened among wild species. In this process, which he called Natural Selection, nature took the place of man: favouring certain characteristics, which gradually became more marked – and more widespread – until what had once been varieties eventually became distinct species.

In this formulation, Darwin's observations during his voyage, his enquiries among pigeon-fanciers and dog-breeders and his wide reading came together in one overarching theory of the origin of all living forms. The resemblance of present-day species to extinct species in South America had convinced him of the fact of evolution. The unique character of related species on the various islands of the Galapagos archipelago had persuaded him that individual species could evolve from a common ancestry, as a result of gradual changes over time. His conversations with gardeners and animal-breeders had satisfied him that the favouring of particular characteristics which were capable of being transmitted to later generations could bring about dramatic changes in the appearance and behaviour of both plants and animals. And his reading of Malthus had opened his eyes to the competition that resulted from the speed at which animals and plants were able to reproduce. Putting all these ideas together, he was led irresistibly to the conclusion that a process of Natural Selection had operated throughout the ages, and was still operating. It was a process that favoured the transmission of advantageous features; that is, features which increased the chances of any living form surviving to the age when it was able to reproduce, and pass those features on. Given sufficient time, this process was capable of yielding an even more dramatic outcome than that which resulted from artificial selection.

At the end of May, he left Emma and the children at Maer, and travelled to Shrewsbury, by himself. There, in the quiet of the house where he was born, he put the finishing touches to a thirty-five-page sketch that summarized his secret thoughts on the origin of species. They were thoughts that had first stirred in Patagonia five years before. He was convinced in his heart that they held the key to the whole history of life on earth. With the sketch completed, he experienced a feeling of wellbeing and mental release. Under its influence, he decided on a little adventure. He had never forgotten the week he had spent with Sedgwick in North Wales in the summer of 1831. He now embarked on a sentimental journey, albeit one with a purpose. He left the Mount in a gig, as he and Sedgwick had done, and took the Holyhead road into the heart of Snowdonia. He walked alone among the hills, and even found the strength to climb a little. He gazed on the same scenes as he had eleven years earlier; but he looked upon them with eyes educated by reading. This time the signs of a past Ice Age were plain to see. The road itself ran through a great U-shaped valley, above which smaller hanging valleys proclaimed their glacial origin. Mountain lakes glistened behind the moraines that had brought them into being. Perched blocks lay where the retreating ice had left them. The geologist in him was ecstatic. Writing to a scientific colleague in London, he rhapsodized about:

scenes . . . which have given me more delight than I almost remember to have experienced since first I saw an extinct crater. – The . . . Inn at which I am writing, must have once been covered by at least 800 or 1,000 ft in thickness of solid ice! Eleven years ago, I spent a whole day in the valley, where yesterday everything but the ice of the glacier was palpably clear to me, and then I saw nothing but plain water and bare rock.

His holiday over, they started house-hunting in earnest. This time their search was successful. Fifteen miles south-east of London, in the Kentish countryside, they found a village of about forty houses, and just outside it, a plain, but spacious, former vicarage in reasonable repair and within their price bracket. The village was called Down, and the house was called Down House.

By mid-September they were established in their new home. They had exchanged the smoke and fogs of London for the clear air of Kent. They were surrounded by fields and woods in which children could run and play, and paths where a naturalist could walk – and think – in peace. He had his country vicarage after all.

Writing to his old servant, and former shipmate, Syms Covington, he headed his letter:

> Down, near Bromley, Kent
> N.B. This will be my direction for the rest of my life.

TEN

Secrets and Sorrows

———————◆•◆•◆———————

Their first months in their new home were not happy ones. The week after they moved in, Emma was delivered of her third child, a girl, who was christened Mary Eleanor. Just three weeks later they buried her in the village churchyard. Writing to her sister-in-law Fanny, Emma said:

> Our sorrow is nothing to what it would have been if she had lived longer and suffered more . . . with our two other dear little things you need not fear that one sorrow will last long, though it will be long indeed before we forget that dear little face.

While coping with this loss, Emma was living with the possibility of another. Her father, Charles's revered uncle Jos, had had a stroke, and with every post she half-expected to hear of his death. He had been frail for a long time, and he and his wife Bessie lay bedridden at Maer. The old house, which had been the scene of so many happy gatherings, now stood hushed and half-deserted. The doctor rode out to visit him, but he was too frail himself now to be of much use, and he broke down when he saw his friend's condition.

For Darwin some distraction from unhappiness was, as always, available in the form of work. He turned to his *Beagle* notes, and started on the second of the proposed volumes, dealing with the geology of the voyage. The first had been the book on coral reefs. The next was to be devoted to the subject of volcanic islands.

In the spring of 1843 they embarked on a programme of improvements. The house was plain, but it was spacious, and it had sufficient land – eighteen acres in all – to provide them with privacy and a setting of their own choosing. They raised a bank outside the front door to keep out the north wind. A lane passing the house was lowered, so that they were not overlooked. An orchard was laid out. And beds were planted, with flowers like those that had bloomed around Emma's childhood home.

One memory of Maer that Darwin particularly treasured was the mile-long Sand Walk encircling the lake. At Down, he rented a strip of land from a neighbour and, using gravel and red clay from a nearby clay pit, he had his own Sandwalk, about a quarter of a mile in length, laid alongside it. Here, rain or shine, he took daily walks, recording the number of circuits by removing a pebble from a previously counted-out heap at the side of the path each time he went round. It was an ideal place for quiet thought. As the children grew, it also became a favourite place for play. He enjoyed their presence, and they took comfort in his, as they listened to his iron-shod walking stick beating out his steps.

One day towards the end of March, he opened his newspaper to read a news item that took him back to his days on the *Beagle*. He had not seen Fitzroy for five years. He knew that he had been a member of parliament. He now learned that his old dining companion had been appointed Governor of New Zealand. It was undoubtedly an honour, but it was not one that everyone would have welcomed. The colony had only recently come under the rule of the British Crown, and the tensions between the indigenous population, the established settlers and the newly arriving, commercially sponsored colonists promised the new Governor an interesting time. Darwin wrote warmly:

Dear Fitzroy,

I read yesterday with surprise and great interest your appointment as Governor . . . I do not know whether to congratulate you on it, but I am sure I may the Colony, on possessing your zeal and energy . . . I cannot bear the thought of your leaving the country without seeing you once again; the past is often in my memory, and I feel that I owe to you much bygone enjoyment, and the whole destiny of my life, which (had my health been stronger) would have been one full of satisfaction to me.

That spring, Emma discovered she was pregnant again. She was due in September; but in July preparations for the future were set aside while she and Charles travelled to Maer to take leave of a part of their past. Her father's life was ebbing away, and she was by his side when the end came. It was clear that her mother would soon follow and that with her death the old house would be sold. Life was moving on. It was now up to her and Charles to try to create for another generation of children the happy environment that Jos and Bessie had provided for theirs.

Shortly after they returned home, Darwin sat down to draft a reply to two letters he had received from George Waterhouse, a fellow naturalist newly recruited to the staff of the British Museum. Waterhouse had sought Darwin's opinion as to the correct basis on which plants and animals should be classified into groups. The accepted framework for classification was the *Systema Naturae* of the Swedish botanist Linnaeus. Linnaeus had based his classification on physical similarities within and between major groups, such as the arms of primates and the wings of bats. Underlying this classification was the idea of a Master Plan embodied in the natural order, which in turn reflected an idea in the mind of God. For Darwin, as he indicated to Waterhouse, this was meaningless drivel:

> Most authors say it is an endeavour to discover the laws according to which the Creator has willed to produce organised beings – But what empty high-sounding sentences these are – it does not mean order in time of creation, nor propinquity to any one type . . . in fact it means just nothing – according to my opinion (which I give everyone leave to hoot at, like I should have, six years since . . .)

classification consists in grouping beings according to their actual *relationship*, ie their consanguinity, or descent from common stocks.

It was a letter that revealed the intellectual distance Darwin had travelled, and the assurance he had gained, since he had returned from his voyage. 'Descent from common stocks' was no longer a speculation: it was the basic assumption underlying his view of the natural world. The great Linnaeus was no longer a towering presence: he was merely a fellow-seeker after truth, to be treated as an equal. And if Darwin was still reluctant to broadcast his ideas to the world at large, he no longer felt any timidity in exposing them to scientists he respected.

On 25 September 1843, just a year after Mary's birth and death, Emma was safely delivered of another daughter. She was christened Henrietta, but her family name was Etty. They now had three children. William, the eldest, was nearly four, and Annie was two-and-a-half. As the family grew, so did the number of people who ministered to their needs. The family of five was supported by a staff of fifteen. There was cooking and cleaning to be done; there were coals to be carried; and in a house with no bathrooms and a sick master there was much fetching of water and changing of linen. There were horses and carriages to be cared for and driven, gardens to be maintained, and children to be nursed and taught. Even at the modest level of wages in the 1840s, it was a considerable expense. But thanks to the Darwin and Wedgwood money that underpinned it, the economy of the house was secure. Like Charles and Emma's own homes of thirty years earlier, it was an island of wealth that stood clear of the sea of poverty and malnutrition surrounding it.

The early 1840s – the 'Hungry Forties' – were years of privation for many people in Britain. Bad weather caused poor harvests, and the Corn Laws prevented the importation of cheap corn. In 1844 there was famine in the Kentish countryside. But for all that it affected the lives of the Darwins and their wealthy neighbours, it might as well have been happening on the moon. For the educated classes, in those early years of Victoria's reign, the mismatch between the needs of a growing population and the available food supply was a vindication of Malthus's dismal prophecies, and the need for a reduction in the birth-rate was self-evident. But, safe on their little islands of prosperity, their own birth-rate raced merrily on.

Free of any need to concern himself with the problem of feeding the growing number of mouths at Down House, Darwin addressed himself to larger matters. During the previous two years, in spite of continued sickness, and while engaged on other work, he had continued to amass evidence bearing upon the subjects of species and variation from his reading and from his correspondence. He was now more than ever convinced that species had changed over time, and that all living creatures shared a common origin. In January 1844 he showed his hand to a new friend, the twenty-six-year-old botanist Joseph Hooker:

> I have been now ever since my return engaged in a very presumptuous work . . . I was so struck with the distribution of the Galapagos organisms . . . and with

the character of the fossil American mammifers . . . that I
determined to collect blindly every sort of fact, which could
bear in any way on what are species . . . At last gleams of
hope have come, and I am almost convinced (quite contrary
to the opinion I started with) that species are not (it is like
confessing a murder) immutable . . . I think I have found
out (here's presumption) the simple way by which species
become exquisitely adapted to various ends. You will now
groan, and think to yourself, 'on what a man I have been
wasting my time and writing to'. I should, five years ago,
have thought so.

His saying that he was 'almost convinced' was, of course, a
front. He was by this time utterly convinced. But being sure
in his mind was one thing; going public was something else.
He was not a natural rebel. The idea of the transmutation of
species was anathema to most respectable scientists, including
many of those he most admired, and some of his closest friends.
'Evolution' and 'transmutation' were words associated with
radical, atheistical pamphleteers. For a respected gentleman
naturalist, there was nothing to be gained by joining them at
the barricades, and much to be lost. It was not just a matter of
his reputation. He had reasons nearer home to make him want to
keep his thoughts to himself. His beloved wife had no interest in
science, and no particular curiosity about his scientific thinking.
Nothing that he said or published was likely to shake her faith
in the religion she had been taught as a child. But to have his
name associated with ideas that challenged the basic teachings

of that religion could only cause her deep distress. He was loath to injure his reputation, and reluctant to hurt her. Publication could wait.

But what if he were to die and his ideas were to die with him? Where would his fame be then? The thought was unbearable. It had been his ambition since he was a twenty-two-year-old student to make an important contribution to scientific knowledge. Now, at thirty-five, that ambition burned more fiercely than ever. He was happy to keep his work secret for the moment, but he was not prepared to take it with him to the grave.

In the spring of 1844 he took down the thirty-five-page sketch he had written in Shrewsbury two years earlier, and set about putting it into publishable shape. When he laid down his pen in July, he had a fully crafted essay of 230 pages. He had it neatly copied out by the village schoolmaster, and then addressed himself to the question of its ultimate publication. Although the implications of the essay would be distressing to Emma, he had total trust that she would carry out his wishes. And while he was reluctant to cause her pain while he was alive, he had less compunction about doing so after he was dead. He sat down and wrote what, to him, was clearly one of the most important letters of his life:

July 5th 1844

My Dear Emma

I have just finished my sketch of my species theory. If, as I believe that my theory is true & if it be accepted by even one competent judge, it will be a considerable step in science.

I therefore write this, in case of my sudden death, as my most solemn & last request, which I am sure you will consider the same as if legally entered in my will, that you will devote 400£ to its publication & further will yourself . . . take trouble in promoting it . . .

He listed the names of possible editors, including Henslow, Lyell and Hooker. He signed the letter 'My dear Wife/Your affect/C.R. Darwin' and, before sealing the envelope, he added:

If there shd. be any difficulty in getting an editor . . . then let my sketch be published as it is, stating that it was done several years ago & from memory, without consulting any works & with no intention of publication in its present form.

He now had the best of both worlds. His respectable reputation remained intact; but he could relax, secure in the knowledge that his bid for immortality had been made.

If he had any doubts about his decision not to go public, they were swept aside by a stunning development just three months later. Towards the end of October he picked up a newly published book entitled *Vestiges of the Natural History of Creation*. The book was not very big, but its scope and its ambitions were huge. It dealt not just with the history of life on earth, but with the whole history of the universe, the solar system, and the origins of mankind. The book's central theme was that there was a Law of Development governing both animate and inanimate matter, and it traced the supposed workings of this law from the first condensation of galaxies out of clouds of gas to its ultimate manifestation in the emergence of the human race. Underlying the science, there was a sub-text that challenged the right of universities, politicians and priests to tell people what they should believe, and how they should order their lives. The book, understandably, was anonymous, and Darwin was unable at first to guess at the identity of the author. He or she was clearly not a trained scientist, and such science as the book contained had obviously been obtained at second hand. But much as Darwin scorned the science, he had to concede the excellence of the presentation. The book was written in a pacy, journalistic style, which swept the reader along, and which filled Darwin with envy. And to his extreme annoyance, amid all the dubious science, it proposed a scheme of evolution of all living creatures from one simple form, which was similar in outline, if not in detail, to the scheme he had himself conceived.

Vestiges, as the book was popularly called, was a publishing sensation. The first edition was an instant sell-out, and was quickly followed by three reprints. The book's name, if not its author's, was on everyone's lips. The English edition was read by Benjamin Disraeli, the American by Abraham Lincoln. But it was not only a talking point at fashionable dinner tables; it was energetically debated in bar parlours and mechanics' institutes. The invention of the steam printing press a decade earlier had

ushered in a new age of cheap mass publishing. The latest ideas
in science and philosophy were no longer the private property
of the respectable classes; they were being eagerly sought out
by a new class of artisan readers, hungry for knowledge. Their
appetite for learning was fed by a new kind of journal, and in
these journals *Vestiges* was extensively reviewed and vigorously
promoted.

As the months went by, the success of the book, and its
perceived threat to established religion – not to mention its
possible effect on the morality and governability of the lower
orders – created a backlash from the scientific and religious
establishment. Scientists and churchmen lined up to denounce
the book's errors and its irreligion. A particularly vicious
denunciation in the *Edinburgh Review* came from the pen of
Darwin's old geology mentor, Adam Sedgwick.

For Darwin the message was clear. If he should ever publish
his own ideas on species and their origins, he would have to
make sure that his evidence was unassailable, and he would
have to steer clear of provocative wider issues. But beyond
this, for someone of his conservative outlook and respectable
connections, it raised the fear of attack, and possible alienation,
from those whose opinion meant most to him. Whatever else
'Mr Vestiges' had achieved, he had made it even less likely that
Darwin would ever voluntarily expose his ideas to the risk of
similar treatment.

The identity of the book's author never became known during
the author's lifetime, although some astute readers made a good
guess at it. It was the work of a Scottish journalist and publisher,

Robert Chambers, who was joint editor of the highly successful *Chamber's Edinburgh Journal*. He never publicly admitted his authorship, even when challenged on his deathbed. When in later life a close relative asked him why he had not done so, he pointed to his house, and said, 'I have eleven reasons,' meaning his eleven children. By this measure, Darwin already had three good reasons for keeping quiet, and, unlike Chambers, he had no need of the money.

In the summer of 1845 he acquired a fourth reason for being cautious, when Emma presented him with a second son, whom they christened George. They now had four children under five. Unlike many couples of their social level, they delighted in their children's company. Emma's father, although he was very reserved in character, had had enlightened views on child rearing, and she had grown up in an exceptionally liberal atmosphere. She applied these same principles to her own children's upbringing, and her placid nature and her notorious untidiness created a children's paradise. She would let their mess accumulate until it became physically necessary to clear it up, and she would then instruct one of the servants to attend to it. Her sturdy style at the piano was ideally suited to musical games. Having inherited her father's reserve, she did not normally participate in the children's other games. This she left to Charles who, when he was not ill or absorbed in work, could sometimes be persuaded to join in. A favourite sport, as the children grew older was sliding downstairs on a specially-constructed 'slide', which could be made to run slowly for little ones and quickly for the more adventurous.

The children were at all times treated with respect, and they comported themselves with confidence. On one occasion Darwin suggested to one of the boys that he should perhaps not jump on and off a new sofa; to which the child replied that if it disturbed him, perhaps *he* should go out of the room.

In his crucial letter to Darwin's own father thirteen years before, which had swung the argument in favour of joining the voyage, his uncle Jos had said: 'Is it not the case that sailors are prone to settle in quiet and domestic habits?' Of no sailor had this been more true than Darwin himself. His five years at sea had accustomed him to routine. Now he maintained a sailor's regular habits. When he was well, he rose early. After a light breakfast, taken alone, and his first walk, he would be in his study soon after eight. He would work for about an hour and a half, and then rest for an hour or so on a sofa, while Emma read to him, either from a novel or from the day's letters. He would then work for another hour and a half. At noon he would reappear, usually with the words 'Well, *I've* done a good day's work', and take himself off, whatever the weather, for his midday round of the Sandwalk. Family lunch, at one o'clock, was followed by another session on the sofa, for his daily reading of *The Times*. He would then write his letters before settling down to a smoke, while Emma read to him again. After a rest in his room he would take his final stroll of the day, and another hour or so of work. An hour of relaxation, another rest, and it was time for family supper. After supper Emma would play to him on the piano, and their day almost always ended with a game of backgammon. By half past ten he was ready for bed. This unchanging pattern was partly the habit of an old sailor, and partly a reflection of his simple character. But it was also an essential element in his strategy for keeping his treacherous health under some degree of control. In his late thirties he was already tied to an old man's routine.

In the summer of 1846 he completed the third and last of the volumes on the geology of the voyage. The five-year journey had taken ten years to write up. He was now a moderately rich man, and there was no monetary reason why he should ever work again. But he was incapable of being idle. His search for knowledge had become an addiction, and he needed a regular fix. But in addition to his craving for knowledge, there was a new factor – intellectual insecurity – driving him on. His reputation as a gentleman amateur was impregnable, but there was another meaning of 'amateur' – a dabbler – that was rather less flattering. His greatest ambition was still to make an original contribution to the study of species; but why should a scientific dilettante expect to be taken seriously in such a controversial area? He had no formal training in zoology, and he had done no systematic work on classification. It was not enough to be right; he had to earn the *right* to be right.

His consciousness of his limited qualifications was intensified by a casual remark by his friend Hooker, who was a botanist of impeccable credentials. Referring to someone else altogether, and having no idea how deeply his words would cut, Hooker wrote to Darwin, saying: 'I am not inclined to take much for granted from someone who . . . does not know what it is to be a specific naturalist.'

That was it. If his thoughts on species were ever to be taken seriously by people who mattered, he would have to win his spurs as a zoologist. But how was this to be done? Among the specimens remaining from the voyage there was a jar containing a tiny creature – a barnacle about the size of a pin's head – which did not fit in to the currently accepted classification of the barnacles, or Cirripedes, as they were known to science. The more closely Darwin examined it, the more unusual and fascinating it seemed to be. It was generally agreed among zoologists that the classification of the Cirripedes was a mess. Everyone he spoke to expressed the opinion that it needed sorting out, and the more illustrious the scientist, the more insistent was the belief that a re-classification was urgent. Here, he thought, was an opportunity to prove himself. It should not take long, and it would give him the standing as a 'specific naturalist' which he craved. It would also enable him to engage in practical microscopy and dissection: activities that had always given him pleasure. He wrote to Hooker, telling him of his plans:

I am going to begin some papers on the lower marine animals, which will last me some months, perhaps a year, and then I shall begin looking over my ten-year-long accumulation of notes on species and varieties, which, with writing, I dare say will take me five years.

In October 1846 he started work on his barnacles, with the happy anticipation of a small boy with a new hobby. He had no suspicion of the magnitude of the project he was embarking on. In the summer of 1847, when he seemed close to finishing the particular group he had set out to examine, he attended a meeting in Southampton of the British Association for the Advancement of Science. One of the speeches was given by Louis Agassiz, who was probably America's greatest naturalist, and who was about to be appointed Professor of Natural History at Harvard. In the course of his speech Agassiz remarked that a complete study of the Cirripides was 'a great desideratum'. Darwin had never contemplated a study of the entire order of barnacles; but here was one of the world's leading naturalists effectively calling upon him to go on to the bitter end. It was a challenge he could not resist; but in accepting it he was committing himself to years of painstaking study.

At least it was work he could do at home. From his study in Down House he built up a worldwide network of scientific contacts and sources of material. He wrote long letters of enquiry about barnacles to scientists around the globe. Where most researchers would have taken it for granted that they had to travel to where material was housed, Darwin coaxed irreplaceable collections out of museums in Britain and abroad, and had them delivered to his door. It was a support system such as had rarely, if ever, been seen in the whole history of science; and while he always couched his requests in appropriately diffident language, it was clear that he considered such co-operation no less than his due.

Around him as he worked the house echoed with the happy noise of his growing family. William, the eldest, was now nine years of age. Annie – the light of his life – was seven. Below them came Henrietta, George and Elizabeth, and in 1848 they were joined by a baby brother, Francis. The house was littered, not only with their books and toys, but with a multitude of specimens and ongoing experiments. For the children, natural history was a part of everyday life, as they assumed it was in other houses. One of the boys, visiting a boy in a nearby grand house, enquired of him: 'Where does your father do his barnacles?' When work became tedious, Darwin would join them in their games, and one of their greatest treats was to be allowed, when they were unwell, to lie quietly on a couch in the study while he worked.

While his children were growing, the world of his own childhood was gradually slipping away. In January 1848 the local Shrewsbury newspaper, *Eddowes Journal*, carried an announcement that: 'We understand that it is in contemplation to alter the town clocks to Greenwich time, in the course of the next few days. The Post Office clock was yesterday put forward ten minutes, in accordance with the new arrangement.' The railway had reached his home town, and timetables required that the clocks in every station told the same story. Never again would arriving coach passengers have to alter their timepieces to Shrewsbury time.

For Darwin, a more important link with the past was about to be severed. His father's life was drawing to a close. He was now eighty-one. Mentally, he remained as alert as ever, but he was confined to a wheelchair and required continuous care from Susan and Catherine, who still lived at home. Grossly overweight, he wheezed rather than breathed, and he who had been such a great talker now found conversation almost impossible. When Charles visited him in May his health was clearly breaking. The strain of seeing his father in this state affected his own health, as such things always did. He experienced fainting and shivering fits, nausea and listlessness. He longed to be back at Down House, in Emma's care. 'Oh Mammy,' his letter home read, 'I do long to be with you & under your protection for then I feel safe.'

One morning in November Robert died quietly, sitting in his chair. Catherine wrote with the news, ending her letter with the words: 'God comfort you, my dearest Charles, you were so beloved by him.' On the day of the funeral, the lowest house at the foot of the hill below the Mount had its blinds drawn, and the children stood at the door crying. The doctor had not practised for many years, but his kindness had not been forgotten.

For the family, Robert's care continued beyond the grave. His will left them all well provided for. Charles's share of the estate came to over £50,000. Added to what he had already received in his father's lifetime, it was more than enough to ensure that his own family, however large it became, would always be comfortable.

During the months while his father was declining, Darwin's own health had taken a distinct turn for the worse. In the winter following his father's death, he became a chronic invalid. Sick and depressed, at times almost unable to walk, he became a cause of concern to all his friends. One day he received a visit from an old shipmate, Bartholomew Sullivan, Fitzroy's former second-in-command. Sullivan was on his way back to the Falklands on a three-year sabbatical to farm there. He had called to pay his respects before leaving. Shocked by Darwin's condition, he suggested that he should try the water cure. Unlike the leisurely 'taking of the waters' in spas like Buxton and Bath, which had been the fashion in Darwin's youth, this was a regime of cold baths, exercise and strict diet. Its leading practitioner was Dr James Gully who ran a hydropathic establishment at Malvern in Worcestershire, 150 miles west of London. When Sullivan's suggestion was endorsed by other aquaintances, Darwin decided to act upon it.

It was not a cure for those of limited means. Not only did it involve a 400-mile round trip from Down, it required a two months' residence in Malvern, with substantial fees for the treatment in addition. There was no way that Darwin could face such a regime, and such a prolonged absence from home, without Emma. Without her, the cure would have been worse than the sickness. But Emma could not leave the children for that long. The only solution was for them all to move to Malvern for the period of the cure. In the summer of 1849 the entire family, plus manservant, governess and children's maids, moved to a rented house in the town, where they remained for nearly three months. For the children, it was a memorable holiday. And fortunately, it paid off. Three months of cold baths, rubbing with towels, cold compresses and long walks resulted in a marked improvement in his condition. So pleased was he with the outcome he returned for two further periods of punishment in 1850. At home, he adopted, on Gully's advice, a regime of strictly limited hours of mental exertion. It might all be quackery, as some of his friends suggested, but there was no question that he was feeling better than he had for a long time.

When he returned from his third visit, the beneficial effects persisted, and as his condition improved, his spirits lifted. He continued with the treatments at home, and it began to look as though he could look forward to a permanent improvement in his health. But no sooner had he got used to the idea of being free of sickness, than it was the turn of another member of the family to give cause for concern.

Charles and Emma had had a bad fright in the previous year, when three of the children – Annie, now nine, and her two younger sisters – had contracted scarlet fever; but they seemed to have made a complete recovery. However, towards the end of June 1850, Annie began to show signs of not being her normal self. From being a notably lively and confident child, she had changed into a sometimes tearful and clinging one. By September her parents could see that there was something physically wrong with her. Thinking that a spell at the seaside would do her good, they sent her and her sister Etty to Ramsgate, thirty miles from Down, in the care of their governess. A fortnight later, their parents joined them, in the expectation of a pleasant family holiday. But within two days of their arrival, Annie was running a fever. Doctors were consulted, but no satisfactory explanation was forthcoming. Early in December, she developed a barking cough.

It now occurred to Darwin that his friend Dr Gully might have some useful advice to offer. He wrote describing Annie's symptoms, and received a prescription for a water cure to be administered at home. From the middle of January, she was subjected to a regime of damp towels and wet sheets, and heavy sweating over a spirit lamp placed under a chair. 2 March was her tenth birthday, and she was well enough to enjoy her first ever ride on a pony. But within a week she developed influenza. Darwin, by now desperately concerned, decided upon drastic measures. As soon as she was able to travel, he took her, with her nurse and her governess, and with Etty for company, on the 200-mile journey to Malvern, with the intention of leaving them there for a month or so, while she underwent whatever treatment Dr Gully recommended. Emma, seven months pregnant, remained behind.

Things now started to go badly wrong. Soon after he returned home, Annie became sick and feverish. Summoned back to Malvern, Darwin saw that she was very ill indeed. Writing to Emma, he said: 'her face lighted up, & she certainly knew me . . . Dr Gully is most confident there is strong hope.' His use of the words 'she certainly knew me' and 'strong hope' were enough to tell Emma how bad things were. Unable to be together, they were suddenly having to think the unthinkable.

While their treasured daughter teetered between life and death, their agonized letters flew back and forth. Desperately concerned that her husband was having to face things alone, Emma persuaded her brother Hensleigh's wife, Fanny, to join him in Malvern. But then a carriage arrived from London, bearing a message from Darwin's brother Erasmus that he had received a telegram to say that Annie had rallied. This was quickly confirmed by a letter from Darwin himself, saying that all trace of fever had gone, and that Gully was convinced she had turned the corner. 'An hour ago I was foolish with delight,' he said, 'and pictured her to myself making custards.'

It was a vain hope. Emma had just finished writing a note, listing the foods she thought would be suitable during Annie's convalescence, when his next, dreadful, letter arrived: 'She went to her final sleep most tranquilly, most sweetly at 12 o'clock today . . . She expired without a sigh. God bless her . . . Do what you can to bear up & think how invariably kind & tender you have been to her.' Their loving, high-spirited daughter, at whose birth he had said 'She will be a solace in our old age', had been taken from them.

In his pain he could not bear to be away from Emma. He left Malvern the next day, leaving Fanny to arrange Etty's transfer to his sister Caroline's home, and Fanny's husband – Emma's brother Hensleigh – to attend to the funeral.

A week after her death, in an attempt to capture his memory of her while that memory was still fresh, he wrote a private memorial. In it, he remembered her way of walking:

All her movements were vigorous, active and graceful. When going round the sand-walk with me, although I walked fast, yet she often used to go before, pirouetting in the most elegant way, her dear face bright all the time with the sweetest of smiles . . .

and he ended it with a sad echo of the comment with which he had greeted her birth:

We have lost the joy of the household, and the solace of our old age: She must have known how we loved her, oh that she could now know how deeply, how tenderly we do still and shall ever love her dear joyous face. Blessing on her.

Over her grave in Malvern, he had a plain headstone erected. It carried no comforting message, no submissive text. It said simply:

ANNE ELIZABETH
DARWIN
BORN MARCH 2 1841
DIED APRIL 23 1851
A DEAR AND GOOD CHILD

After her death, he still walked to church with the family every Sunday morning. But he left them at the church door.

ELEVEN

Forced into the Open

———— ◆•◆ ————

Three weeks after Annie's death, Emma gave birth to a son, who was christened Horace. She had hoped that caring for a new-born child might take away some of the pain; but if anything, it was made worse by the thought that Annie was not there to take pleasure in the new baby's arrival. In the same way that Darwin had written his note, in an attempt to preserve something of Annie's memory while it was still fresh, she too reached out for some link with their lost child. She gathered together a few small keepsakes and a lock of Annie's hair and placed them in a box which she would keep until she died.

For both of them, the pain of Annie's loss was overwhelming, and their need to share it was real. But their reaction to their loss was different, and the difference made talking difficult. For her, it was a bitter test of her faith; but that faith still provided consolation. Her beloved daughter had been taken from her, but her religion told her that they would one day be reunited. For him, no such prospect was conceivable, and Annie's death was a demonstration of the cruel and capricious chance that governed the life of every living creature.

But if he had no religion to provide consolation, he had his work to provide distraction. He immersed himself in his study of barnacles and, by the end of the year, he had two thick volumes – one on fossil barnacles, and one on living species – ready for publication. During the next three years, he produced two follow-up volumes. On 9 September 1854 he recorded in his journal the completion of his monumental task: 'Finished packing up all my Cirripedes . . . distributing copies of my work, &c . . . Began Oct 1, 1846. On Oct 1 it will be 8 years since I began! But then I have lost 1 or 2 years by illness.'

The major part of his working day, for eight years, had been devoted to the minute examination and classification of a single group of marine crustaceans. He had studied, and described, 10,000 different varieties. It was an undertaking of which the very thought would have been enough to make most zoologists' brains hurt. For a non-scientist, both the activity itself, and its point, was beyond comprehension. He even had doubts about it himself: 'my work was of considerable use to me when I had to discuss . . . the principles of a natural classification. Nevertheless, I doubt whether the work was worth the consumption of so much time.'

But his scientific peers entertained no such doubts. His volumes on barnacles were universally acclaimed. Those who were best qualified to judge were the most fulsome in their praise. Even before the work was fully published, it had gained him the Royal Society's Royal Medal. And most important of all, those eight years of painstaking work had fulfilled the purpose for which they had been embarked upon. He was now a time-served zoologist, whose qualifications to pronounce on the subject of species and their relationships could never be called into question. He had covered his flank, and now, at forty-five years of age, he was ready to move forward to the completion of what he had never ceased to believe would be his greatest achievement.

He took down his files of notes, and examined the evidence he had accumulated during the previous eighteen years. As he identified gaps in his understanding of variation in plants and animals, he fired off letters to whoever he thought was best qualified to answer his questions. Many of his enquiries were addressed to eminent scientists, in Britain and abroad. But he had no narrow view of where knowledge was to be found. If his questions concerned variation in domesticated plants, they were addressed to gardeners, or to landowners who had conducted agricultural experiments. If they were about domesticated animals, they were addressed to gamekeepers or dog-breeders. He visited agricultural shows. He frequented pigeon clubs which met in gin palaces, and when he got home, he would keep the cabdriver standing while he plied him with questions about horses. The servants, the children, his neighbours and their children were all roped in to look for specimens, and to seek out answers to his questions. He took it for granted, as he had on the *Beagle*, that people would be happy to help him, and his charm usually achieved the desired result.

He did not, however, content himself with second-hand knowledge. While his acquaintances and his correspondents toiled to find answers to his questions, he kept himself busy with a multitude of experiments and observations. He kept and bred unusual varieties of domestic fowl. He begged the cadavers of interesting specimens from his friends, and boiled them down, so that he could examine their skeletons. While other men of science lived among, and got their ideas from, their books, Darwin and his family shared an ambience that was sometimes part greenhouse, part charnel house and part menagerie, with smells to match. A good example of his correspondence, and his preoccupations, at this stage of his life was the letter he wrote to an old school friend, and one-time shooting companion, Thomas Eyton, in November 1855:

My Dear Eyton
As you have had such great experience in making skeletons, will you be so kind as to . . . give me some pieces of information . . . I have been making a few, & when I took them out of the water, the smell was so dreadful that it made me reach awfully . . . pray tell me how do you get the bones moderately clean, when you take the skeleton out, with some small fragments of putrid flesh still adhering. It really is most dreadful work.

In addition to his massive correspondence, and his practical experiments, he kept up the programme of systematic reading he had started on his return from his voyage. Every so often he would hit upon something of particular relevance to his own researches. Round about the time that he wrote this letter to Eyton, he came across a paper in the *Annals and Magazine of Natural History* that revealed that he was not the only person toying with ideas of descent by variation. The article was entitled 'On the Law that has Regulated the Introduction of New Species'. Its author was a thirty-two-year-old traveller named Alfred Russell Wallace. Fourteen years younger than Darwin, Wallace was no gentleman amateur. He was a self-trained naturalist, of modest origins, who had begun his working life as a builder's apprentice, and had subsequently been employed as a land surveyor and as a schoolteacher. At twenty-five, inspired, like Darwin, by Humboldt's *Narrative*, but also by Darwin's own *Journal*, he had invested his meagre savings in a four-year expedition to the Amazon jungle with the naturalist Henry Bates. For a collector such as Wallace, without private means, the main point of such an expedition was the prospect of being able to dispose of his specimens to eager buyers on his return to England. Unfortunately, he had lost a large part of his collection when fire broke out in the ship in which he was returning. With great resilience, he had subsequently set out for the Malaysian archipelago, with the intention of accumulating another collection, and it was on the island of Sarawak that he had written the paper that Darwin now read. It had been brought to Darwin's attention by Lyell, who knew he was working on species, but who was not yet aware of the revolutionary nature of his theory.

Like Darwin, Wallace had been influenced by Lyell's *Principles of Geology*, and his evolutionary train of thought had been reinforced by his reading of Chambers' *Vestiges of the Natural History of Creation*. His paper drew attention to the varieties of domestic animals that had resulted from artificial selection, and to the similarity between present-day and extinct species in various regions of the world. It invoked the same image of a 'tree of life' that Darwin had employed in his notebook eighteen years before. And it ended with the words: 'Every species has come into existence coincident both in space and time with a pre-existing closely allied species.' Had Darwin had his wits about him, he might have been jolted out of the stately pace at which he was moving towards the writing of what he was now calling his 'big species book'. But he was misled by the cautious way in which Wallace developed his argument, and he read the paper as implying successive *creation* of new species, rather than their evolution. As a result, he perceived no threat to his priority, and he continued with his own thorough, but leisurely, investigations.

But if he thought he could continue to build up his case at a pace of his own choosing, and to continue to put off the date when he would present his ideas to the world, he was deceiving himself. Science does not stand still while individual scientists decide whether the time is ripe to let the world into their secret thoughts. If Darwin could not see this, he had friends who could. In April 1856 he invited Lyell to Down House, ostensibly to see his pigeons, but in reality to test his reaction to the theory for which those pigeons formed part of the evidence. He had always maintained that his own ideas had 'sprung half out of Lyell's brain'. Now it was time to submit those ideas to the scrutiny of that brain. As they toured the cages in which the pigeons were kept, he drew attention to the varieties that human intervention had created from the domestic pigeon's wild forebears. Having thus prepared the ground, he changed the subject to the origin of varieties in a state of nature, and he suggested ways in which geographical isolation and changing conditions might cause new species to arise by descent from the same common stock.

Lyell was shaken. He had not until now realized the full import of Darwin's theorizing, and the magnitude of the challenge it presented to current thinking. He could not bring himself to accept it there and then. He could see too plainly where Darwin's road led. If species were not fixed, but derived from common stocks, then this must be true of *all* species, man included. To abandon all ideas of a special status for man, to treat man as just one animal among others – as Darwin clearly already did – was for him a step too far. But although he could not accept all the implications of his friend's theory, nevertheless he was still his friend, and as his friend, he was concerned for his scientific status. Wallace's paper was fresh in his mind, and even if Wallace should be heard of no more, others would arise to claim priority. Chambers' *Vestiges of the Natural History of Creation* might not have packed a sufficient scientific punch to win the day for transmutation, but the book had ensured that the subject would not go away. It could only be a matter of time before someone else – someone of real scientific stature – would steal Darwin's thunder, and what would he have to show then for nearly twenty years' work on species and their origins?

Darwin was nonplussed. He had wanted Lyell's opinion, and it was sweet to hear him admit that he had a case. But the thought of going public still gave him the shakes. He found it particularly difficult to come to terms with the idea of a short essay, which was what Lyell was suggesting. Yet the thought of being forestalled, and seeing all his work go for nothing, was even more painful to contemplate. On this point, at least, Lyell was right. He had to publish soon, or risk having to abandon for ever his youthful dream of making a great contribution to scientific knowledge. On 14 May 1856 he sat down and began to write his 'big book'. He had decided to call it *Natural Selection*.

By the middle of October he had two chapters ready. A rare trip to London for a Royal Society meeting gave him an opportunity to show them to Hooker. Hooker's reaction was gratifying. 'I have never felt so shaky about species before,' was his comment after reading them. It was music to Darwin's ears. The two men whose opinion he valued above all others were taking his ideas seriously. If Hooker was already half-convinced, after reading only a fraction of his book, if Lyell believed that his thoughts were worth publishing, what had he to fear?

By Christmas, he was into the heart of his subject. Writing to Hooker on Christmas Eve, he said:

I have just been comparing definitions of species . . . It is really laughable to see what different ideas are prominent in various naturalists' minds when they speak of 'species'; in some, resemblance is everything and descent of little weight – in some, resemblance seems to go for nothing, and Creation is the reigning idea – in some, descent is the key – in some, sterility is an unfailing test, with others it is not worth a farthing. It all comes, I believe, from trying to define the undefinable.

If the 'experts' could not agree on what constituted a species, what remained of the concept? And if the concept itself was questionable, was his battle not already half won?

He should have been enjoying himself. He was embarked upon what promised to be the crowning achievement of his scientific career. The friends whose opinion mattered most to him were encouraging. His evidence had been assembled, and his line of argument was clear. Yet within six months of starting on his book he was miserable. After five years of comparatively good health, his old symptoms had come back to trouble him.

Earlier that year Emma had discovered that she was pregnant – for the tenth time. It was unexpected, and unwelcome, news. Her husband did not believe in contraception. It was his belief that the multiplication of the British middle classes was one of the best guarantees of the advancement of civilization. But at forty-seven years of age, and five years after the birth of her youngest child, Emma had assumed that her childbearing years were over. As her pregnancy progressed, Darwin reacted in the way he always did. He experienced palpitations and depressed feelings. Intensifying his usual reaction to Emma's pregnancies was a concern which had always been at the back of his mind, but which was now more insistent. In the light of his own miserable health, and against the background of a cousin marriage – and other cousin marriages that had gone before – he had always worried that his children might fall victim to hereditary defects. In the context of a late pregnancy, and after Annie's death, these fears were accentuated. The combination of these fears, the stress of the pregnancy and the burden of his big book played havoc with his bodily condition. The baby was born in December, and christened Charles. Within a few months, Darwin's worst fears were confirmed. The child displayed the symptoms of what a later age would know as Down's Syndrome.

In February 1857 Darwin received a visit from Fitzroy. They had not met for fifteen years, and they were now middle aged. Darwin was nearly fifty; his old friend was fifty-four. Time had not been kind to Fitzroy. His personal life had been marked by tragedy, having suffered the deaths, first of his wife, and then of his daughter. His professional career had also had its ups and downs. He had not lasted long as Governor of New Zealand. The situation there would have been a challenge for the most patient and politic of men. For a man of Fitzroy's high-minded but imperious character the appointment had been a disaster. Within two years he had been recalled and replaced. His short tenure of the governorship had not only injured his reputation, it had incurred significant expense, making further inroads into a private fortune already depleted by the losses he had suffered as Commander of the *Beagle*. After a spell as Superintendent of the Royal Naval Dockyard at Woolwich, he had resigned from active service in 1850. Things had taken a turn for the better in 1851, when he was elected a Fellow of the Royal Society, on the recommendation of thirteen existing Fellows, including Darwin himself. In the following year he had been appointed, on the Society's recommendation, as Meteorological Statist at the Board of Trade, charged with creating Britain's first Weather Service. He had recently remarried, and been gazetted as a Rear-Admiral, and the purpose of his visit on that February day was to introduce his new wife and his eighteen-year-old son to his old shipmate. Darwin, simple character that he was, was thrilled to have an Admiral in the house. Emma, who had grown up among famous people, and cared nothing for rank or appearances, was amused by his excitement.

Emma had not been well since the birth of baby Charles, and in the spring of 1857 she took a sickly thirteen-year-old Etty off to the seaside for a month's holiday, in the hope that they would both benefit from the sea air. With his nurse gone, and the demands of his book overwhelming him, Darwin's condition deteriorated. Remembering how his health had benefited from his water treatment six years earlier, he decided to repeat the experiment. There could be no question of returning to Malvern – the associations were too painful. He had never seen Annie's grave, and he had no wish to go near it now. He therefore booked himself in for a fortnight's treatment at a hydrotherapy establishment at Moor Park in Surrey, a mere forty miles from Down. It was run by a young doctor called Edward Lane, who had no doubt that Darwin's sufferings were real. 'I cannot recall any [case],' he later said, 'where the pain was so truly poignant as his. When the worst attacks came on he seemed almost crushed with agony.' Like everyone who ministered to Darwin's health, Lane was entranced by the sweetness and stoicism of his character. The regime at Moor Park was gentler than that at Malvern. The house was peaceful and its surroundings were beautiful. Calmed and cared for, Darwin's physical condition, and his animal spirits, showed a rapid improvement. Writing to Hooker, he said:

> having been here a week, and having already received an amount of good which is quite incredible to myself and quite unaccountable. I can walk and eat like a hearty Christian, and even my nights are good. I cannot in the least understand how hydropathy can act as it certainly does on me. It dulls one's brain splendidly; I have not thought about a single species of any kind since leaving home.

If it was true that he had 'not thought about a single species' since leaving home, it was a state of mind which did not last long. By the end of that first week, he had written a very detailed letter to one correspondent, seeking answers to questions about the behaviour of a particular group of crustaceans. Before the second week was out, he had penned a similar letter to Wallace. As well as rattling off the usual list of questions which all his correspondents had learned to expect, he fired a warning shot across the bows of this traveller who seemed to be venturing into waters he regarded as his own preserve:

May 1 – 1857

My Dear Sir

I am much obliged for your letter of Oct. 10th from Celebes received a few days ago . . . By your letter & even still more by your paper in Annals, a year or more ago, I can plainly see that we have thought much alike & to a certain extent have come to similar conclusions. In regard to the Paper in Annals, I agree to the truth of almost every word of your paper . . .

This summer will make the 20th year (!) since I opened my first notebook, on the question how and in what way do species & varieties differ from each other – I am now preparing my work for publication, but I find the subject so very large, that though I have written many chapters, I do not suppose I shall go to press for two years –

. . . It is really *impossible* to explain my views in the compass of a letter on the causes and means of variation in a state of nature; but I have slowly adopted a distinct and tangible idea . . .

This is a very dull letter, but I am a good deal out of health; & am writing this, not from home . . . but from a water-cure establishment.

With most sincere good wishes for your success in every way I remain/My Dear Sir/Yours sincerely/Ch. Darwin

It was, to put it charitably, a somewhat evasive letter. Was it really impossible to explain his views 'in the compass of a letter'? Did his state of health really prevent him from writing a more interesting one? It had not prevented him from stuffing this one with questions he would like to have answered for the purposes of his own researches. He had been given a glimpse of Wallace's hand, but he was keeping his own cards close to his chest.

Two months after writing this letter, he added to his credentials as a pillar of the establishment by accepting an invitation to serve as a Justice of the Peace for the county of Kent. While he secretly continued to lay the charges which threatened to dynamite the religious underpinning of Victorian society, he was swearing on its holy book to keep its peace and to deal with the felons who threatened its security.

As his confidence in his theory increased, his fear of publication abated. But a new fear was ready to take its place. Lyell's concern was that he might be forestalled. His brother Erasmus had issued the same warning. This now became his own concern also. His big book was going to take him two or three years to finish, at the very least. He did not think that Wallace represented any real threat. And as far as he could see, no one else was on the same track. But his reading told him that ideas of evolution were in the air. His own theory was not yet public knowledge. How could he be sure that there was not some other naturalist, at this very moment, putting the finishing touches to a book that would pre-empt his? Scientific discovery was a sport in which there were no prizes for coming second. If he waited until his big book was ready, he would have no defence to the charge of plagiarism, should someone else publish first. He wanted to keep his secret until he was ready to reveal it. But he needed evidence that his theory was indeed *his* theory. He needed someone he could trust, someone of impeccable reputation, who would, if required, be able to vouch for his priority.

There was one person of sufficient scientific standing, who was far enough removed from his own circle to be above any suspicion of collusion. That person was Asa Gray, Professor of Natural History at Harvard University. A year younger than Darwin, Gray was an authority on the international distribution of plants, a subject on which he and Darwin had been corresponding. On 5 September 1857 Darwin sent him a letter, specifically for the purpose of establishing his priority in the event of anyone publishing before him. He had already shown his hand to Gray in a letter written in July of the previous year. In that letter he had said:

I *assume* that species arise, like our domestic varieties with *much* extinction . . . to my mind to say that species were created so and so is no scientific explanation, only a reverent way of saying it is so and so . . . I have come to the heterodox conclusion, that there are no such things as independently created species . . .

Now, for the first time in his life, he was offering a detailed outline of his theory to a fellow scientist. Surprisingly, he now found that it *was* possible to explain his views 'in the compass of a letter', or at least, in the same envelope:

Down Bromley Kent
Sept 5th

My Dear Gray

I forget the exact words which I used in my former letter, but I daresay I said I thought you would utterly despise me, when I told you what views I had arrived at . . .

As you seem interested in the subject, & as it is an *immense* advantage to me to write to you & to hear *ever so briefly*, what you think, I will enclose the briefest abstract of my notions on the *means* by which nature makes her species.

Enclosed with the letter was a thousand-word summary of his theory of Evolution by Natural Selection. This was built around four propositions:

1 Artificial selection has had a marked effect on the form of domesticated plants and animals, although it has only been systematically applied for a small number of generations.

2 Imagine the changes which might be effected if there were a similar force acting in nature over millions of generations.

3 There is such a force: the selective action of the struggle for existence between species, and within species, in the circumstances of a tendency for population growth to out-run the rate of growth of the means of sustenance. Only a few of those annually born can live to propagate their kind.

4 If a change occurs in the physical environment, individuals will be exposed to new circumstances, and competition from a different set of inhabitants. These changes will favour the transmission of features that are advantageous in the new conditions.

To these four propositions, which had formed the basis of his 1844 essay, he now added a fifth, to which he attached the greatest importance:

5 All species are characterized by variation between individuals. In any new environment there will be different conditions from place to place. Individual variations will be favoured by particular sets of circumstances, and this will give rise to a tendency for varieties to become more distinct through successive generations. This *Principle of Divergence* is the most important factor in the evolution of new species.

Nearly twenty years after he had opened his first transmutation notebook, the conceptual framework of his theory was at last complete:

Species arose by *Common Descent*, as a result of *Divergence* from a *Common Stock*. *Divergence* was made possible by *Isolation*, which was usually a matter of geography, e.g., separation by stretches of water, or mountain ranges; but which could take the form of differing habits of life, e.g., breeding at different seasons.

An analogy was the divergence of two daughter languages from a parent language in geographically isolated populations. The *Common Stock* was the parent language or species. *Common Descent* was what characterised languages or species with shared parentage.

Natural Selection was the process by which new species were brought into existence. It was a process of interaction between:

a) *changes* in the environment

b) *competition* between, and within, species

c) the *variation* naturally occurring within species

and it was driven by

d) the *excess* of procreation over the numbers the environment can support

His thinking was done. It was all perfectly clear in his mind. All he needed now was the time, and the strength, to put it into publishable form.

In December 1857 Darwin received a letter from Wallace containing two questions. These were, firstly, why had his own paper in the *Annals* aroused so little interest and, secondly, was Darwin's book going to tackle the subject of human origins? In reply to his first question, Darwin reassured him that, although his paper had not given rise to public discussion, some serious scientists, such as Lyell, had paid it very close attention. In response to the question about human origins, his answer was: 'I think I shall avoid the whole subject, as so surrounded by prejudices; though I fully admit that it is the highest and most interesting problem for the naturalist.' They both knew that

Darwin aged 31, by George Richmond RA

Emma aged 31, by George Richmond R A

Down House

Darwin's study at Down House where *The Origin of Species* was written

(Above) The Sandwalk – where Darw
did his thinking

(Left) The child who played there –
Annie Elizabeth (Annie),
age 8

The Coming Man: Darwin aged 40 in 1849

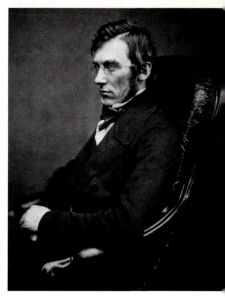

Friends and sparring partners:

(Above left) Charles Lyell, geologist

(Above right) Joseph Hooker, botanis

(Left) Thomas Huxley, biologist

Two allies and an adversary:

(Above left)   Asa Gray, Harvard botanist and American champion

(Above right) Alfred Russell Wallace, co-discoverer

(Right)   Samuel Wilberforce, Bishop of Oxford

Darwin in old age – dressed for the Sandwalk

this was the killer question. Darwin was quite clear in his mind that challenging the fixity of species, and suggesting a common origin for distinct groups of plants and animals, was going to involve him in a battle royal. To extend the argument to include humanity's place in the natural order would make that battle impossible to win.

In regard to his own theory, he was still giving nothing away:

> Though agreeing with you on your conclusions . . . I believe I go much further than you; but it is too long a subject to enter on my speculative notions . . . I have got about half written; but I do not suppose I shall publish under a couple of years.

Through the winter of 1857–8, he continued to work away at his big book. He occasionally took time off to attend to other matters. One of these was the education of his eldest son William who was now of an age to go to university. At the end of February he wrote to him on the subject of his choice of college. The question of choice of university did not arise. Darwins went to Cambridge. Conservative as ever, he had decided that his son should go to his old college:

> My Dear William
> The more I think of it, the more clear I am that you had better go to Christ. Coll. So I will write and enter you tomorrow . . . I think there would be more temptation

in many ways to be idle at Trinity, & it is hard enough for the young to be industrious. You must see that when my fortune is divided between 8 of you, there cannot be enough for each to live comfortably & keep house, and those that do not work must be poor (though thank God with food enough) all their lives. You may rely on it, habits of industry at the University will make all the difference in your success in after life.

He refrained from adding 'as my own case proves'.

His book was going well, but it was playing havoc with his health. In April he was back at Moor Park for another dose of the water cure. Writing to Lyell, he said: 'I have come here for a fortnight's hydropathy, as my stomach had got, from steady work, into a horrid state.' The quietness and the undemanding regime worked their magic once more. A new calmness entered the letter he wrote home:

the weather is quite delicious. Yesterday . . . I strolled a little beyond the glade for an hour and a half . . . at last I fell asleep on the grass, and awoke with a chorus of birds singing around me. And squirrels running up the trees, and some woodpeckers laughing . . . and I did not care one penny how any of the beasts or birds had been formed.

The beginning of May found him back at Down: refreshed, and ready for another attack on the mass of notes in his portfolios. He was now more than halfway towards the book's completion.

As each chapter was started and finished, he recorded its title, and the relevant date, in his journal. On the page for 14 June he entered the title of his next chapter: 'Pigeons'. A little lower down the page he wrote '(interrupted)'.

'Interrupted' was a mild term to describe what happened that week. His mail on 18 June had looked enticing. It included a substantial package from the East Indies, which was clearly another communication from Wallace. Whatever it was, it could hardly fail to be of interest. But he was not prepared for what he found inside. It was only a sheaf of papers – about twenty pages – but if it had been a bomb, it could hardly have had a more devastating effect. As he unfolded the contents, he could see that it was an extended essay. Its title alone was enough to freeze his blood: 'On the Tendency of Varieties to Depart Indefinitely from the Original Type'. As he read it, surprise gave way to dismay. It was like looking into a mirror. There on the page was an outline of his own theory, proceeding by the same steps, and in many places using almost the same words.

What Darwin did not know as he read Wallace's paper was that its conclusions did not simply mirror his own, they had received their inspiration from the same source. In February of that year Wallace had been ill with malaria on the island of Ternate in the Moluccas. During his convalescence, turning over his evolutionary ideas in his mind, he had recalled a book he had read some years earlier. It was Thomas Malthus's *Essay on Population*, the book that had provided Darwin with the key to Natural Selection. In a moment of insight, uncannily like Darwin's own, Wallace had made the connection between

Malthus's 'struggle for existence' and the competition for the means of survival in the natural world.

When Darwin turned to Wallace's covering letter, his dismay began to verge on despair. In this letter Wallace asked Darwin, if he thought the paper was any good, to pass it on to Lyell. He did not mention publication, but that was the logical next step.

Darwin was in turmoil. The letter could hardly have come at a worse time. His daughter Etty was seriously ill with diphtheria. In the village nearby, children were going down with scarlet fever, and the first deaths had already occurred. Annie's death was still fresh in his mind. He could not cope with the thought of losing another child *and* losing the reward for twenty years of mental struggle. In his distress, he turned to the two men – Lyell and Hooker – who had been his intellectual soulmates and sounding boards for so long. Within hours of reading Wallace's paper, he had written to Lyell what was not so much a letter as a cry of pain:

Your words have come true with a vengeance – that I should be forestalled.

. . . I never saw a more striking coincidence: if Wallace had my MS. Sketch written out in 1842, he could not have made a better short abstract! Even his terms now stand as heads of my chapters. Please return me the MS., which he does not say he wishes me to publish, but I shall, of course, at once write and offer to send to any journal. So all my originality, whatever it may amount to, will be smashed . . .

I hope you will approve of Wallace's sketch, that I may tell him what you say . . .

Five days later the next blow struck. Baby Charles, eighteen months old, came down with scarlet fever. In his fog of worry and confusion, Darwin managed another note to Lyell:

I should be extremely glad now to publish a sketch of my general views in about a dozen pages or so; but I cannot persuade myself that I can do so honourably . . . I would far rather burn my whole book, than that he or any other man should think that I had behaved in a paltry spirit.

By now, he was past being able to decide what he should do. Four days after this second letter was written baby Charles died. In the face of this loss concerns about priority were ceasing to matter. He wrote a short note to Hooker:

I have just read your letter, and see that you want the papers at once. I am quite prostrated, and can do nothing, but I send Wallace, and the abstract of my letter to Asa Gray . . . I dare say it is all too late. I hardly care about it. I send my own sketch of 1844 solely so that you can see by your own handwriting that you did read it . . . God bless you my dear friend. I can write no more.

In his moment of need, his two friends took charge. By chance, an extra meeting of the Linnaean Society of London had been scheduled before the summer recess, and they contrived at the last moment to have the topic included in the agenda. Wallace's paper and Darwin's 1844 Essay (the only copy) were delivered by hand to Hooker on the evening of 29 July. His wife spent the next two days transcribing key extracts, and on 1 July they were read to the meeting as a joint paper, along with Darwin's 1857 letter to Asa Gray. Darwin was not there. While his friends were submitting his ideas for the consideration of his scientific peers, he was burying his infant son.

The reading of the papers generated no particular excitement. It was a warm day, and it had been a long meeting. In any case, the fact that the papers were presented by Lyell – Britain's most illustrious geologist – and Hooker – the country's leading botanist – discouraged dissent. When the President of the Society came to review the year's activities some months later, he allowed himself the observation that it had not 'been marked by any of those striking discoveries which at once revolutionise, so to speak, the department of science on which they bear'.

But if the events of that summer had not caused any great stir in the outside world, they had changed Darwin's own perception of the task confronting him. He realized now that his freedom to decide the scale and timing of his big book was gone. His ideas were leaking into the outside world at an alarming rate, and other people were getting in on the act. He had had a narrow escape. If Wallace had sent his paper direct to a journal, rather than to him, he would have been completely wrong-footed. If the publication of his theory was not to be an anticlimax, he would have to publish very soon.

TWELVE

The Deed is Done

A s he walked back from the churchyard on that July day, Darwin had more pressing concerns than how his ideas had been received in London. They had a houseful of children, and the infection which had carried off their infant son was still rampant in the village. The day after the funeral, they sent all the children, except the fourteen-year-old Henrietta – Etty – to the safety of Emma's sister's house in Sussex. Writing to Hooker a few days later, he said:

> We are become more happy and less panic-struck, now that we have sent out of the house every child, and shall remove H., as soon as she can move. The first nurse became ill with ulcerated throat and quinsy, and the second is now ill with scarlet fever, but, thank God, is recovering. You may imagine how frightened we have been. It has been a most miserable fortnight.

It could have been worse. Before the end of July six children in that tiny village had died of scarlet fever. By then the family had moved to the seaside resort of Shanklin, on the Isle of Wight. On 20 July he received copies of the papers that had been presented in London, and on the same day he commenced work on what he was now referring to as the 'Abstract' of his big book. At first, he assumed that it would be a paper of thirty or so pages, to be published in a scientific journal. But as the weeks went by, he began to realize that he would never be able to bring himself to publish his theory without a substantial body of supporting examples and argument. By October he was informing Hooker that: 'it will be a small volume, which will have to be published separately.'

The 'small volume' continued to grow, and the effort involved began to play familiar tricks with his health. Only a week later, he was writing to say that: 'I am quite knocked up, and I am going next Monday to revive under Water-cure at Moor Park.'

This visit established a pattern that persisted for the next eighteen months. The stress of writing such controversial material played havoc with his digestive system. A few weeks of steady work would reduce him to near total exhaustion, from which the only escape was another period of water treatment. On 24 December he was writing to Hooker to say that the book was going to run to at least 400 pages.

In January he was relieved to receive a letter from Wallace expressing his complete satisfaction with the way his paper had been dealt with. In return, Darwin graciously acknowledged Wallace's role in forcing him into publication:

Though I had absolutely nothing whatever to do in leading Lyell and Hooker to what they thought a fair course of action, yet I naturally could not but feel anxious to hear what your impression would be. I owe indirectly much to you and them; for I almost think that Lyell would have proved right, and I should never have completed my larger work, for I have found my Abstract hard enough in my poor health, but now, thank God, I am in my last chapter but one.

Passing Wallace's letter on to Hooker, he commented: 'He must be an amiable man.'

A few weeks later, Darwin was the victim of what could have been a disaster, but luckily was only a minor misfortune. He had sent a chapter of his neatly copied manuscript to his friend Hooker for his comments. By an oversight, it had found its way into the drawer in which the Hooker children's drawing materials were kept, and they had fallen upon it with delight. By the time the mistake was discovered, much of the manuscript had either been destroyed, or scribbled on beyond recall. Hooker's wife was able to copy out two of the less mutilated pages, but a mortified Hooker was forced to write to his friend to inform him that two-thirds of the chapter was lost. Fortunately, Darwin still had his much altered original, and he was able to comfort his friend with the news that 'I have the old M.S, otherwise the loss would have killed me!'

By the end of March, he was within sight of the end. Writing to his cousin Fox, he said:

I can see daylight through my work, and I am now correcting chapters for the press . . . I am weary of my work. It is a very odd thing that I have no sensation that I overwork my brain: but facts compel me to conclude that my brain was never formed for much thinking . . . You do me an injustice when you think that I work for fame; I value it to a certain extent; but, if I know myself, I work from a sort of instinct to try to make out the truth.

Although he was 'correcting chapters for the press', he had not in fact done anything about finding a publisher. Once again, it was Lyell who took things in hand. Acting as Darwin's agent, he persuaded the Edinburgh publisher John Murray, who had published Lyell's *Principles of Geology* and Darwin's *Journal*, to take the book unseen, and on generous terms.

Darwin was delighted with the terms offered, but he was worried that Murray would regret his decision when he realized what the book contained. He accepted the offer, but did so on the explicit understanding that Murray would have the right to retract after seeing the manuscript. When Murray did see it, in May, he was dismayed. He was an amateur geologist himself, and he thought the book's central thesis was 'as absurd as though one should contemplate a fruitful union between a poker and a rabbit'. He sought a second opinion from the Rev. Whitwell Elwin, editor of *The Quarterly Review*. Elwin suggested that Darwin should recast the book, concentrating on his studies of pigeons. Everybody, he said, was interested in pigeons, and a book about them was sure to have a good sale. The idea appealed to Murray; but Darwin was not amused, and the suggestion was dropped. But Murray did insist on one change. He was prepared to risk an initial print run of 500, but he blanched at Darwin's proposed title: *An Abstract of an Essay on the Origin of Species and Varieties through Natural Selection*. After some negotiation, they settled on the rather more digestible *On the Origin of Species by Means of Natural Selection*.

On 18 May, Darwin collapsed and retreated to Moor Park for another bout of hydrotherapy. Ten days later he was able to tell Hooker that 'entire rest, and the douche, and "Adam Bede", have together done me a world of good.' *Adam Bede* was George Eliot's latest novel, and Darwin was reading it hot from the press.

In June, he felt well enough to face the task of correcting proofs. This soon became a nightmare. Through the summer his corrections accumulated, until the manuscript was barely legible. As he worked, his headaches, his vomiting and his prostration got worse. By September his condition was so bad that he could only work for a couple of hours each morning, and was forced to rest for the remainder of the day. When the task was completed, he was as shocked by his alterations as he had been by the quality if his writing. The bill for the corrections came to £72. Ashamed of this imposition on his publisher, he expressed his readiness to foot most of the bill; but Murray magnanimously declined the offer. He had revised his estimate of the likely demand, and was now planning a print run of 1,250, with a publication date in November, and a cover price of fifteen shillings. Darwin did not share his publisher's optimism, and expressed the hope that Murray would not lose money as a result of the book's publication.

On 30 September, sick and depressed, he sent off the last corrected proofs. The book had taken him fifteen months, during which he had hardly known an hour free of sickness. On 3 October he fled. His destination was a hydropathic establishment in the Yorkshire town of Ilkley. He was at the end of his tether. The stress of bringing the book to completion, and the added stress of anticipating its reception, had taken away the last of his strength and brought physical and mental turmoil. This time the peace of Moor Park was not haven enough. It was too near to London. Ilkley was 200 miles further away, and he planned to remain there, not only until his health was restored, but until the book's launch was out of the way. Two weeks after his arrival in Ilkely, he was writing to Huxley: 'I am . . . coming to life again, after having finished my accursed book, which would have been easy work to any one else, but half-killed me.'

On 22 November 1859, twenty-two years after he had opened his first transmutation notebook, the *Origin* went on sale. To his amazement, the book trade had taken up the entire print run in advance of publication. It had in fact been oversubscribed, the advance orders amounting to 1,500. In the days following its publication, his delight in its success was increased by the appreciative letters that reached his Yorkshire hideaway from the people whose opinions meant most to him. One of the first to write was his friend and champion, Joseph Hooker, whose own *Himalayan Journal* had appeared under the same imprint:

My Dear Darwin

I am a sinner not to have written you ere this, if only to thank you for your glorious book . . . it is capitally written, and will be very successful. Lyell, with whom we are staying, is perfectly enchanted, and is absolutely gloating over it.

From another botanist, Hewett Watson, came a letter such as Darwin could hardly have imagined in his wildest dreams:

My Dear Sir,

Once commenced to read the 'Origin', I could not rest till I had galloped through the whole . . .

Your leading idea will assuredly become recognised as an established truth in science, i.e. 'Natural Selection'. It has the characteristics of all great natural truths, clarifying what was obscure, simplifying what was intricate, adding greatly to previous knowledge. You are the greatest revolutionist in natural history of this century, if not of all centuries.

Particularly gratifying was a letter from Thomas Huxley, a gifted anatomist who was in the process of establishing himself as Britain's most brilliant biologist. They had known one another for eight years, and they shared a close friendship with Hooker. Huxley was a Fellow and Gold Medallist of the Royal Society, and he was one of a group of Young Turks who were intent on wresting control of British science from an older generation who they felt were a drag on scientific progress. For all his iconoclasm, Huxley had never been a friend to advocates of transmutation, and Darwin himself had been shocked at the viciousness of a review of Chambers' *Vestiges* that Huxley had written. Huxley was bowled over by the *Origin*:

> My Dear Darwin,
>
> . . . Since I read Von Bar's essays, nine years ago, no work on Natural History Science I have met with has made so great an impression upon me . . . I trust you will not allow yourself to be in any way disgusted or annoyed by the considerable abuse and misrepresentation which, unless I greatly mistake, is in store for you. Depend upon it you have earned the lasting gratitude of all thoughtful men. And as to the curs which will bark and yelp, you must recollect that some of your friends, at any rate, are endowed with an amount of combativeness which (though you have often and justly rebuked it) may stand you in good stead.

And he closed his letter on a note of relish at the thought of the fight to come: 'I am sharpening up my claws and beak in readiness.'

Perhaps most welcome of all was the letter from his brother Erasmus, the intellectual man-about-town, and his loyal friend and soulmate since their teenage experiments in the garden laboratory at the Mount:

For myself I really think it is the most interesting book I ever read, and I can only compare it to the first knowledge of chemistry, getting into a new world, or rather behind the scenes . . . the a priori reasoning is so entirely satisfactory that if the facts won't fit in, why so much the worse for the facts is my feeling.

On the day the book went on sale to the public, Darwin was amazed to receive an urgent request from Murray for changes to be incorporated in the next print run. He started work on them the same day. Wary of upsetting his health again, he kept the number of alterations small. But the war between his obsessive character and his fragile constitution continued. Within a month, he was writing to Asa Gray at Harvard, asking him to organize an American edition.

Three weeks after the *Origin* was published, he felt well enough – and safe enough – to return home. On 26 December he opened his copy of *The Times* to discover a long and enthusiastic review of his book. Writing to Hooker, he said: 'Have you seen the splendid essay and notice of my book in the Times? I cannot avoid a strong suspicion that it is by Huxley; but I never heard that he wrote in the Times. It will do grand service.'

It was a good guess. By a lucky chance, the member of the *Times* staff to whom the book had been passed for review had no scientific education. On asking for help, he had been recommended to Huxley, and he had offered him the review, on condition that he was allowed to insert a couple of paragraphs of his own at the beginning. When the review appeared, Huxley derived much amusement from being told by various people that they knew it was by him from the style of the opening paragraph.

On 7 January a second printing of 3,000 copies hit the bookstalls. As the book was more widely read, opposition mounted from those who disapproved of its science or feared for its influence on religious belief and even the moral fibre of the nation. Darwin's one-time hero, the astronomer Sir John Herschel, was open in his contempt. William Whewell, Past President of the Geological Society and Master of Trinity College, Cambridge, refused to allow the book into the college library. A scathing review, anonymous as most were, but written by Darwin's old geology mentor, Adam Sedgwick, appeared in the *Spectator*. He had written a long letter to Darwin at Christmas in a tone more in sorrow than in anger. In that letter he had said that, 'parts of it I admired greatly, parts I laughed at until my sides were sore; other parts I read with absolute sorrow, because I think them utterly false and grievously mischievous.' In his *Spectator* article, he expressed his 'detestation of the theory, because of its unflinching materialism', and he condemned the book's methodology. 'Each series of facts,' he said 'is laced together by a series of assumptions, and repetitions of the one false principle. You cannot make a good rope out of a string of air bubbles.'

Many reviews and comments were even sharper than Sedgwick's. Behind the most bitter attacks were two principal concerns. The first of these was that Darwin's Natural Selection left no place for Divine Purpose or Divine Intervention. The second, and for many people the more important, was that a process which embraced the whole animal kingdom must also apply to man. No matter that Darwin had studiously avoided the subject: in the end the debate always came round to the relationship between man and monkey. It was this that prevented people like Lyell, who were otherwise sympathetic, from being able to go all the way with Darwin. And it was this, more than any other factor, that drove the opposition that manifested itself in the spring and summer of 1860.

As scientists, intellectuals and religious spokesmen took up their public positions, they began to look more and more like rival armies drawing up their lines of battle. It was not a simple matter of science versus religion. There were men of undoubted faith, such as the Rev. Charles Kingsley, author of *The Water Babies*, who were sympathetic to Darwin's ideas. And there were men of science for whom those ideas were an abomination. To a considerable extent the disagreement was part of an ongoing war between two generations. For many younger scientists, even those who had reservations about the concept of Natural Selection, the *Origin* was a banner under which they could continue their fight to gain control of science from the old men who were holding it back. And at the heart of the debate there were personal enmities that grew like crystals on the seed that Darwin had provided.

The most important of these rivalries was that between the thirty-four-year-old Huxley, who was a Professor at the Government School of Mines in London, and the fifty-six-year-old Superintendent of the Natural History Collections at the British Museum, Richard Owen. Owen was the uncrowned king of British Zoology. It was he who had coined the term 'dinosaur' in 1842, and had organized an immensely exciting exhibition of dinosaur remains at London's Crystal Palace in 1854. It had been Owen who had identified Darwin's South American fossils on his return from his voyage, and he had even been suggested by Darwin as a possible editor of his 1844 essay, in the letter he had left for Emma, in the event of his death. But such goodwill as had existed between them had long since evaporated, and Owen was now someone for whom the normally gentle and courteous Darwin was ready to admit unmitigated loathing. Owen and Huxley had already had a number of spats and in 1860 they were spoiling for another fight.

Given these swirling animosities, it was not a question of whether battle would be joined between the rival camps, it was a question of when and where. In June 1860 they finally met in a set-piece confrontation. The occasion was the Annual Meeting of the British Association for the Advancement of Science, which that year was being held in Oxford, in the magnificent new university museum. No formal session on 'Darwinism' had been scheduled, but the *Origin* and its author were on everyone's lips, and it was clear that, if an opportunity arose, the issue would be debated. Two of the advertised lectures promised just such an opportunity. The first of these, on Thursday, 28 June, was to be given by the university's Professor of Botany, Charles Daubeny, who was a partial supporter of Darwin's theory. Daubeny had chosen for his subject 'The Final Causes of the Sexuality of Plants, with Particular Reference to Mr Darwin's Work on the

Origin of Species'. The second paper, to be given on Saturday 30th by Professor John W. Draper of New York University, bore the snappy title of 'On the Intellectual Development of Europe, considered with Reference to the Views of Mr Darwin and others, that the Progression of Organisms is determined by Law'.

Darwin had always enjoyed the Association's annual get-together, when his health had allowed him to attend, and he had hoped to be present at both of these sessions. But his health had once more let him down. On the day that the Professor of Botany gave his lecture on the sexuality of plants, Darwin checked in at a hydropathic establishment in Richmond, on the south-west fringes of London, for another session of the water cure. As he lay under his wet towels, he waited, impatient and queasy, for the reports from Huxley and Hooker, who were in Oxford to do battle on his behalf. Some consolation for missing the excitement was provided by the news from America, where, thanks to Asa Gray's efforts, the *Origin* had just been published in an edition of 3,000 copies. His inability to travel to Oxford was less of a disappointment for Emma, who, much as she loved her husband and liked to see him enjoying himself, found such events hard to take. On one of the occasions when they were able to attend, her lack of interest was so evident that even her husband noticed. 'I am afraid you must have found that very boring,' he had said afterwards, to which she had replied, in her usual no-nonsense fashion, 'No more than all the rest.'

Had they been able to attend on this occasion, even Emma might not have been totally bored. By coincidence, the Thursday meeting was chaired by Darwin's old tutor, Henslow, who was now sixty-four, but still Professor of Botany in Cambridge. Both Huxley and Owen were in the audience. When Henslow offered Huxley the opportunity to speak, he declined, on the grounds that he would rather not initiate a discussion before 'a general audience, in which sentiment would unduly interfere with intelligence'. Owen had no such scruples. When the chair extended a similar invitation to him, he launched into a categorical rejection of Darwin's theory, and in particular its implied bearing on the relationship between humanity and the great apes. Owen, who had been the first person to describe the gorilla, supported his assertion of an unbridgeable gap between human beings and other primates by invoking an organ called the Hippocampus Minor, which he had identified in the human brain, but which, he claimed, the gorilla did not possess. This was too much for Huxley, who considered himself something of an expert on the organ in question. Rising in his seat, he said, in effect, if not in so many words, that Owen was talking hogwash, and he gave notice that he would be delivering a total demolition of his rival's case at an early date, but in a more appropriate forum.

Inside and outside the formal sessions, there was now only one topic that anyone wanted to talk about. When it was rumoured that Owen and his ally Samuel Wilberforce, Bishop of Oxford, were planning a demolition job at Saturday's meeting, the atmosphere in Oxford began to resemble that of ancient Rome on the eve of a great gladiatorial encounter. As the advertised time for Professor Draper's lecture on 'The Intellectual development of Europe' drew near, it became clear that the designated lecture room was too small to accommodate all those trying to get in. The venue was therefore changed to the museum's library, which in turn was soon filled to overflowing, partly with the massed supporters of the rival factions, and partly with spectators who were simply out for a good time. The latter included a leavening of students, whose presence guaranteed that any opportunity for partisan display would be suitably exploited. As the room began to heat up, a gentle fluttering of fans and handkerchiefs rose from the ladies in the audience. By the time the proceedings began, more than 700 people had managed to squeeze in.

The meeting was to have been chaired by Owen, but he had cried off, and once again it was Henslow who was called upon to preside. The bishop made a dramatic last-minute entrance. Pushing his way through the packed crowd, he made his way to the platform. Huxley and Hooker were in the audience. Neither of them had intended to be present. Hooker, who was bored with the subject, had walked to the meeting with a friend, with the intention of leaving him at the door; but the atmosphere had proved too enticing for him to be able to tear himself away. Huxley had planned to leave Oxford that morning, but had been waylaid on the previous day by Robert Chambers, the still anonymous author of *Vestiges*. Chambers had told him that Owen, who was spending the night at the bishop's palace, was coaching the bishop, and begged him to stay and fight for the cause. Chambers had his own reasons for wishing to see the bishop confounded, having been verbally thrashed by him at a still remembered meeting of the Association fourteen years earlier. If some Celestial Producer had been making the day's arrangements, he or she could hardly have set up a more piquant chain of events.

History does not record whether Professor Draper of New York was aware that he was playing the part of warm-up man for the main event. He could not have been accused of trying to steal the show. His less-than-thrilling discourse was listened to politely for the hour or so that it lasted; but the audience was getting restless, and the speakers who followed him were interrupted by impatient catcalls. The third of these, a Mr Dingle, provided a much needed release of tension when he advanced to the blackboard with a piece of chalk and the words: 'Let this point A be the man, and this point B be the mawnkey.' This was too much for the assembled undergraduates, who set up a gleeful chorus of 'Mawnkey, Mawnkey'.

It was into this supercharged atmosphere that the Right Rev. Samuel Wilberforce, DD, Bishop of Oxford, now launched himself. He was not intimidated by the occasion. He was the son of the great anti-slavery campaigner William Wilberforce, who had coached him in public speaking as a child, and he was a considerable orator. He was also a man of great intelligence, and he was beyond argument the most influential churchman of the age. Ironically, his father had been a friend, and fellow-campaigner, of both of Darwin's grandfathers, but the son's intention on this Saturday afternoon was to trample the name of Darwin in the dust.

As well as his intellect, Wilberforce was noted for his ingratiating manner. He now proceeded to use his charm and his rhetorical skills to persuade his audience that Darwin's theory was as unscientific as it was irreligious. Judged by style and form alone, it was a brilliant performance; but the longer he spoke, the more certain Huxley and Hooker became that the only ideas in his head were those that Owen had placed there. There was no doubt that he had a large section of the audience on his side. But just before he started his peroration, he made the mistake that was to cost him his moral advantage. Turning to Huxley, he enquired whether it was on his grandfather's or his grandmother's side that he claimed descent from an ape. He rounded off his speech with a resounding declaration that Darwin's theory was contrary to divine revelation, and sat down to rapturous applause. As the noise abated, voices were raised, demanding that Huxley be called to speak. Henslow acceded, and Huxley began his dissection of Wilberforce's performance. He drew the audience's attention to the contrast between the speech's confident manner and its absence of solid matter. His most cutting comment was made in response to Wilberforce's tasteless question. The excitement that followed his speech left those present with conflicting memories of the precise words he used, and the exact point at which he used them. But the essence of his reply was remembered by all who heard it. If he were asked to choose, he said, between an ape for a grandfather, and a man of great gifts, who used those gifts for the purpose of introducing ridicule into a serious discussion, he would unhesitatingly affirm his preference for the ape.

He sat down to at least as great applause as Wilberforce had done, and it was some minutes before the noise calmed down.

During the commotion, it was noticed that one member of the audience – Lady Jane Brewster, wife of the inventor of the kaleidoscope – had fainted dead away; but whether she had done so from excitement, or from the heat, was not clear. When order was restored, and Lady Brewster had been carried out, a few more speakers were able to make a contribution. By a twist of fate, one of these was Admiral Robert Fitzroy, one-time Captain of the *Beagle*, who was in Oxford in his capacity as the Head of the British Government's Meteorological Service, to present a paper on storms. He recalled his shipboard discussions with his old travelling companion, and then, holding a Bible above his head, he denounced his anti-scriptural teachings.

At length it was Hooker's turn. Cooler than Huxley, he delivered a measured refutation of all that Wilberforce had said. He listed the errors his speech had contained, which he said could only be explained on the assumption that the bishop had not read the book. He demonstrated the emptiness of the charge that Darwin's thesis was a mere hypothesis, by pointing out that this was equally true of the belief that species had been individually created. Of the two, he considered that Darwin's was the more plausible hypothesis, and on that basis, he was prepared to accept it until a better one came along.

In retrospect, people's views of the day's events depended upon where their loyalties lay, and whose report they paid most attention to. Darwin's friends remembered it as a famous victory. Their opponents were equally sure the battle had gone their way.

Darwin was in no doubt. As he read the reports in the press, and re-read his champions' accounts of the part they had played, he was sure his party had carried the day. He marvelled at his friends' audacity in taking on such a mighty opponent in public combat. And he thanked his stars that it had been they, and not he, who had had to fight for his ideas.

THIRTEEN

The Battle Rages

⸻

I f there was anyone in the audience on that summer day in Oxford who had been raised outside the Christian faith, they must have been more than a little bemused. Why, they would have wondered, should a scientific theory that proposed a common origin for all living forms generate such passion? Was this not the British Association for the Advancement of Science? Was this how science was supposed to be advanced? Why were so many people so very upset?

The reason was, of course, that it had not merely been a debate about science. It had also been about religion. That is why the star speaker for the opposition had been a bishop, rather than a layman. For fearful people it even seemed to threaten the prospects of sustaining morality and social order. That such concerns should have been the driving force behind an ostensibly scientific dispute shows the tangle that Victorian England had got itself into. For a parallel, one would have had to go back to sixteenth-century Italy, and the cauldron of hot water that Galileo fell into when he published his ideas on the movements of the heavenly bodies. In publishing his theory, Darwin had done what Galileo had done: he had challenged the authority of the Church to explain the workings of the natural world. This was bad enough; but by doing so, he had in effect challenged the right of the Church to lay down the law on anything. If the right of the Church to direct people's thinking on the origins of life could be successfully challenged, where would that leave its claim to pronounce on matters of morality and social organization? All these claims, after all, ultimately derived from the same source: the Bible, and the Church's role as the interpreter of the Bible. No one with a sense of history should have been surprised at the violence of the reaction. And none of Darwin's supporters who possessed a sense of history need have been depressed. The Church had, after all, eventually come to terms with Galileo. All it had needed was time to think things through, and to set the boundaries of its authority in a different place. And unlike Galileo, Darwin was not in danger of being burned at the stake. He wasn't even in danger of excommunication – except from a few dinner tables, most of which he would not have wanted to sit at anyway.

But in the England of 1860, Darwin's theorizing threatened more than the authority of bishops and the curriculum of Sunday Schools. In the eyes of some of his contemporaries it threatened the foundations of civil society. It was one thing for his book to be offered, at a price of fifteen shillings, for the intellectual diversion of the well-to-do. It was another thing altogether for his ideas to be promoted by radical magazines, whose anything-but-secret agenda was to undermine what they saw as an unholy alliance between the Church and the governing classes. The problem was encapsulated in what was to become Victorian England's best-loved children's hymn, 'All Things Bright and Beautiful'. Its first verse echoed the Creation story in the Book of Genesis:

> All things bright and beautiful,
> All creatures great and small;
> All things wise and wonderful,
> The Lord God made them all.

But a later verse carried a very different message:

> The rich man in his castle,
> The poor man at his gate:
> He made them high and lowly;
> And ordered their estate.

The trouble was that evolutionary theory offered an alternative, secular religion that could be used to challenge not only creation myths, but the basis of civil society. This was certainly the belief of the radical pamphleteers who embraced Darwin's ideas so enthusiastically, and it was a danger that concerned many members of the ruling classes. It was a view summed up in the reaction of one well-bred lady reader of the *Origin*, who said: 'Let us hope that it is not true; and if it is true, that it does not become widely known.' Even those who did not fear for the social order were in many cases fearful for their own peace of mind. Where a literal view of Genesis and a religious faith had been imbibed together in the course of the same childhood instruction, it was difficult to feel sure that the one could be rejected while still keeping a firm hold upon the other.

One question above all others lay at the heart of the debate, and it was this question that generated the bitterest arguments. There were people who were troubled on religious grounds who could have gone along with a theory that implied a common origin for 'lower' forms of life. There were many who were quite happy to treat the Creation story in the Bible as a symbolic account, rather than a literal narrative of seven days' work. But there were far fewer who were prepared to relinquish their belief in humanity's special status. The belief that man had been created in the image of God was for many the article of faith above all others that they were not prepared to surrender. Darwin had studiously avoided the question, but he could not hide the logical conclusion of his argument. His theory joined man to monkey as surely as it joined the lion to the tiger. And it was this implied linkage that fired the debates that now raged in university common rooms and public houses alike.

In the years following the publication of the *Origin*, there was an insatiable interest in the subject of evolution, and hundreds of books and pamphlets were published on the subject. There was also a ready audience for lectures on it, especially among those who could not afford to buy the book. One man in particular set himself the task of meeting this demand, and of spreading the Darwinian gospel. That person was Darwin's friend and confidant, Thomas Huxley. But before he could start on his self-appointed crusade, Huxley had to negotiate a personal crisis of his own. Three months after the Oxford meeting, he was devastated by the death of his adored four-year-old son. Writing to the philosopher Herbert Spencer, he said:

> we have lost our poor little boy, our pet and hope. You who knew him well, and know how his mother's heart and mine were wrapped up in him, will understand how great is our affliction. He was attacked with a bad form of scarlet fever on Thursday night, and on Saturday night effusion of the brain set in suddenly and carried him off in a couple of hours . . . as the little fellow was our greatest joy, so is the recollection of him an enduring consolation. It is a heavy payment, but I would buy the four years of him again at the same price.

The death of his beloved child brought him to the verge of a total breakdown, but with the help of his friends he pulled through. His recovery was assisted by the birth a few weeks later of another son, bringing joy that partly assuaged the grief. But he had passed through the fire, and he came out of it with a fierce determination that his life henceforth would be one of which his dead son could have been proud. Revolted by the words that had been recited over his child's grave, he resolved to dedicate his efforts to counteracting what he considered to be the more pernicious teachings of the Church of which he otherwise remained a loyal member. A few days after his son's death, he wrote a long and moving letter to the Rev. Charles Kingsley, Professor of Modern History at Cambridge University, in which he expressed his new-found determination:

> I may be quite wrong, and in that case I shall have to pay the penalty for being wrong. But I can only say with Luther, 'Gott helfe mir, Ich kann nichts anders.' [God help me, I can do no other.]
>
> . . . One thing people shall not call me with justice, and that is – a liar . . . if ever the occasion arises when I am bound to speak, I will not shame my boy.

By the spring he felt strong enough to begin to put his words into effect. He embarked on a lecture tour in which he expounded Darwin's theory, with particular reference to its implications for human origins, to enthusiastic audiences of working men throughout the length and breadth of Britain. His devotion to Darwin, and to Darwin's cause, was total, and it was to his efforts, as much as to any other factor, that Darwin owed the widespread acceptance of his ideas. This was in spite of reservations Huxley himself still entertained. He was captivated by the power of Darwin's theory to explain the similarities between related species, and to make sense of the fossil record. But he was too good a scientist to accept it unconditionally. In his eyes, until the theory could be proved, it remained a hypothesis, and it would not be proved until Natural Selection could be shown to have produced separate species which were infertile with one another, and with their parent species. In 1860 such proof could not be produced. He was also of the opinion that Darwin was mistaken in holding so rigidly to the principle of *Natura non fit saltum* – that nature did not make jumps. He was prepared to accept that the gradual process of Natural Selection was the principal agent of evolution, but he still believed that it was only possible to make sense of the fossil record by assuming that, occasionally, evolution received a boost from more dramatic events.

While Darwin was delighting in Huxley's despatches from the battlefront, he was saddened to receive news that his former tutor, and scientific godfather, John Henslow, was dying. Darwin sent his apologies for not visiting him. 'I should not like to be in the house,' he said, 'as my retching is apt to be extremely loud.' He felt badly about not going, but his embarrassment about his treacherous stomach, and his fear of the stress created by such occasions, made him reluctant to leave his den. Earlier that month, a few minutes' speaking at a Linnean Society meeting had been punished by twenty-four hours of vomiting.

In between bouts of illness he continued with new projects. There was no question of resting on his laurels. His habits of work were too deeply ingrained, and his curiosity was too restless. He had been working on a book dealing with the variation of animals under domestication, but the pleasures of boiling the flesh off chickens were beginning to pall, and he was open to distraction. In the summer of 1861, on a visit to the seaside resort of Torquay, in Devon, he was taken by the beauty of the wild orchids and fascinated by the behaviour of the insects which visited them. When he returned home he sought out more orchids to study in the woods and fields around Down House. He put his chicken bones to one side and settled down to produce a monograph on his new interest. Off went the letters of enquiry to orchid-fanciers around the country, and back came the rare flowers he wished to examine. He had not lost his touch as a solicitor of favours.

In May 1862 the product of his labours was in the bookshops. It was called *On the Various Contrivances by which British and Foreign Orchids are Fertilised by Insects*. It was not the catchiest of titles, but it found a ready demand. Orchid-growing was a rich man's hobby, and its practitioners were happy to fork out for such a fascinating book on their pastime. Nor was it as far removed from Darwin's still unfinished labour on evolution as its title might have suggested. He had been able to show that the apparently functionless patterns, colours and shapes that orchids displayed were anything but functionless. They performed quite explicit functions, which could be demonstrated, and which could be explained as the result of interaction during the simultaneous evolution of orchids and the insects that fertilized them. It was more telling evidence in support of his evolutionary theory.

He had been glad of the distraction his orchids provided. His health was deteriorating again. In addition to his familiar afflictions, he was now troubled with a condition that was causing his skin to come off in layers. Writing to his friend Asa Gray at Harvard, when he was suffering, and two members of the family had scarlet fever, he said: 'We are a wretched family, and ought to be exterminated.'

His correspondence with Gray had, in the past year or so, acquired a new dimension. In 1861 Abraham Lincoln, who happened to have been born on the same day as Darwin, had been inaugurated as President of the United States, and the prospect of a possible war between the North and the South had revived Darwin's anti-slavery enthusiasm. In one of his letters, his feelings bubbled over:

> I never knew the newspapers so profoundly interesting. North America does not do England justice; I have not seen or heard of a soul who is not with the North. Some few, and I am one of them, even wish to God, though at the loss of millions of lives, that the North would proclaim a crusade against slavery. In the long run, a million horrid deaths would be amply repaid in the cause of humanity.

It was a startling opinion for such a gentle man to express. The Darwin family prejudices clearly ran very deep.

In the years since the publication of the *Origin*, Gray had been a loyal advocate of Darwin's theory in America, even though, like Huxley, he had strong reservations about some aspects of it. Having seen the American edition through the press, he had exploited every opportunity to promote it, including taking part in a series of debates with Darwin's leading transatlantic opponent, the great Louis Agassiz, whose expressed opinion was that Darwin's theory was a 'scientific mistake, untrue in its facts, unscientific in its methods, and mischievous in its tendency'. In spite of the interest raised by these debates, the *Origin* had not caused as great a stir in America as it had in some other countries, notably Germany and France. Americans, in the years following Lincoln's inauguration, had rather more pressing matters on their minds.

In January 1863 Darwin received news of an exciting find. The fossil of a strange creature, half-bird, half-reptile, had been uncovered at Solenhofen in Bavaria, and it had been purchased for the British Museum by the Museum's Director, Richard Owen. As details emerged, Darwin's excitement mounted. The creature, which Owen had christened Archaeopteryx, had discernible feathers; but it also had teeth, a long bony tail and vestigial claw-like fingers on the front of its wings. It seemed to provide powerful evidence in favour of a reptilian origin for birds, or a common origin for birds and reptiles. Darwin was delighted. 'The fossil bird,' he said, 'is a grand case for me.'

As the year progressed his health got worse, to the extent that for long periods at a stretch he could find the strength neither to read nor to write, and was forced to rely on others to do these things for him. Other chores, such as shaving, became intolerably burdensome and were abandoned. For the rest of his life, the face he turned to the world would be a bearded one. In the autumn of 1863, his health became so bad that Emma was able to persuade him to pay another visit to his old friend Dr Gully in Malvern, who was still practising his water cure on the rich and gullible. Much as Darwin craved relief from his sickness, he was not keen to revisit Malvern. It was now eleven years since Annie's death, but the memory was still painful. While they were there, Emma sought out Annie's grave, which neither of them had ever visited. Darwin did not accompany her.

Dr Gully's prescription included six months' rest. In Darwin's condition, it was a superfluous recommendation. All that winter, and into early spring, he lay on his sofa in Down House. Sick after every meal, vomiting several times a night, and unable to work, he found himself wishing that his life might be short. Fortunately, in April, his health began to improve. As it did so, a new interest was waiting to engage his attention. In the previous summer his American champion, Asa Gray, had sent him a packet of wild cucumber seeds. Darwin, confined to his sofa, had observed their daily progress with fascination as they wound their way around the supports he had provided for them. Any invalid would have been grateful for the distraction. But this invalid could not just watch; he needed to understand. As his health improved, he began to experiment with other kinds of climbing plants. Soon every window-sill was crowded with pots. He went out into the Kentish hop-fields to observe hop plants *in situ*, and brought them home to study them more closely. He wrote to Hooker at Kew, to beg more exotic specimens. By September he had competed a 118-page monograph, which he persuaded the Linnean Society to publish under the title of 'The Movements and Habits of Climbing Plants'. He had not lost either his obsessive curiosity or his ability to face down physical infirmity.

Two months later his morale was lifted by the news that the Royal Society had awarded him its coveted Copley Medal. The decision had been a close one: ten votes to eight. The number of votes cast against him was a sign of the opposition to his theories among the older generation of British scientists. The majority in favour revealed the success that Huxley and his friends had had in infiltrating this bastion of scientific rectitude. The tide of scientific opinion was clearly flowing his way.

In April 1865 an assassin's bullet ended Lincoln's life. Two weeks later, while the newspapers were still turning over the implications of this violent death, they found space to report another, that of Darwin's shipmate, Admiral Robert Fitzroy. Fitzroy's later career had been one of disappointment and frustration. He had been passed over for the post of Chief Naval Officer in the Marine Department of the Board of Trade, in favour of his former subordinate on the *Beagle*, Lieutenant, now Admiral, Bartholomew Sullivan. In his post of Meteorological Statist, he had been striving for years to establish a national system of weather forecasting, in the passionate belief that it could save lives at sea. He had had to contend with inadequate resources and widespread scepticism, and not always kindly comment in the press. The stress created by these problems in his professional life, and his tendency to overwork, was intensified by the internal struggle which had been going on for years between his scientific intelligence and his religious faith, as his beliefs were assailed by the public theorizing of his former friend.

Earlier that year, as he approached his sixtieth birthday, Fitzroy's health had begun to crack, and his concerned wife had consulted doctors as to his mental condition. He was given leave of absence from his meteorological duties, but a prescription of total rest was something his over-zealous temperament found difficulty in accepting. On 29 April, a Saturday, he returned home late in the evening after a day in London in an agitated and distracted state. The next morning he rose at about a quarter to eight, and made his way to his dressing room, stopping on the way to kiss his young daughter. A few minutes later, he took a razor to his throat, and ended his agony of mind. It was a sad end for a man of such intelligence, human sympathy and noble aspirations.

A year later, another link with the past was broken by the deaths, within a few months of one another, of two of Darwin's sisters. His sister Catherine, his childhood playmate, and the possessor of a bright intelligence that had never found an outlet, died early in 1866. His sister Susan, the one who had tried unsuccessfully to improve his youthful spelling, and whose later years had been devoted to the care of their sister Marianne's orphan children, died in October. His brother Erasmus travelled to Shrewsbury to supervise the disposal of the household furniture and effects. There was no need for Darwin to make the journey, and every reason for him not to do so. His health was still fragile, and the stress of seeing his childhood home broken up could have had unpleasant consequences.

As 1866 drew to a close, he parcelled up a huge pile of papers and despatched it to his publisher. It was the almost-complete manuscript of his longest book to date. It was called *The Variation of Animals and Plants under Domestication*. It was the second instalment of the big book which he had always planned to write, and of which the *Origin* had been the first. He had started it within months of the *Origin*'s publication, but had found it difficult, and he had twice put it on one side to tackle subjects that gave him more pleasure, and involved less struggle. Now, after seven years, it was nearly finished. It was largely concerned with the variations that arose as a result of the efforts of animal- and plant-breeders, but it also contained an important chapter on 'Pangenesis'. Pangenesis was the concept he had developed to answer the most persistent criticism of the ideas he had put forward in the *Origin*.

In the years since the publication of the *Origin*, many scientists, and almost all the younger ones, had come round to the idea of evolution, and had relinquished belief in the separate creation of individual species of plants and animals. But Darwin's theory of how evolution had occurred – Descent by Natural Selection – had not met with anything like the same degree of acceptance. It fitted the facts well enough, but something more was required of such an ambitious theory than merely fitting the facts. Darwin had proposed that species had originated as a result of the pressure of environmental changes on populations, of which some members displayed characteristics that gave them an increased chance of surviving to propagate their kind. But nowhere in the *Origin* had he offered any suggestion as to what biological processes made Natural Selection possible. This had not been an oversight on his part. Like the rest of his contemporaries, he had no idea how inherited characteristics were passed down from generation to generation.

His inability to provide a plausible explanation of how Natural Selection actually worked meant that his friends remained unconvinced, and it gave his critics licence to reject his theory out of hand. Natural Selection was perfectly plausible as a description of a process that *might* be operating in the natural world; but until Darwin could explain what it was that that process *operated on*, no one was under any obligation to accept that it was a correct description. Neither he nor anyone else had any idea what the mechanism of heredity was. How variations arose in the first place, and how they were passed on from one generation to the next, were equally mysterious.

Darwin's concept of Pangenesis was conceived by necessity out of desperation. It was a Just So story that represented Darwin's best shot at providing a mechanical underpinning for the process he called Natural Selection. What he suggested was that every organ in the body produced units he called 'gemmules'. These gemmules, which contained information concerning the structure and functioning of the organs in which they had originated, migrated to the organs of procreation, where they supplied the templates from which the seeds of the next generation were produced. Variations existing in one generation were thereby passed on to the next, and if a variation gave a competitive advantage in the struggle for survival, it would be more likely to be reproduced, and would gradually become established as the norm in succeeding generations. He could offer no evidence that any such mechanism actually existed, and his description of it was greeted with dubious looks from friend and foe alike.

It was in writing *Variation* that he used for the first time an expression that would later be inseparable from public discussion of his ideas: 'Survival of the Fittest'. The phrase had been coined two years earlier by the philosopher Herbert Spencer. Darwin was attracted to it because it avoided an implication carried by the term Natural Selection. As used by Darwin, Natural Selection was a shorthand expression to describe the process whereby environmental pressures favoured the survival of individuals displaying particular characteristics. He had intended it to be understood as being analogous to the process of artificial selection practised by animal- and plant-breeders. On reflection, he had come to the conclusion that this analogy was open to the interpretation that there was a Selector overseeing the process, which was the very last thing he wished to imply. Had he thought harder about the many interpretations to which 'Survival of the Fittest' was open, he might have stuck with his original expression. And had he done so, he would have given a lot less scope to people who wished to invoke the prestige of his name to promote their own very different agendas.

Variation was published on 30 January 1868. It was a huge book – twice the size of the *Origin* – which filled two volumes, each 400 pages long. In spite of this, it sold well. The name of Darwin was a sufficient recommendation. The first printing of 1,500 copies went within a week, and a second printing two weeks later found an equally ready sale. It was well enough reviewed; but its publication was a quiet event compared with the reception that met *The Origin of Species*. This was not surprising, since it was really a second bite at the same cherry. For the most part, it was an exhaustive reinforcement of the evidence and the arguments contained in the earlier work, to which was added a powerful rebuttal of the idea that Natural Selection left any room for Intelligent Design in the process of evolution. Darwin, as always, was apprehensive about his book's likely reception. He was particularly concerned as to how his friends would react to his latest brainchild, Pangenesis. He attempted to fend off their half-expected scorn by downplaying the book's worth. To one of his German champions, Fritz Muller, he wrote: 'The greater part, as you will see, is not meant to be read; but I should very much like to hear what you think of "Pangenesis", though I fear it will appear to *every one* far too speculative.'

Writing to Hooker, he was even more modest: 'About my book I will give you a bit of advice. Skip the whole of Vol. 1, except the last chapter . . . and skip largely in the 2nd volume; and then you will say it is a very good book.'

Any reader of *Variation* who remembered the promise implied by the sentence in the *Origin* – 'Light will be thrown on the origin of Man and his history' – and who was hoping to find that promise redeemed would have been disappointed. The subject of human origins did not figure in its pages. At a late stage, Darwin had once again funked the big question. The only crumb he had offered to his impatient readers in the nine years since the *Origin* had first appeared had been to change the sentence in later editions to read: '*Much* light will be thrown on the origins of

Man and his history.' Human evolution, he had decided, would be better treated as the subject of a separate 'short essay'. It was an ominous phrase. *The Origin of Species* had begun life as a short essay. It was beginning to look as if his big book was going to run to a third instalment.

FOURTEEN

Late Harvest

————— ◆ —————

Two weeks after the publication of *Variation*, Darwin celebrated his fifty-ninth birthday. He was able to look back with some satisfaction. He had led a rich life, both physically and intellectually. His youth had been filled with comfort and affection, and the joy of his favourite sports. His twenties had been illuminated by the experience of his five-year voyage, which had been as great an adventure of the mind as it had been of the body. His thirties and forties had brought the happiness of a good marriage and joyful parenthood; a home that was both a pleasure garden and an impregnable fortress; and the discovery of an idea that provided endless fascination, and the possibility of fulfilling his adolescent dreams of scientific fame. In his fifties, he had seen the world of his contemporaries convulsed by the publication and refinement of that idea, and he had seen his name go round the world, as he himself had once gone round it. If he was reviled by many he did not care about, and many more he had never met, he was honoured and revered by those he himself most respected, and he had the love and unshakeable loyalty of a band of trusted friends.

For most people, this would have been adventure and achievement enough. But this was a man who was constitutionally incapable of sitting back and contemplating his achievements. While there was breath in his body, and questions still unanswered, he had to keep working, and the compulsion to communicate the results of his enquiries was as great as the compulsion to conduct them.

No sooner had this second massive instalment of his big book appeared in the shops, than he was at work on the preparation of the third. This time there would be no evasion. He had published his thoughts on the origins of plant and animal life, and the heavens had not fallen. With that experience behind him, he was ready to face the ultimate challenge: the integration of humanity into his grand scheme of Descent by Natural Selection. 'Descent', not 'Ascent', would be the operative word. He was not going to erect a ladder of evolution leading up to 'Man'. He was going to trace humanity's family tree, looking for the clues that would establish beyond argument man's kinship, not only with the apes, but with the whole of the animal world.

Early in 1869 he took time off from this task to make some changes to the text of the *Origin*. It had been no nine-day wonder. It had remained in steady demand for ten years, and his publisher was now calling for a fifth edition. In making his revisions, he adapted the book's arguments so as to meet some criticisms that had emerged from a very powerful quarter.

In the 1860s the name of William Thomson stood pre-
eminent in British science. A brilliant mathematician and
physicist, he had been appointed Professor of Natural Philosophy
in the University of Glasgow in 1846, at the age of twenty-two.
While still in his twenties, he had shot to fame with his
formulation of the First and Second Laws of Thermodynamics.
In 1867 his standing had been recognized by the conferring of
a knighthood, and it was as Sir William Thomson, leader of the
scientific establishment, that he had turned his guns on Darwin
and his theory. An attack from this quarter was unexpected.
That geologists, botanists or anatomists might take issue with
his thesis of Evolution by Natural Selection was something
Darwin took for granted. It was in the hope of pre-empting
such opposition that he had worked so hard to support his
arguments with a mass of evidence from the world of nature.
But physics was not only a discipline he had not suspected was
relevant, it was one he knew nothing about. His consciousness
of his ignorance intensified his concern, as he realized the power
of the argument this new adversary had put together.

Darwin's argument in the *Origin* had been rooted, as all his
thinking was, in the concept of gradualism that pervaded Lyell's
Principles of Geology. His process of Natural Selection depended
upon the accumulation of small changes in plant and animal
populations through countless generations. This in turn required
enormously long periods of time to achieve the huge changes
implied in the evolution of modern species from their assumed
common ancestors. He had estimated that the wearing down of
the chalk deposits of the Weald – the low-lying plain to the

south of his home in Down – had taken 300 million years. And this was only a modest fraction of the extent of geological time that seemed to be implied by the fossil record. Thomson had poured scorn on such numbers, and the theory that needed them. His argument was based on his own estimate of the rate at which the earth had cooled since it had first solidified, and the period over which the sun could have maintained its current rate of heat output. These estimates suggested a much shorter history for the solid earth, and its source of heat, than Darwin had assumed, and implied a geological time scale which he accepted was too short to allow his accumulation of small changes to produce the range of life forms then existing. It was an argument that Darwin's opponents seized on with glee, and it was one that filled him with dismay.

As it happened, he had a tame physicist in the family, who was perfectly at home with such calculations. His son George had just graduated from Cambridge with a glamorous degree in mathematics. His position in the honours list – second place, or Second Wrangler – was the same as Thomson himself had achieved fourteen years earlier. Unfortunately, George's message to his father was that Thomson's calculations were unassailable, unless the sun and the earth possessed sources of energy unknown to nineteenth-century science.

Huxley was not fazed by the great man's sums, and publicly stated that if physics produced answers that were incompatible with Natural Selection, so much the worse for physics. Darwin, however, was sufficiently intimidated to revise his arguments in the next edition of the *Origin*. Clutching at straws, he suggested that characteristics acquired during an individual creature's lifetime might perhaps be passed on to the next generation, thereby speeding up the rate of evolutionary change. Giraffes, in other words, might acquire longer necks by straining to reach the tops of the trees, and then pass this characteristic on to their offspring. It was an unfortunate lurch in the direction of the theories of the Frenchman Lamarck, with his belief in the inheritance of acquired characteristics, which Darwin had hitherto treated with scorn, and it was a sad, if understandable, failure of intellectual nerve.

Two days after this latest edition of the *Origin* went on sale, he celebrated his sixtieth birthday. For some men it would have been an excuse to slow down, but for Darwin it was a reminder that time was passing and an incentive to press on even harder. Fortunately his health was on the mend, and this particular birthday marked the beginning of a long period of greatly improved health. He was once again able to attend dinner parties; to visit relatives and friends; to spend days at the Zoo; and even to take holidays at the seaside. He was also able to attend scientific gatherings, including meetings of the Royal Society in London. Hitherto, such gatherings, when he had dared to venture forth, had had to be planned like a military operation to ensure the minimum of stress and the maximum of privacy. His embarrassment over the levels of noise that emanated from his digestive tract had meant that meals were usually taken in his hotel room. Now at last he was able to travel and mix in society, almost as other people did.

His improved health also meant that he was able to work for

longer periods at a stretch, and his output increased accordingly. Between the ages of sixty and seventy he produced a series of books that would have been impressive had they represented the work of an entire lifetime. The first of these was his book on man, which was the third and last instalment of his big book. He worked on it for most of 1869 and 1870. In February 1871 it went on sale, in two heavyweight volumes adding up to a thousand pages. Its title was *The Descent of Man, and Selection in Relation to Sex*. Despite its length and its cost, it was an instant bestseller. It could hardly have been anything else. With Darwin's name on the cover, and monkeys and sex on the inside pages, it was a publisher's dream. A second edition followed within three weeks of the first. By the end of March 4,500 copies had walked out of the shops, and an already wealthy Darwin had banked another handsome cheque.

As its name suggested, *Descent* was really two books in one. The first section, entitled 'On the Descent of Man', dealt with the evidence for, and the manner of, the evolution of human species from the 'Lower Animals'. It also contained Darwin's speculations on the origins of what he called 'the Intellectual and Moral Faculties'. The second part, entitled 'Sexual Selection', discussed in great detail what he termed 'the Secondary Sexual Characters' of insects, birds, fish, mammals and humans, and the role of sexual competition and sexual selection in creating and perpetuating variation.

The *Descent*, formidable as it was, did not have the grandeur and sweep of *The Origin of Species*. The *Origin* had been a manifesto, written by a younger man, working against the clock, and fuelled by the excitement of presenting the product of twenty years of thought to an unsuspecting and probably hostile world. The result had been a masterpiece. The *Descent* was a different kind of book altogether. It took the *Origin* as its point of departure, and applied its arguments to the special case of human origins. Most of it was the work of the same acute scientific observer who had created the *Origin*; but some of it read as if it had been written by another Darwin altogether: someone who inhabited the same body, but lived in a cosy world of unquestioned social assumptions. The result of this 'dual authorship' was that the finished book contained observations which, while they would not have raised many eyebrows in the Reading Room at the Athenaeum, would have seemed rather smug and unscientific to readers with a different racial or social take on the book's subject-matter. Readers in County Galway were probably less pleased than readers in Perthshire to come across the following passage, which Darwin quoted with apparent approval from another writer:

The careless, squalid, unaspiring Irishman multiplies like rabbits: the frugal, foreseeing, self-respecting, ambitious Scot, stern in his morality, spiritual in his faith, sagacious and disciplined in his intelligence, passes his best years in struggle and in celibacy, marries late, and leaves few behind him.

And not every female reader would have warmed to an author who was capable of saying that:

[while] it is generally admitted that with woman the powers of intuition, of rapid perception, and perhaps of imitation, are more strongly marked than in man . . . some, at least, of these faculties are characteristic of the lower races, and therefore of a past and lower state of civilisation.

Elsewhere, he allowed himself the observation that:

The chief distinction in the intellectual powers of the two sexes is shewn by man attaining a higher eminence, in whatever he takes up, than woman can attain – whether requiring deep thought, reason, or imagination, or merely the use of the senses and hands.

It is not recorded whether he blushed when George Eliot's masterpiece *Middlemarch* appeared a few months later.

Fortunately such lapses from intellectual rigour were few in number. The book as a whole was a powerfully reasoned investigation of the affinities between human beings and other mammals, and the evidence for their common origin. A particularly striking feature of the book was its uncompromising tone. There was no question of trying to persuade the reader of the plausibility of its thesis. That human beings had evolved from ancestors they shared, not only with apes, but with elephants, was taken as given. The object of the book was not so much to persuade the reader that this had happened, as to explore the way in which it probably *had* happened. An additional objective was to extend the realm of Natural Selection beyond the merely physical, and to demonstrate that it could also have been the process by which humanity's mental and moral faculties had originated.

As a work of literature, and as an example of elegant argument, *The Descent of Man* was in a lesser league than *The Origin of Species*, but its impact was as great, if not greater. This was partly because of the confident terms in which its arguments were couched. But it was chiefly because the argument struck at the heart of many people's most cherished assumptions. Man's animal ancestry was no longer something to be coyly hinted at; now it was being baldly stated. And the evidence that Darwin had amassed put the burden of proof on those who would disagree with him. He had taken a long time to summon up the courage to tackle the big question; but his timing had been proved right, and the case he had built up during the period of waiting looked pretty well unassailable. So although the impact of the book was profound, the criticisms were more muted. His enemies still growled, but not many of them now dared to bark. Some readers would have been reassured to discover that having an ape for a grandfather was not so terrible after all. What mattered was, not where they had started from, but where they had finished up. And the scientific Darwin's other self – the rich white gentleman who bore the same name – assured them that, as well-bred Englishmen, they really were the topmost twigs on the evolutionary tree.

Darwin now addressed himself, at his publisher's suggestion, to the needs of a less well-bred, and less well-heeled, readership. Murray was planning a sixth edition of the *Origin*, at a price calculated to bring it within the reach of the better paid working man. For this edition Darwin made some substantial changes. In the course of these, the word 'evolution' found its way into the text for the first time. The new edition went on sale early in 1872. To the great joy of author and publisher, the volume of sales immediately quadrupled.

No sooner was this book in the shops, than another was in the pipeline. Amazingly, even after writing the *Origin*, *Variation*, and *Descent* – nearly three thousand pages in all – there were still some bits of his big book left over. In the portfolios behind his desk in Down House, there was a file of notes dealing with the way in which humans, and other animals, displayed their emotions. He had started it more than thirty years before, when he had taken notes on the behaviour of Jenny the orang-utan, and his tiny first-born son. The son was now a partner in a bank; but his first smiles and tears were still on record, along with notes on the behaviour of the family pets, waiting to be worked into a book. In the intervening years, Darwin had added to the file the replies he had received to letters addressed to missionaries and colonial civil servants concerning the mannerisms of other races, and notes on the behaviour of both wild and domestic animals. In the autumn of 1872 *The Expression of the Emotions in Men and Animals* became the latest in his list of bestsellers. Five thousand copies were taken up on the first day. Once again, the combination of the name of Darwin and an enticing title had proved a winning formula, adding to the Niagara of royalties that was cascading over him.

When he came to send out his complimentary copies, he

remembered a friend he had not seen for many years: Fanny Owen's sister Sarah, once a 'most prodigious friend' of his sister Susan. Writing to her under her married name, he said:

Down, November 1 [1872]

My Dear Mrs Haliburton,

I dare say you will be surprised to hear from me. My object in writing now is to say that I have just published a book on the 'Expression of the Emotions in Man and Animals', and it has occurred to me that you might possibly like to read some parts of it . . . Although I have had no communication with you or the other members of your family for so long a time, no scenes in my life pass so frequently or vividly before my mind as those which relate to happy old days spent at Woodhouse. I should very much like to hear a little news about yourself and the other members of your family, if you will take the trouble to write to me.

I have had many years of bad health . . . and now I feel very old . . . I am able to do some daily work in Natural History, which is still my passion, as it was in old days, when you used to laugh at me for collecting beetles with such zeal at Woodhouse. Excepting from my continued ill-health, which has excluded me from society, my life has been a very happy one . . . With sincere feelings of gratitude and affection for all bearing the name of Owen, I venture to sign myself,

Yours affectionately,

Charles Darwin

He was rewarded with an equally affectionate reply, which drew from him a further letter, ending with the words:

How kind you all were to me as a boy, and you especially, and how much happiness I owe to you.

He was sixty-three years of age, and a Grand Old Man of Science; but among the bulging portfolios in his study there was a bundle of letters: the letters that Fanny had written him in those carefree days nearly half a century before. They had not met for thirty-five years, and she too was getting old; but the memory of past happiness remained bright. And in years to come his daughter Henrietta would recall the look on his face when, and the exact spot where, he recounted the story of how Fanny had not flinched, although the recoil from her gun had left her shoulder black and blue.

In the summer of 1873 he and Emma were the house-guests of friends in nearby Surrey. It was their first such visit outside the family for the best part of twenty years. By a coincidence, the estate on which they were staying had recently been the scene of a tragic accident, involving a figure from Darwin's past: Samuel Wilberforce, the former Bishop of Oxford. Wilberforce, who was an expert horseman, had been staying at the house; he had suffered a fall while riding, and been killed outright. The inquest on his body had been conducted in the very room where Charles and Emma learned of his misfortune. In spite of the bishop's public attacks on the *Origin*, there had never been any personal animosity between the two men, and Darwin was distressed to hear of his old adversary's fate. Huxley was less forgiving. When he heard what had happened, his comment was that, 'for the first time in his life, Sam's brain had come into contact with reality, and the shock had proved fatal.'

In his improved state of health, Darwin was now better able to cope with visitors. As his fame spread, an increasing number of people, from Britain and abroad, expressed a desire to visit him in his country retreat. He was still wary of the physical upsets that followed any unusual excitement, and Emma was as protective as ever; but he had a genuine love of company, and those who were admitted to his presence could rely upon a friendly and considerate reception. Typical of the impression he made upon his visitors were the comments of the Harvard philosopher and scientific popularizer, John Fiske, who visited Down in November 1873:

old Darwin is the dearest, sweetest, loveliest old grandpa that ever was ... There is a charming kind of quiet strength about him and about everything he does. He isn't burning and eager like Huxley. He has a mild blue eye, and is the gentlest of gentle old fellows.

At home at Down, in the autumn of his years, this 'gentle old fellow' maintained the routine he had established when he had moved there thirty years before. He still paced the Sandwalk, before breakfast, before lunch and in the late afternoon. He and Emma still played their nightly game of backgammon, as they had for the past twenty-five years. Competitive as ever, he kept a running total of how many games they had each won. The house was quieter now. The children were grown up, and all, save Elizabeth, had flown the nest. His intellectual life was quieter too. His species work was finished, and his reputation was secure. Writing to Wallace, he added a P.S.: 'I have taken up old botanical work and have given up all theories.'

As he approached old age, he had returned to the study of plants, the plants he had loved since his father had introduced him to them half a century before. But this was no mental pottering around the flower garden. The curiosity, the minute and patient scrutiny, the ability to make connections were as powerful as ever, and the books he produced in the seventh decade of his life provided an information resource, and a collection of insights that botanists would turn to for inspiration long after he was dead. Healthier in his body, and happy in his researches, he was now able to produce a book a year. And his gift for unearthing interesting facts was matched by his talent for picking subjects that people wanted to read about. In 1875 he published *Insectivorous Plants*, which was a study of the devices which sundews and other plants employed to capture their insect prey. 1876 saw the publication of *The Effects of Cross- and Self-Fertilisation in the Vegetable Kingdom*. No sooner was this book out of the way than he began to assemble the notes for another two.

It was a series of books such as might have been written by someone who had found a winning formula and was determined to milk it for all it was worth. But Darwin was no hack writer with an eye for current publishing fashions. He had no need of the money, and he had no craving for public attention. He was simply following his interests, and writing up the results of his researches in order to share them with fellow-scientists. When the public queued up to buy the finished article he was always genuinely surprised. He was delighted too, of course; but the pursuit of popular success had never been part of his plans.

The success of his botanical books, although unlooked for, was no lucky accident. Output on this scale, and of this quality, did not just happen as the by-product of a satisfying hobby. His research was always meticulously planned and carried through, and it tapped into the knowledge and experience of a wide circle of friends and correspondents. And it was backed up by a ruthless organization of his life, so as to maximize the time available for his researches and his writing. His health, or rather his lack of it, helped in this regard, as he himself freely admitted. It made it easier to decline invitations, to avoid the distraction of unwelcome visitors, and to retreat from the company of even the welcome ones. It also made it easier for him to escape those chores, such as the membership of committees and boards of governors, which were the usual lot of a distinguished man of science. His freedom to pursue his botanical researches, and the reputation which came from his publications, must have been envied by his friend Hooker who sat on fifteen committees of the Royal Society, while holding down the job of Director of the Royal Botanic Garden at Kew. It would not have helped the advancement of science if everyone had behaved as Darwin did, but he could reasonably have said that he was doing what he was best at.

In the summer of 1876, he took a break from his botanical researches to record some reminiscences. This was not an attempt at autobiography. It would not have been in his nature to make much of his personal history. It was a collection of recollections and reflections written for the private information of his family. Much of it was an expression of gratitude for a fulfilled and happy life, and it reflected the pattern of his life, divided as it was into two distinct parts. Up to the moment when the family moved to Down, his recollections are full of incident. At that point the reader is brought up sharply with the words:

> My chief enjoyment and sole employment throughout my life has been my scientific work; and the excitement from such work makes me for a time forget, or drives quite away, my daily discomfort. I have therefore nothing to record during the rest of my life, except the publication of my several books.

The words give no impression of having been chosen for effect; but they forcefully convey how his life changed when his ship tied up in that little village in the Kentish countryside.

He may have had nothing more to record concerning external events after his move to Down, but he had something very particular to say about the course of his inner life. As he approached his seventieth birthday, he had a growing feeling that his race was nearly run. These notes he was writing for his children were not only a chance to tell them what he had done; they might be his last chance to tell them who he was.

There was one matter he had never written about in any of his books, and seldom talked about to his friends. This was the nature of his religious beliefs. He had never felt any great need to talk about such matters, because religion had, in truth, never meant very much to him. He had acquired certain beliefs as a child, in much the same way as he had learned his table manners. As he moved through his twenties, and particularly in the two years following his return from his voyage, he had gradually cast off these beliefs, as he came to regard them as a superstitious encumbrance. But, unlike his father and his father's father, he had never been outspoken about his lack of belief. His was a cautious, calculating, trouble-avoiding temperament and he had always stepped carefully around other people's religion. He had never felt any need to take up a public position on such matters, and he had a cherished wife who would have suffered distress had he done so. His friend Huxley had invented a word – 'agnostic' – which fitted him perfectly, and he used it to fend off questions whenever impertinent people tried to get inside his head. But as he reflected on his life, for the enlightenment of the family he held so dear, he felt a need to put the record straight. He worked through the arguments that had caused him to slip away from the religion in which he had been raised, and he made it plain that it had left no trace behind: 'disbelief crept over me at a very slow rate, but was at last complete. The rate was so slow that I felt no distress, and have never since doubted even for a second that my conclusion was correct.'

Turning to his scientific career, he expressed himself amazed at the influence he had had. He considered what qualities he possessed that might explain his success. He was sure he had 'no great quickness of apprehension or wit', but:

> On the favourable side of the balance, I think that I am superior to the common run of men in noticing things which easily escape attention, and in observing them carefully . . . my love of natural history has been steady and ardent. This pure love has, however, been much aided by the ambition to be esteemed by my fellow naturalists. From my early youth I have had the strongest desire to understand . . . whatever I observed, – that is, to group all facts under some general laws. These causes combined have given me the patience to reflect . . . for any number of years over any unexplained problem . . .
>
> My habits are methodical, and this has been of not a little use for my particular line of work. Lastly, I have had ample leisure from not having to earn my own bread. Even ill-health, though it has annihilated several years of my life, has saved me from the distractions of society and amusement.

He concluded with one of the most disarming comments any man of science ever made on his own achievements:

> With such moderate abilities as I possess, it is truly surprising that thus I should have influenced to a considerable extent the beliefs of scientific men on some important points.

It sounds as if he had forgotten the young man who set out with such a fierce determination to make his mark in the world of science. Perhaps he truly was surprised at his own success. Perhaps not.

FIFTEEN

Last Days

During those summer days of 1876, as he worked quietly on his Recollections, he and Emma were looking forward with pleasurable anticipation to a landmark in their lives: the birth of their first grandchild. Their son Francis – or Frank, as he was known in the family – had been married for two years, and he and his twenty-six-year-old wife Amy lived nearby. Amy was expecting her first child. The child, a boy, was born at Down on 7 September. He was christened Bernard. The joy that accompanied his birth was short-lived. His mother fell victim to puerperal fever and died just four days after he was born.

The shock of Amy's death devastated the household. Frank was heartbroken and remained in shock for months afterwards. For Emma, who had been especially fond of her daughter-in-law, the blow was one of the most severe she had ever suffered. The young father and his infant son moved into Down House. Emma attended to the baby's welfare, while Frank found employment as his father's assistant. Darwin, as always, could find refuge in his work; but he was older now, and conscious of his own mortality. He found it hard to fight off the feelings of depression that Amy's death had triggered. The suffering of his widowed son brought home to him how impossible his own life would be if he were to lose Emma.

In the summer of 1877 another of his botanical books went on sale, *The Different Forms of Flowers on Plants of the Same Species*. By the time it appeared he was already busy with the next, which was to be a study of the movement of plants. There had never been anything like it. He was throwing off botanical knowledge like a Catherine wheel.

That November his old university finally recognized his achievements by awarding him an honorary doctorate. It was long overdue, and the delay in honouring him was a sign of the strength of feeling against him that still lingered in academic backwaters. Huxley publicly denounced the university's foot-dragging, but Darwin was not sulking. He travelled to Cambridge to receive the degree in person. With his lifelong delight in pageantry and uniforms, he revelled in the ceremony. The Senate House was packed. The main body of the building was filled with academics and their ladies, and the window-sills and galleries were crowded with students, eager to catch a glimpse of the great man. Someone had strung a monkey-puppet from one gallery to another. In his red silk Doctor of Laws gown, with Emma by his side, he walked through streets he had first walked through fifty years before as a young student. On the day following the ceremony, he and Emma were the guests of honour at a splendid luncheon at Trinity College, hosted by their son George.

This tribute from his old university had a special significance; but similar marks of distinction and respect were now showering upon him from academic and scientific institutions around the world. In the 1860s he had received the Prussian order 'Pour le Merite', and honorary degrees in medicine from the Universities of Breslau and Bonn. He had been elected to membership of the Royal Swedish Academy of Sciences, the Imperial Academy of Sciences in St Petersburg and the American Philosophical Society in Philadelphia. Now every week's post brought news of some fresh honour, as learned societies in country after country lent lustre to their own names by adding his to their lists of members. From one list only was his name conspicuously absent: the Honours List of his own country. No knighthood came his way. There were still people close to the centre of power and patronage who were determined that the authorship of *The Origin of Species* would never receive that particular endorsement.

Despite the modest noises he made, Darwin had always wanted scientific fame, and these marks of esteem gave him great pleasure. But they were not a reason to stop work. His mental powers were still intact, and the natural world still contained unsolved puzzles. Some of these puzzles were tackled in letters to journals, on topics that indicated the range of his curiosity. The readers of the *Gardeners' Chronicle* were treated to his reflections on 'The Scarcity of Holly Berries and Bees'; the readers of *Nature* shared his thoughts on 'Rats and Water Casks' and 'The Sexual Colours of Certain Butterflies'. But Darwin was not content with letters and articles. He still had a book or two in him yet.

Through 1878 and 1879, with the assistance of his son Frank, he conducted a follow-up programme of research to his earlier study of climbing plants, extending his investigations into the movements of plants of all kinds. The outcome was his most substantial botanical text of all, which ran to 400 pages and 200 illustrations, and was entitled *The Power of Movement in Plants*.

As he had approached his seventieth birthday, he had returned to a subject that had first aroused his curiosity as a teenager. On one of those golden days on his uncle Jos's estate at Maer, more than fifty years before, his uncle had drawn his attention to the way in which worms were able, by their continued disturbance of the soil, to bury quite large stones. It was a conversation he had never forgotten. When he returned from his voyage, one of the very first papers he had presented to his scientific peers had been one that he had read before the Geological Society, entitled 'On the Formation of Mould'. He had maintained his interest in the subject ever since, and after forty years of note-taking and experiment, he had enough material in the portfolio marked 'Worms' to form the basis of one last book. He had no idea whether anyone would want to buy it, but it was a labour of love, and he settled down with pleasure to the task of describing the part that these tiny creatures played in the economy of nature.

He tackled the subject in the only way he knew: exhaustively. Worms were animals, and he wanted to know how their abilities and their sensations compared with those of other animals. As always, his questions and his experiments went far beyond what would normally be regarded as the appropriate course of a scientific investigation. He brought worms into the house and had Emma play the piano to them, and Frank play the bassoon, to see if they responded to music. He shouted at them, blew tobacco smoke over them, and threatened them with a red-hot poker. He went into the garden after dark, and shone red and blue lights into their faces. He offered them salads to see whether they preferred red cabbage to green cabbage, and he eavesdropped on them, studying their sexual behaviour. He tested their intelligence: offering them leaves of different shapes and sizes, and observing the way they solved the problem of manoeuvring them into their burrows. To anyone who did not understand what he was up to, his behaviour would have appeared certifiable. But by the time he had finished he was an honorary worm himself, with an insight into their abilities and their instincts which enabled him to explain for the first time the huge contribution which worms made to the well-being of humanity. The result was a little gem: *The Formation of Vegetable Mould, through the Action of Worms, with Observations on their Habits*. It was a publishing phenomenon. Within two years of its publication it had sold 8,000 copies.

It was his swan song, and the book summed up the man. It displayed all the qualities that had made him the scientist he was: the total commitment to a problem that had caught his interest; the patience to carry an investigation to a successful conclusion years after it had first been embarked upon; the refusal to be confined by any narrow definition of how a scientific enquiry should be conducted; the ability, amounting to genius, to frame questions, and to make the connections that led to the answers; and most important of all, the childlike sense of wonder, that was a source of delight when he was seventy as it had been when he was seven.

Unfortunately, it was the last such challenge to engage his mind and, with his worm book finished, he experienced a feeling of emptiness. He had never been without at least one demanding project for forty years and, without work, there was a greyness about his world which even the love of his family could not entirely dispel. In the summer of 1881 Emma had persuaded him to take a family holiday in the Lake District. They had rented a large house in Patterdale for a month, and most of the family had been there at some time or other during the month. He had delighted in the scenery and he and Emma, and their little grandson Bernard, had had happy walks together. But the weather had been dreary and Darwin, who had always been sensitive to the cold, found it hard to stay in good spirits. In the past, a cold and rainy day could have been shut out by an absorbing piece of work, but that escape door was now no longer open.

Back at Down, in the warm Kentish sunshine, his spirits revived. Music and laughter and hours on the veranda, or under the trees, reminiscing about old times, created a late summer idyll. He travelled up to London to sit for his portrait, and he joined the Prince of Wales and the German Crown Prince as a guest of honour at the opening dinner of the International Medical Congress. But with the first whiff of autumn came a reminder that old times were slipping away. His brother

Erasmus, the companion of his youth and the intellectual soulmate of his early manhood, was grievously ill in London. On 26 August he died, and on 1 September the whole family turned out to see him buried in Down churchyard. The funeral was conducted by the Rev. John Allen, the same cousin who had officiated at Charles and Emma's wedding, more than forty years before.

Eras had left half his estate to Charles, and half to their surviving sister Caroline. When the sums were done, Charles was stunned to discover that he was now worth over a quarter of a million pounds. Those old worries about his family's financial future had not been necessary after all.

In December 1881 he and Emma travelled to London to visit their daughter Etty and her husband. On 15 December, on his way to pay a call on an old scientific colleague, he was taken ill in the street with pains in his chest. He clung momentarily to a railing, but then succeeded in hailing a cab which took him back to his daughter's house. A doctor was called the next morning, but could find no reason for concern. As Darwin seemed none the worse for the experience, they went ahead with their pre-Christmas plans. During the course of the next few days, he was cheered by a stream of visitors who called to pay their respects, including, most welcome of all, his old comrades in arms, Huxley and Hooker.

He got through the winter with nothing worse than a bad cold. He was still pacing the Sandwalk; but he was much slower now, and he no longer had to kick stones on to a pile to keep count of his circuits. One day in March 1882, he was walking there, alone and far from the house, when he experienced severe chest pains. He managed to stagger home and insisted that there was no need to call the doctor. When Emma finally sent for the doctor a few days later, he diagnosed angina.

On 15 April, a Saturday, he was sitting at the dinner table when pain struck again – this time in his head. Complaining of dizziness he collapsed on to a sofa. A tot of brandy revived him, and he passed a reasonable night. During the next two days he seemed to be making a good recovery, and even managed a short walk in the garden. But just before midnight on the Tuesday he was struck by an agonizing pain, and slumped temporarily into unconsciousness. When he came round, he clasped Emma's hand, saying, 'I am not the least afraid to die.' After an unquiet night, and a little breakfast, he managed to sleep for a while, but when he wakened, he was seized by violent retching, which continued on and off for several hours. His son Frank arrived from London at ten a.m., and his daughter Etty arrived at one. At half past three, he said, 'I feel as if I should faint.' Emma, who had been resting, was called and cradled him in her arms. Soon afterwards he lost consciousness, and at four o'clock, he breathed his last, his head still resting on the breast that had comforted him for forty-three happy years.

SIXTEEN

A Nation Says Goodbye

———————•·◆·•———————

It had always been his assumption that he would be buried in the village churchyard at Down, alongside his infant children and his brother Erasmus. On Thursday, the day after his death, the family began to make the necessary arrangements. But his scientific colleagues had other ideas. Prompted by Huxley and Darwin's cousin Francis Galton, the President of the Royal Society wrote requesting the family's permission for his interment in Westminster Abbey. On the Friday, Darwin's friend and neighbour, Sir John Lubbock, collected a petition of fellow members of parliament in support. On Saturday, *The Standard* published a powerful leader in favour of an Abbey burial:

> one who has brought such honour to the English name, and whose death is lamented throughout the civilised world . . . should not be laid in a comparatively obscure

grave. His proper place is amongst those other worthies whose reputations are landmarks in the people's history.

In response to the pressure, the family agreed to a change in the arrangements, and hurried preparations were made for an Abbey funeral on the following Thursday. While these preparations were going ahead, tributes poured in from around the world, and the length and fulsomeness of the obituary notices in Britain and elsewhere bore witness to the universal recognition of his stature.

The Times was in no doubt that it was marking the passing of a very great man indeed:

It has been said . . . that one must seek back to Newton or even Copernicus, to find a man whose influence on human thought . . . has been as radical as that of the naturalist who has just died . . . whatever development science may assume, Mr Darwin will in all the future stand out as one of the giants in scientific thought and scientific investigation.

The *Morning Post* was of a similar mind:

Yesterday saw the quiet ending of Mr Darwin's life. He passed that life in elaborating one central idea, and he remained in the world long enough to see the whole course of modern science altered by his speculations.

In Paris, the readers of *France* opened their paper to read that: 'Darwin's work has not been merely the exposition of a system, but . . . the production of an epic – the great poem of the genesis of the universe, one of the grandest that ever proceeded from a human brain.' In Vienna, the *Allgemeine* apologized for mentioning politics: 'on a day when humanity has suffered so great a loss. It seems to us that the world has become gloomier and grown greyer since this star ceased to shine. Our century is Darwin's century. We can now suffer no greater loss, as we do not possess another Darwin to lose.'

All the American journals devoted much space to the news of his death and reviews of his life and work. There had been talk of his visiting America in the following year, and there was much regret that he should have died before he could become personally known to scientists there. The *Sun* said that his foes as well as his friends would always award him the highest praise for original and profound investigation of the phenomena of Nature. The *Tribune* called him 'a giant among his fellows'. The *Herald* said that 'his life was like that of Socrates, except in its close.'

On Wednesday afternoon, the funeral carriage, drawn by four horses, set off on its sixteen-mile journey to London. As the evening shadows fell, the coffin was borne through the Abbey cloisters, to lie overnight in the chapel of St Faith. At eleven o'clock the next morning, draped with black velvet, edged with white silk, and covered with wreaths of white flowers, it was carried into the Chapter House, where those who were to follow it were assembling. At twenty minutes to twelve, the procession of ambassadors, members of parliament, university chancellors and professors and presidents of learned societies made its way through the west and south cloisters to the West Door, where the family was waiting. Emma was not there. She had chosen to remain at Down, with her memories, in the home they had shared for forty years.

Inside the Abbey every seat was filled, and people without tickets stood along the walls. The choir sang a specially composed anthem to words from the Book of Proverbs: 'Happy is the man that findeth wisdom, and getteth understanding. She is more precious than rubies, and all the things that thou canst desire are not to be compared unto her . . . Her ways are ways of pleasantness, and all her paths are peace.'

As the organ played music by Beethoven and Schubert, the coffin was carried to the north-east corner of the nave, next to the grave of Darwin's early hero, Sir John Herschel, and beneath the monument to Sir Isaac Newton. As it was lowered into the grave, the choir sang 'His body is buried in peace, but his name liveth for evermore.'

The Established Church, which had blessed his infant body, had received his mortal remains. But it had done so on his terms. His fellow-scientists were in no doubt as to the significance of the day's events. He was no lost child, returning home. He was a hero, entering into his nation's Hall of Fame. As *The Times* said, reflecting on the final destination of his body: 'The Abbey needed it more than it needed the Abbey.'

A Backward Look

———— •◆• ————

As the tributes quoted in the previous chapter demonstrate, Darwin's reputation at the time of his death stood about as high as it was possible for a scientist's reputation to stand. He could not have timed his departure better. During the forty years after his death his reputation went into a decline. He was still regarded as a great scientist. His contributions to the study of geology, botany and zoology could not be ignored, and no one wished to devalue them. But as the nineteenth century drew to a close, the central propositions of the work for which he would most have wished to be remembered – *The Origin of Species* – came increasingly to be questioned. It was not that many scientists at the end of the nineteenth century doubted the reality of evolution. The evidence presented in the *Origin* had, for most of them, settled that argument once and for all. And as the years went by, the fossil record yielded more and more evidence to support it. Archaeopterix, the fossil bird with reptilian features, had been discovered within two years of the publication of the *Origin*. As more and more fossils were uncovered, a striking pattern was revealed. Rocks from successive geological periods were characterized by their own associated plant and animal types, which differed from those in rocks which were older, and from rocks which were younger. A picture was revealed of whole categories of living creatures which had disappeared, and been replaced by new ones. But this striking confirmation of the truth of evolution was not enough to ensure a special status for the author of the *Origin*. Paradoxically, as the fact of evolution became more widely accepted, Darwin began to appear less special. The man who had once seemed a giant came to be regarded less as the architect of a revolution, and more as just the most significant in a long line of evolutionary theorists, which included his grandfather Erasmus, the Frenchman Lamarck and Robert Chambers, author of *Vestiges of the Natural History of Creation*.

Had he lived to witness this devaluation of his great work, his distress would have been acute. He did not write the *Origin* to convert people to the idea of evolution. He wrote it to persuade them of the validity of his theory of how evolution had come about. Had his ultimate achievement been merely to sell the idea of evolution, he would have considered his book to have been a failure, and the years of toil that preceded it a waste of time. Twenty years after his death, it was beginning to look as though that might be the verdict of history. The hole in his theory that he himself recognized – its inability to explain how Natural Selection was possible – was now a yawning gap.

What he had described – or rather, postulated – was a process. It fitted the facts, as they were then known. But so had any number of scientific theories that had had their day and then been discarded, as new thinking, and new evidence, rendered them redundant. It was not enough that his theory fitted the facts of evolution. To be convincing, it had to be able to identify the mechanism that drove evolution onward. It was Darwin's inability to identify the mechanism underlying his process of Natural Selection that left scientists free to deliver a verdict of Not Proven, and made it possible for non-scientists to treat his theory as a collection of unsupported speculations. By 1922 it was so little regarded that it was possible for a reputable biologist (John T. Cunningham) to tell a joint meeting of the Botanical and Zoological sections of the British Association for the Advancement of Science that 'Natural Selection is as extinct as the dodo.'

Ironically, one of the most important clues to the explanation he sought was discovered not long after the *Origin* was published; but he never got to hear of it. Just over a year after that famous Oxford debate, Huxley wrote a letter to Hooker, in which he said: 'Why does not somebody go to work experimentally, and get at the law of variation for some one species of plant?' Even as he wrote, a thousand miles to the east, someone was doing exactly that.

In a monastery garden in Brunn (Brno), in what is now the Czech Republic, in the 1850s and 1860s, a monk called Gregor Mendel, with a background in biology and mathematics, conducted a series of experiments on the processes of inheritance in plants. He traced the pattern of inheritance of a number of variable characteristics through successive generations of peas and sweet peas. By repeated crossing of different varieties, and breeding from the resultant offspring, Mendel established the crucial fact that inheritance was *particulate*, not blending. What his experiments showed was that characteristics inherited from individual parents were not lost in a mixing process, but passed from parent to offspring in discrete little parcels, which could then be passed on to later generations. Had Darwin known this, he would have been greatly encouraged, because it was only if inheritance worked in this way that the process he called Natural Selection could have any suitable raw material to work on. Mendel reported his discovery in a paper delivered to the Natural History Society of Brunn in 1865, but it did not make waves. He was the son of a poor peasant farmer, and while the monastery of Brunn was a respectable centre of scientific learning, it was a long way from the Athenaeum. Those scientists who did comment on Mendel's paper during the next thirty years seem to have regarded it as an interesting novelty, rather than as a vital piece of evidence. As a consequence, news of it never reached Darwin's ears. Almost unbelievably, a copy of the paper, which Mendel had sent him, still lay unopened on his study shelf on the day he died.

The significance of Mendel's paper was not recognized until 1900, when it was simultaneously rediscovered by researchers in Britain, Holland and Germany. In 1909 the Danish botanist Wilhelm Johannson coined the term 'gene' to describe the tiny packets of inheritable material that Mendel had called 'hereditary elements'. The next two decades saw the development of the science of genetics, which employed the concept of the gene to analyse the processes of inheritance as they were illustrated by the results of Mendel's experiments, and the findings of an army of researchers who followed in his footsteps. In the 1930s, the marriage of genetics and Darwinian Natural Selection created what became known as Neo-Darwinism, or the New Synthesis. Evolution by Natural Selection now had a credibility it had hitherto lacked, and Darwin's reputation began to rise once more.

When Francis Crick and James Watson described the double helix structure of DNA in 1953, it became possible for the first time to understand exactly what happened when genetic material from two parent organisms was combined. Almost a hundred years after the publication of *The Origin of Species*, the mechanics of inheritance were at last exposed, and what was revealed was a process that provided a perfect vehicle for Darwin's Natural Selection.

Thanks to these discoveries, we know now that plants and animals carry within them a mass of genetic information that retains its identity from generation to generation, and that the recombination of this genetic material at each conception creates the variety that makes Natural Selection possible. These differences between individuals of the same species give some a better chance, in a changing environment, of generating offspring, which in turn display further variety, and so on.

When Darwin laid such heavy emphasis on the signifi-cance of inheritable variation in the first edition of the *Origin*, he possessed no understanding of how that variation arose. And when he suggested a close family relationship between chimpanzees and human beings in *The Descent of Man*, he could not have imagined that scientists would one day be able to quantify the closeness of that relationship as a ratio of 98 per cent of shared genetic inheritance. He spent much of the twenty years that followed the publication of the *Origin* flailing around in an unsuccessful search for a biological under-pinning for his theory. But the failure of his search does not invalidate his theory; nor does it lessen the magnitude of his achievement. He created the conceptual framework within which evolutionary biologists still operate, and the more we learn, the more we come to appreciate the power of his concept of Natural Selection to explain the wonderful variety of the living world.

When Isaac Newton published his *Principia*, in which he set out his Theory of Universal Gravitation, it was greeted by the English poet Alexander Pope with the words:

> Nature, and Nature's laws, lay hid in night:
> God said 'Let Newton be', and all was light.

Substitute Darwin for Newton in that famous couplet, and it would not be extravagant as a description of the position which Darwin occupies in the history of biological science. He did not give us all the answers, any more than Newton did. To the end of his days, he was the creature of Lyell's brain, and as a disciple of Lyell, he was consumed by the concept of gradualism. Natural

Selection was for him overwhelmingly the explanation of the origin of species, and Natural Selection was a gradual process that achieved massive change by the repeated favouring of tiny advantages. Only the most devoted of his followers would now go all the way with him on this. Many biologists, much as they may admire or even worship him, would insist that he underestimated the importance of climate change and natural catastrophes in creating extinctions, and thereby dramatically altering the environment – in the sense of competition from other species – within which the development of surviving species takes place. And many would insist that his analysis does not sufficiently allow for the speed at which small changes can accelerate, and be followed by massive consequences, if they provide significant advantages in an environment which is itself changing. There are also reputable scientists who believe that evolution is best understood as a history of long periods of species stability interrupted by short periods of rapid change – a concept known as Punctuated Equilibrium. But the battles being fought within evolutionary biology are being fought on the field that Darwin laid out.

There are, of course, still some people who are unable to accept the picture which evolutionary biologists have drawn of the history of life on earth. This is particularly true of some Christian communities, especially in the United States. For such people, the 'truth' of scripture, literally interpreted, is still superior to the 'truth' of science, as portrayed by the followers of Darwin. This is not a gap that can be bridged by argument, and people who think that it can are missing the point. Belief in the inspired nature of the scriptural record is a matter of faith, and faith is not something one works out: it is something one either has or doesn't have. To have it is a basic human right, as is the right to attempt to convert other people to one's faith. But within the Christian community there has been a steady redefining of what are considered to be the proper concerns of religion, and what are the proper concerns of science. As long ago as 1927, an English bishop, William Barnes, the Bishop of Birmingham, was happy to go on record as saying that: 'Darwin's assertion that man has sprung from the apes has stood the test of more than half a century of critical examination. The stories of Adam and Eve have become for us folk-lore.'

More significantly, Pope John Paul II, in his Message to the Pontifical Academy of Sciences in 1996, delivered himself of the opinion that:

new knowledge has led to the recognition of the theory of evolution as more than a hypothesis. It is indeed remarkable that this theory has been progressively accepted by researchers, following a series of discoveries in various fields of knowledge. The convergence, neither sought nor fabricated, of the results of work that was conducted independently is in itself a significant argument in favour of the theory.

The Catholic Church, which had anathematized the evolutionary writings of Darwin's grandfather Erasmus, had finally done what it had done with Copernicus, and with Galileo: it had allowed a decent interval of a century or two to pass before redrawing the boundaries between its own authority and that of the natural sciences.

The need to be sensible in setting these boundaries had already been emphasized by the Lutheran World Federation in its Statement on Evolution in 1965:

> evolution's assumptions are as much around us as the air we breathe and no more escapable. At the same time theology's affirmations are being made as responsibly as ever. In this sense both science and religion are here to stay, and the demands of either are great enough to keep most (if not all) from daring to profess competence in both. To preserve their own integrity both science and religion need to remain in a healthy state of tension of respect towards one another and to engage in a searching debate which no more permits theologians to pose as scientists than it permits scientists to pose as theologians.

In expressing these sentiments, these official statements were following the trail blazed by the distinguished British biologist, Sir Ronald Fisher, whose book, *Genetical Theory of Natural Selection*, which was published in 1930, was one of the key documents in the creation of the Neo-Darwinian synthesis. Fisher, who was a thoroughgoing Darwinian in his science, was also a devout Christian and a political and moral conservative in his private and public life, and a living, breathing proof of the fact that there is no necessary connection between a person's scientific beliefs and his or her religious or moral outlook.

Outside the scientific community, quite apart from religious considerations, Darwin's theory is still widely misunderstood. Many people who accept that evolution is a proven fact still have in their mind's eye the eighteenth-century image of a ladder of evolutionary progress from lower to higher, with human beings on the highest rung. Even those who, like Darwin, think in terms of a tree, sometimes talk of the top of the tree. In Darwin's mental universe, there was no ladder, no higher or lower. And his tree had no top; it had only branches, and those branches ended in twigs. Many of these twigs were dead. They were the extinct species. And among those that were still green – the living species – none was 'special' when looked at from an evolutionary point of view.

But most important of all, in his universe there was no drive, and no direction. Whatever confusions he may have been guilty of on his off days, when his brain was firing on all cylinders he understood that giraffes did not have long necks because their grannies had stretched to reach the highest leaves. They had long necks because they had grannies who had been lucky enough to have inherited longer necks than other giraffes, giving their offspring an edge in the survival stakes, when giraffes were plentiful and leaves were in short supply. There was no purpose involved. It was just a lottery of interaction between variable inheritance and changing circumstances.

If there is one phrase which has distorted Darwin's message more than any other it is the one thought up by the English philosopher Herbert Spencer: 'Survival of the Fittest'. It would be difficult to think of another group of four words which has so misled seekers after truth, and given so much rope to those who would abuse it. 'Fittest' is a weasel word. It has a multitude of meanings, and it winds and twists its way through discussions of evolutionary theory, changing its meaning as it goes, and corrupting the discussions in which it is employed. When Darwin adopted Spencer's phrase in later editions of the *Origin*, he was quite clear in his own mind as to the sense in which he was using it. For Darwin, 'fittest' meant simply that the individual in question was best suited to survive and reproduce in a given environment, and it meant no more than that. A dark-coloured moth on the sooty trunk of a tree in a wood near a smoky industrial town in the closing years of the nineteenth century had a better chance of not being eaten than a light-coloured one had. It fitted its environment better, and as a consequence had a better chance of having descendants. During those years the proportion of dark-coloured moths in the woods around Manchester did increase, providing one of the best-known and most elegant demonstrations of the workings of Natural Selection. In that sense, and in that sense only, the phrase 'survival of the fittest' embodies a legitimate interpretation of Darwin's theory. Unfortunately, the phrase was too useful, and too persuasive, to be left in the hands of clear-thinking Darwinians. Capitalists needing justification for their wealth; social engineers with an urge to restrict the breeding habits of the poor; racist thugs seeking to legitimise the murder of 'inferior' peoples; all have employed it in their propaganda. It is a tribute to the prestige attaching to the name of Darwin that the proponents of so many dubious arguments have used it as a prop. And it is a delicious irony that the phrase should have been used by, and in the name of, a man whose whole life was a demonstration of its inapplicability to human affairs. If the rich, pampered and hideously sick Charles Darwin can be said to have survived, and procreated on such a heroic scale, because he was 'fit', then perhaps the moon really is made of green cheese.

If one looks for those aspects of Darwin's character and intellect on which one might pin the label 'the Secrets of His Success', one has to give pride of place to his seeing eye. He had an almost superhuman ability to see things that other people did not notice. His powers of observation were as different from the average person's as a hawk's are from a mole's. He also had a quite breathtaking ability to see, not only the thing itself, but its significance. This derived in turn from his ability to make connections that just would not have occurred to many good scientists confronted with the same phenomenon. His ability to make these connections was not a sign of exceptional brilliance. Powerful though his intelligence was, it was not quick or flashy. He usually had to work hard to achieve his insights. His ability to see connections where other people saw only disparate facts was the consequence of possessing an open mind. His thinking was not compartmentalized. He did not regard some knowledge as scientific, and other knowledge as non-scientific. For Darwin, knowledge was knowledge, whether it was a pigeon-fancier's knowledge or a professor's knowledge.

As a result, he was simply much better informed than anybody else. And he had no preconceptions as to what was relevant and what was not relevant. He did not wear academic blinkers. His belief was that all knowledge was potentially relevant. He went through life asking questions, and looking for answers, like a pig smelling for truffles. And every so often he turned up a beauty.

It helped that, in some ways, he never grew up. He kept to the end a childlike wonder at the magic and mystery of the natural world. And there was another characteristic that may have had its roots in childhood. In his autobiography, he used the word 'dogged' to describe his childhood resistance to the moralizing pressure exerted by his loving older sisters, and 'dogged' certainly describes his lifetime attitude to scientific enquiry. He just never gave up. It was an attitude that sometimes caused him to persist in errors that a less obstinate mind would have conceded much earlier. The most notable example of this was his reluctance to admit his mistake over the parallel roads of Glen Roy. These striking terraces along the sides of the Scottish valley of that name were a puzzle for years. Darwin suggested that they were raised beaches, resulting from changing levels in an arm of the sea. Long after they were correctly identified as being the consequence of the damming-up of an inland lake by glacial moraines, he stuck to his theory; and it was many years before he finally conceded his error. He was similarly reluctant to abandon his belief that erratic boulders resulted from the action of floating ice, rather than transport by glaciers. But the triumphs that came from his refusal to let go of a question that puzzled him far outweighed the few mistakes he made on the way.

Darwin was utterly obsessive about the things that caught his interest. A less wealthy man who displayed the same degree of obsession with matters that had nothing to do with his family's welfare would have been condemned as a good-for-nothing, whose probable, and deserved, destination was the workhouse. The beauty of Darwin's situation was that he could be as self-absorbed as he liked, and that his self-absorption would not only be accepted by those around him, but praised as high-minded by the people whose opinion he valued most.

Of all the people who ministered to his needs during a long life, the most important were three who deserve to be called his guardian angels. The first of these was his father. Robert Darwin was an angel to many, both within the family circle and outside it. Towards his son Charles, whom he never ceased to love, his indulgence was total. He set him in the way of medicine because it was the trade he himself knew, and because he genuinely believed his son possessed the qualities needed to succeed as a doctor. He let him idle away two years of supposed medical studies without any attempt to monitor his progress, and without any pressure to perform. When his son finally confessed his uselessness in that endeavour, he remembered that he himself had been forced into medicine, and accepted the situation without recrimination. He then pointed that son towards the Church, because he possessed no discernible ambition, and it seemed the calling in which he would be able most easily to pursue his interest in natural history. While his son was supposedly preparing for that vocation, he continued his policy of non-interference and unlimited generosity. All he ever wanted was that his son should be a useful member of society, in spite of being rich.

In relation to the most important experience of his son's life – the *Beagle* voyage – his attitude was one of total commitment and fierce pride. The possibility of an Admiralty salary was rejected out of hand; every extravagance was accepted without complaint, and every word of praise for his son's achievements and promise was kept and treasured. When the voyage ended, he immediately, and unconditionally, made over the income needed to enable that son to live an independent existence away from home. And when Darwin married, his father ensured that he would be able to support a wife and family without any need to be gainfully employed. When Darwin's sister Catherine wrote on their father's death, 'God comfort you, my dearest Charles. You were so beloved by him', she was speaking the simple truth, and it was Darwin's great joy to have known that truth while his father was still alive.

The second of Darwin's guardian angels was his host and travelling companion Robert Fitzroy. People who like their history simple have focused upon one powerful image: Fitzroy standing before that crowded Oxford meeting, brandishing his Bible, and crying, 'The Book, the Book.' From this image they have constructed a character for Fitzroy – the character of an unimaginative bigot – that bears about as much resemblance to the real man as a seaside donkey bears to a thoroughbred racehorse.

Darwin himself said that the *Beagle* voyage was 'by far the most important event in my life, and has determined my whole career'. Those five years operated on Darwin's mind like a pressure cooker. Almost every day, for 1,800 days, at an age when his mind was at its most receptive, he was exposed to new experiences. He travelled slowly enough to absorb these experiences, but fast enough to be able to make comparisons between changing environments. Throughout this period, when he was not engaged in collecting, or observing, or experimenting, he was talking science, or reading about it. This remarkable opportunity, which had such tremendous consequences for Darwin personally, and for the history of science, was not the result of any initiative on the part of the British Admiralty, or any member of the scientific establishment. It was created by the passion for scientific enquiry of a naval officer of outstanding intelligence and imagination.

But Fitzroy's contribution to Darwin's achievement did not end there. Had he not, through five difficult and demanding years, provided unstinting physical and emotional support, adapting his arrangements to suit his passenger's every need, and all with almost unfailing courtesy and consideration, it is questionable whether Darwin would have stuck it out, given that he was free, and could afford, to leave the ship at any port en route.

Fitzroy did not merely provide Darwin with an infrastructure; he also supplied intellectual stimulus. When the *Beagle* left Plymouth, he was at least as well informed in scientific matters as his passenger. He was certainly as excited about the possibilities of scientific discovery. Throughout the voyage, but particularly during the first three years, he was Darwin's intellectual sparring partner, without whose stimulus and response the *Beagle* would have been little more than a travelling library. It is amazing that so little credit has been given to those thousands of hours of shipboard conversation in published accounts of Darwin's intellectual development.

Even in the matter of religion, the popular image of Fitzroy's character is woefully adrift of historical reality. When they left England, and during the first year or so of the voyage, there was little difference in their religious outlook. In Patagonia, it was Fitzroy who expressed doubt as to the ability of scripture to explain the geological evidence that confronted them. It was not until after his return from the voyage that he adopted such a literal belief in the Bible record; just as Darwin was coming to the conclusion that the account in the Book of Genesis was a picturesque irrelevance.

It is true that as the years went by Fitzroy, as a result of his own reflections and almost certainly the influence of a devout wife, became more entrenched in a traditional religious view of earth history. And there can be no doubt that the growing difficulty, for an honest and acute intelligence, of reconciling scripture and scientific discovery – both of which he cared passionately about – caused him mental agony. And unlike the younger Darwin, he remained a man of action, who needed a public role in which he could serve his fellow men. This exposed him to the slights which politicians and jacks-in-office deliver to those who lack political nous. He felt very keenly the reproof implied in his removal from the Governorship of New Zealand, when political expediency made his removal desirable. He smarted under the snide comments, in the press and elsewhere, which greeted his efforts to establish his country's first weather forecasts. He wasn't helped by his impetuosity, which was always getting him into scrapes, or by his aristocratic hauteur, which may have helped to run a ship, but was a decided handicap in running a country like New Zealand, or in obtaining support for his weather service. In the end, the combination of internal conflict and external struggle became too much for a sensitive temperament to bear. But the tragedy of his end has no relevance to a just assessment of his part in Darwin's achievement.

The third of Darwin's guardian angels was his wife Emma. Provided that one takes care not to credit her with any direct contribution to his work, it is difficult to overstate the importance of the part she played in making that work possible. At the time they married, he was in serious danger of coming completely unstuck. He really was not capable of managing both his physical life and his mental life without subjecting himself to escalating stress. But from the day of his marriage the mundane business of daily existence was taken out of his hands. Not only that, but he acquired a companion and a nurse, whose first concern would always be to protect him from worry and to smooth his path through life. His luck in marrying Emma was breathtaking. He did not have to go looking for her. She was there waiting, within the extended family circle. She brought him love and laughter and lifelong security and protection, with a handsome dowry as icing on the cake. She had no needs that conflicted with his; or if she had, he never knew about them. And she accepted his monstrous, albeit sweet-natured, scientific self-absorption, and his mid-Victorian masculine prerogatives, as if they were the most natural things in the world. She had no interest in science, and she played no part in his work, except as an amanuensis and an improver of his style; but she was the rock on which his working life, and therefore his scientific reputation, was founded. He was an unreconstructed, hidebound, conservative country gentleman, and he kept the keys to every cupboard in the house. But she kept the key to his heart and, to his credit, he spent his life singing her praises and acknowledging the debt he owed her.

His luck in marrying Emma was equalled by his luck in hanging on to her. This was an age in which childbearing was a high-risk activity. Many women died in childbirth, and many more died when their children were young, as his own mother, and his father's mother, had done. Emma by contrast, not only outlived her husband, but after a move to Cambridge, lived long enough to know the love of nine grandchildren. That his beloved wife survived ten pregnancies, and remained fit and active enough to care for his children, and to nurse him into old age, was a crowning piece of good fortune in a lifetime of lucky chances.

If these three people – his father, Fitzroy and Emma – were the most important in making his achievements possible, there were others whose contributions to his scientific work were considerable. One was his Cambridge tutor, John Henslow, who not only encouraged his early enthusiasms, and put the *Beagle* opportunity his way, but acted as his agent and publicist while he was abroad, ensuring that, when he returned from his travels at the age of twenty-seven, he was able instantly to assume a leading position among the men of science of his day.

In his scientific maturity, he incurred an enormous debt to three friends – Charles Lyell, Joseph Hooker and Thomas Huxley – who provided his intellectual sounding-board, and who helped to stiffen his resolve when fear might have defeated him. It was Lyell whose books inspired his early thinking, and helped him to make sense of the experiences the voyage afforded. It was Lyell, along with Hooker, who supplied an ever-ready audience and a friendly, but critical, reception for any ideas he needed to toss around, no matter how outlandish. And uncomfortable as it was for him personally to have to consider the implications of Darwin's 'mental rioting', Lyell never let his own feelings influence the advice he gave.

Joseph Hooker was the closest, and most trusted, of Darwin's scientific colleagues. His botanical expertise was on call whenever it was needed, and his wider scientific knowledge made him an ideal confidant. But beyond this, there was a like-mindedness that nourished Darwin's theorizing, underpinned by a mutual regard that could quite properly be described as love.

Darwin's trio of loyal friends was completed by Thomas Huxley, 'Darwin's Bulldog', as he later came to be called. A valued colleague before the *Origin* was published, it was he who assumed the role of Darwin's champion: facing down his detractors and promoting his theories, in books and articles, and in a tireless programme of public lectures.

Another person to whom Darwin owed a considerable debt, albeit of a different kind, was Alfred Russel Wallace. He contributed almost nothing in the way of ideas to the writing of the *Origin*. Darwin's theory was almost completely worked out by the time he read Wallace's paper. But if that paper had not been written, there is a real possibility that Darwin's masterwork would never have seen the light of day. He was extremely reluctant to expose his theory to public view. In so far as he was really intending to publish at all, it was his big book that he had in mind: a book that he might never have finished. Even if he had managed to complete it, it could never have had the impact of *The Origin of Species*. It would have been such heavy going, and so expensive, that its argument would have been buried under a mountain of examples, and its readership would have been confined to the wealthy and highly educated.

Wallace saved Darwin from himself. What he gave Darwin was not ideas, but a fright: the fright he needed to force him into publication. It was Darwin who made, and threw, the bomb; but it was Wallace who lit the fuse. And that was all he ever claimed to have done. He probably could not have done more. Had there never been a Darwin, Wallace might have been the first person to go public with a theory of Evolution by Natural Selection. But he would not have made the same impression. He was on the fringe of scientific society. Darwin was at its heart. His scientific reputation made his ideas difficult to brush aside. And he packed a punch that Wallace could not deliver. Darwin had spent twenty years accumulating the evidence and the arguments that made his theorizing difficult to refute. It is silly to try to diminish Darwin's achievement on the grounds that another man had the same idea. Anyone with intelligence can have an idea. Having an idea is hardly more praiseworthy than having hiccups. It is the labour and the skill that go into developing and applying an idea that turns chance thought into great science.

Darwin is one of the best documented people in the history of science. First of all, there are his letters – 15,000 of them. Then there is his *Beagle* diary, which runs to over 150,000 words, and a stack of notebooks. In addition, there are the letters and other documents accumulated by a family that seems to have had difficulty in throwing away a toffee wrapper. The problem for the Darwin biographer is not what to put in, but what to leave out.

With so much material to hand, it would seem unnecessary to make things up; but that has not prevented some biographers from putting a very questionable spin on some of the material in question. This is particularly true of the subject of Darwin's health – or rather, his ill-health. One of the astounding things about the amount of work that Darwin got through in his life was that so much of it was produced while fighting off sickness of one kind or another. When one contemplates the books he wrote, and the work behind them, and one considers that he lost the equivalent of several years of working time to illness, one can only marvel at the industry and determination implied.

Much – too much – has been written about Darwin's medical history, and about the possible causes of his illnesses. Given that it is 120 years since he died, and that he lived at a time when medical knowledge was more limited than it is today, some caution is called for in attempting a diagnosis. His symptoms are well-documented: palpitations, sweating and fainting feelings; violent retching, often for hours on end; boils in uncomfortable places, sometimes half-a-dozen at a time; and terrible flatulence.

Up to the age of twenty-two, when he sailed on the *Beagle*, he was a fit and active youth and young man. He did suffer from eczema, and on the Darwin side there was a history of allergies. But his health gave no particular cause for concern. During the voyage, thanks to his previous sporting history, and the exercise and good food associated with his long periods on shore, he was probably the fittest man on board. He certainly displayed exceptional fitness and stamina on several occasions. He did, however, suffer periods of appalling seasickness throughout the entire five years. And whatever it was that laid him low for six weeks in Valparaiso was clearly serious, and it may have had long-term consequences. His chronic invalidism began within a year of his return, and its first onset coincided with an intense period of overwork. Thereafter, he was a sick man, on and off, for the rest of his life. He worked with several possibly deleterious chemicals. And any exceptional stress, either personal, or connected with his work, could be relied upon to stop him in his tracks. Beyond these indisputable facts, all is speculation, and speculation has run riot.

One of the more bizarre by-products of the Darwin industry has been the myth of Robert Darwin, the oppressive father, and the alleged legacy of psychological turmoil he bequeathed to his son. This stream of analysis has flowed in two channels. The first of these, and the one that has involved the greatest outpouring of unbridled speculation, is that concerned with the search for a psychological basis for Darwin's illnesses, on the assumption that these were rooted in childhood experience. The second, which takes us close to the limits of rational debate, is that which categorizes the formulation of the theory of Evolution by Natural Selection as an act of Rebellion Against the Tyrant Father.

On the evidence available at the present day, it stretches words to breaking point to describe Darwin's father as a tyrant. Every action of which we have record, and every comment by his contemporaries, tell the same story of love and care and tireless attention to the needs of others. It is true that some of his poorer patients feared him; but it is also true that he cultivated an intimidating manner towards those he thought needed such an approach to keep them in the ways of health and sensible behaviour. Against these cases, one has to set the people who revered him for his many kindnesses: the confidential loans and gifts of money; the gifts of food in times of need; the medical care provided free of charge, taking up time that could have been given to wealthy patients; the infants' school he established, at which his daughter Caroline taught. If Robert Darwin was a despot, he was one of the most benevolent despots who ever drew breath.

In the relationships that concern us here – within the family – it is difficult to think of a single occasion when he imposed his will on anyone. He was a facilitator, whose constant concern was to enable those who depended upon him to lead their lives to the full. He got rich by hard work, and by being clever and careful; but no man ever had less of the skinflint about him. He spread his protective wings about his family, and they never knew what it was to want for anything that his money could provide.

How did all this father–son business get started? It is in part attributable to over-seriousness on the part of some past biographers. Two remarks have been seized on time and time again. One is the comment his father made about him that Darwin recorded in his autobiography: 'You care for nothing but shooting, dogs and rat-catching; and you will be a disgrace to yourself and all your family.' The other is a description of the wait for the doctor to return from his rounds recorded by one of the Wedgwood girls as a teenager: 'Sunday we dined at half-past one, drest afterwards, and sat about 3 hours expecting the tide to come in about dark, and rather stiff and awful the evening was.'

The first of these remarks is supposed to typify the doctor's behaviour towards his son, the second, his effect on people generally. Two such throwaway comments seem a rather precarious foundation on which to construct either a character portrait of a father or a psychological profile of a son.

How then does one account for the caricature that has found its way into the Darwin literature? To some extent, it is simply a misunderstanding. Because *The Origin of Species* initiated one of the greatest revolutions in the history of science, and one that had profound implications for religious belief, there is an assumption that its author must have been some sort of rebel. If one starts with this assumption, it is natural to seek the sources of that rebellion, and followers of Freud will not need any encouragement to look to the father. Unfortunately for psychoanalysts, this approach is founded on a total misconception. To understand Darwin, it is necessary to understand that he never looked for trouble. On the contrary, he tried most strenuously to avoid it. He wasn't a rebel. He was an obsessive, whose obsession just happened to turn the world of his contemporaries upside down.

If there is no case to answer in regard to Darwin's supposed rebelliousness, there is even less foundation for the suggestion that his feelings towards his father were responsible for his lifelong experience of illness. That there was a psychological element in his afflictions is beyond argument. His prostration whenever his wife was about to give birth; the crippling sickness and headaches at times of emotional or intellectual crisis, such as his father's death, and the publication of the *Origin*, all speak of a temperament exceptionally susceptible to stress. But to attribute this to the father–son relationship requires more substantiation than mere assertion by psychoanalysts, and that substantiation is nowhere to be found in the voluminous records we have of Darwin's life and family history.

The more one studies Darwin's life, the more one realizes how lucky he was. But this realization should not lessen our admiration for what he accomplished. One can only properly understand the achievements of people like Darwin if one understands the background of their lives and times, and the contribution which others made to those achievements. The alternative is to adopt a view of history that sees a great man or a great woman as some sort of force of nature that asserts itself in spite of circumstances, and achieves its results unaided, by virtue of something called genius. Such an approach is as naïve when it is applied to scientific history as it is when applied to any other kind of history. But when every allowance has been made for luck, and the contributions of others, we are always left with the x factor: that combination of personality and intellect that enables one person to make so much more of their opportunities than others could have done, and which explains why some people tower over their times, while others, equally advantaged, are not remembered.

The comparison with Newton is irresistible. Newton formulated a theory that enabled people to understand the universe in a radically different and more fruitful way. The fact that scientists have moved beyond him does not diminish his stature. And 300 years after his death, we can handle the idea of living in a self-regulating universe, in which the Earth has no special place. So it is, and will be, with Darwin. Biologists still argue about the exact role of Natural Selection in the overall process of evolution, and schoolchildren nowadays know things about evolution that he had no knowledge of. But none of this diminishes him. And by the time *he* has been dead for 300 years, people will no doubt be perfectly comfortable with the idea of being part of a natural order in which humanity holds no special place.

APPENDIX 1

List of Dates

1809, February 9th	Birth in Shrewsbury
1825, October	Enrols at Edinburgh University
1828, January	Enters Christ's College, Cambridge
1831, December 27	The *Beagle* leaves Plymouth
1835, Sept 15–Oct 20	Survey of the Galapagos Islands
1836, October 2	The *Beagle* docks at Falmouth
1838, September 28	Reads Malthus on *Population*
1839, January 29	Marriage to his cousin Emma
1839, July	Publication of *Journal of Researches*
1842, June	First sketch of Evolutionary Theory
1842, July	*The Structure and Distribution of Coral Reefs*
1842, September	Moves to Down House
1844, March	*Volcanic Islands*
1844, July	Converts 1842 sketch to 270-page essay
1846, October	Begins work on Barnacles
1848, November	Father's death
1851, April	Death of his daughter Annie

1854, September	Finishes work on Barnacles
1858, June 18	Receives Wallace's essay
1858, July 1	Joint presentation to the Linnean Society
1859, November 22	Publication of *The Origin of Species*
1860, June 30	Huxley v. Wilberforce in Oxford
1862, May	Publication of his *Orchids* book
1865, April	Death of Fitzroy
1868, January	*The Variation of Animals and Plants*
1871, February	*The Descent of Man*
1872	*The Expression of the Emotions*
1875	*Insectivorous Plants*
1876	*The Effects of Cross- and Self-fertilisation*
1877	*The Different Forms of Flowers*
1877, November	Honorary LL.D. (Cambridge)
1880	*The Power of Movement in Plants*
1881	*The Formation of Vegetable Mould*
1882, April 19	Death at Down House

Down House

———————•◆•————————

D own House, Darwin's home for the last forty years of his life, and the place where he wrote *The Origin of Species*, is situated on the edge of the village of Downe, sixteen miles south-east of London, close to the town of Sevenoaks. The house and the village shared the same name in Darwin's day, but the name of the village was changed in the nineteenth century, to meet Post Office concern that it might be confused with Down in Northern Ireland.

The house is in the care of English Heritage and it is open to the public from Wednesday to Sunday every week, except for the period from late December to early February. Both the exterior and the interior of the house are much the same as they were in Darwin's lifetime, and the furnishings give a faithful impression of the surroundings in which he lived and worked. This is particularly true of his study, which is powerfully evocative of his working day. The house contains a fascinating collection of pictures, books and maps, and many interesting geological and zoological specimens. The story of his life and work is told in a superb series of displays, which lead visitors from room to room, supported by an accompanying audio commentary. Admission to the house also admits to the Sandwalk, where it is possible to walk in Darwin's footsteps in an essentially unchanged environment.

Address: Down House, Luxted Road, Downe, Kent BE6 7JT.
Tel: 01689 859 119

Further Reading

—————————◆•◆•◆—————————

A Biographies

Darwin has been the subject of two excellent full-length biographies:

1 *Darwin* by Adrian Desmond and James Moore (Penguin, paperback, 1992)

   This book is particularly good on the historical and social context. It gives added depth to the story of the life by relating it to the political and intellectual history of nineteenth-century Britain.

2 *Charles Darwin* by Janet Browne, volume 1 (Pimlico, paperback, 1996); volume 2 (Jonathan Cape, 2002)

   Janet Browne's two volumes concentrate on the detail of Darwin's life, and on his intellectual development.

Together they constitute one of the finest scientific biographies ever written.

B The Historical Context

Early Victorian Britain, 1832–51 by J.F.C. Harrison (Fontana, 1988)
This small volume paints a fascinating portrait of the changing face of British society during the time that Darwin was developing his theory.

C Nineteenth-Century Science

The Heyday of Natural History by Linn Barber (Jonathan Cape, 1980)
A survey of nineteenth-century natural history, and the people who created it. Superbly researched and beautifully illustrated. It is unfortunately out of print; but no enthusiast for the subject will rest until they possess a copy.

D The *Beagle* Voyage

The reader who wishes to retrace Darwin's five-year voyage has several choices:
1 *Voyage of the Beagle* edited by Janet Browne and Michael Neve (Penguin, paperback, 1989)
This edition reproduces about 60% of Darwin's *Journal of Researches*, the account he published two years after his

return to England. It also includes a first-class introduction, describing the background to the voyage.

2 *Charles Darwin's Beagle Diary* edited by R.D. Keynes (Cambridge University Press, paperback, 2001)
The full text, immaculately edited, of the day-to-day diary which Darwin kept during the voyage.

3 *Fossils, Finches and Fuegians* by R.D. Kenyes (HarperCollins, 2002)
This is Darwin's *Beagle* diary, retold in the form of an illustrated narrative.

4 *A Narrative of the Voyage of H.M.S. Beagle*, edited by David Stanbury (The Folio Society, 1977)
This is a compilation of interwoven extracts from the on-board diaries kept by Darwin and Fitzroy, with colour reproductions of pictures painted by the ship's artist, Conrad Martens. A joy to possess, it is now out-of-print; but it is obtainable from second-hand-book websites.

E Family Life

1 *Emma Darwin, the Inspirational Wife of a Genius* by Edna Healey (Headline, 2001)
Emma's story in full, including her family background, her marriage and her life after her husband's death.

2 *Annie's Box* by Randal Keynes (Fourth Estate, 2001) (published in the USA in 2002, by Riverhead, as *Darwin, His Daughter, and Human Evolution*)
The moving story of Annie's short life and tragic death.

3 *Period Piece* by Gwen Raverat (Faber, 1952)
A book of reminiscences by one of Darwin's grand-daughters, recalling a child's view of life at Down House in the closing years of the nineteenth century. Sweet and funny, it has never been out of print in fifty years. A gem.

F The Masterwork

The Origin of Species is one of the few classics of science that can be read with pleasure by non-specialist readers. Both of these editions contain first-class introductions.

1 *The Origin of Species* by Charles Darwin, edited by J.W. Burrow (Penguin, 1985)
The full text of the first edition.

2 *The Origin of Species*, by Charles Darwin (Harvard University Press, 1964)
A facsimile edition of the first edition, with an introduction by Ernst Mayr.

G The Development of Darwin's Thought

Darwin on Evolution by Thomas F. Glick and David Kohn (Hackett, 1996)
A selection of Darwin's writings on evolutionary topics, from the *Journal of Researches*, through the 1842 *Sketch* and the 1844 *Essay* to the *Origin* and *The Descent of Man*. Includes the full text of Wallace's 1858 *Essay*, and an extract from Malthus. Not for recreational reading, but

accessible to anyone wishing to follow the development of Darwin's evolutionary thinking.

H Evolutionary Theory from Darwin to the Present Day

1 *The Blind Watchmaker* by Richard Dawkins (Penguin, Illustrated edition, 2001)

A lucid and impassioned exploration of the concept of Natural Selection. Richard Dawkins has taken on the role of 'Darwin's Bulldog' that was once filled by Thomas Huxley. Like Huxley, he is a superb popularizer, and like Huxley, he takes no prisoners.

2 *Ever Since Darwin* by Stephen Jay Gould (Norton, 1977; Penguin, 1980)

A selection of Gould's entertaining and instructive monthly essays in *Natural History* magazine. Most of the essays in this particular collection are directly concerned with the subject matter of this book.

3 *Darwin* edited by Philip Appleman (Norton, 3rd edition, 2001)

A wide-ranging anthology, comprising extracts from Darwin's works, the writings of his contemporaries, and those of later commentators. A magnificent source-book for students, but also a treasure chest for anyone wishing to read widely, rather than deeply. Seriously good value for money.

4 *One Long Argument* by Ernst Mayr (Harvard University Press, 1991)

A masterly exposition of Darwin's theory, and an assessment of his significance, by the doyen of evolutionary biology. Lucid, elegant and very readable.

5 *What Evolution Is* by Ernst Mayr (New York, Basic Books, 2001; London, Weidenfeld, 2002)

Probably the best available outline of the mechanics of evolution, from a Darwinian standpoint. Although written for non-scientists, it is not light reading; but anyone prepared to make the effort required to master its contents will be richly rewarded.

J General Introductions

1 *Get a Grip on Evolution* by David Burnie. (Weidenfeld and Nicolson, 1999)

This looks like a comic book, but it is actually an excellent survey of the whole subject, packed with information, and impressive in the clarity of its explanations.

2 *Evolution: The Triumph of an Idea* by Carl Zimmer (HarperCollins, 2001; William Heinemann, 2002)

An illustrated overview, written as a companion text to the seven-part WGBH television series *Evolution*. An ideal book for anyone who wishes to know more about evolution, but who does not want an academic text.

K Field Studies

The Beak of the Finch by Jonathan Wiener (Jonathan Cape, 1994)

A fascinating account of evolution in progress, among the bird population of the Galapagos Islands, and a lucid exposition of the meaning of Natural Selection. A modern classic.

L Genetics

The Language of the Genes by Steve Jones (Flamingo, Revised Edition, 2000)
A clear and lively introduction to the history and present state of the science of genetics.

M Botany

Darwin and His Flowers by Mea Allan (Faber, 1977)
A study of Darwin's lifelong love of plants, and of the relevance of his botanical work to the development of his evolutionary theories. Full of interest and very readable.

Index